HIGHLAND GOLD & SILVERSMITHS

←

HIGHLAND GOLD & SILVERSMITHS

G P Moss & A D Roe

NMS Publishing

Published by NMS Publishing Limited, Royal Museum,
Chambers Street, Edinburgh EH1 1JF

British Library Cataloguing in Publication Data

A catalogue record of this book is available from the British Library

ISBN 1 901663 25 6

Designed by NMS Publishing Limited
Printed in the United kingdom by Henry Ling, Dorchester
Photographs not otherwise marked are © G P Moss

Throughout this book personal names have been spelled as they were found in the
sources.

OATH OF TRADE

I shall be faithfull just & true to all the Incorporate Trades of this Burgh & in a more
special manner to the Hammermen Craft, of which I am to be a member, I will
Conceal theire lawfull Secreets (sic), advance theire Lawfull Interests & be ready to
offer my best Council & advice when it is ask'd. I will likewise Inform them of any
unjust plots or malicious designs that may be privately intended against them or
theire Interest, if you know of it all those things you promise answer to God.

Inverness Hammerman Incorporation Minute Books

Front cover inset: *Inverness quaich by Thomas
Borthwick*. Private collection. Ewen Weatherspoon

Front cover detail: *Mug by John Sellar, Wick,
later decorated to Victorian taste*. Private collection.
Ewen Weatherspoon

Back Cover: *Brooch by Daniel Ferguson, Nairn*.
National Museums of Scotland

CONTENTS

ACKNOWLEDGEMENTS

Our sincere thanks to: the Staff of the Inverness Library, especially Mr Norman Newton and the Staff in the Reference Room; Highland Council Archivist Mr Robert Steward and his assistant Miss Fiona MacLeod; Mr Alistair Macleod, Highland Council Genealogist and his assistant Ms Anne Wood; Mrs Catharine Niven and in particular Mrs Lorna Cruickshank of Inverness Museum and Art Gallery; the staff of the Information Services Dept of Elgin Library, notably Mr Graeme Wilson; the Forres Archivists Dr Iredale and Mr Barrett. A very special thanks to Miss Violet Murray of the Aberdeen and NE Family History Society, and Mr Ron McGregor.

We are also grateful for the assistance of the following:

University of Aberdeen, Queen Mother Library, Aberdeen

Assay Master, Edinburgh Assay Office

Dumfries Museum

The General Register Office for Scotland

The Northern Health Services Archives, Aberdeen (Archivist Miss F R Watson)

The Highland Photographic Archives (Ms Lesley Junor)

The Registrar, Inverness

The Scottish Record Office

Nairn Library

Wick Library

Mr & Mrs D Adamson

Mr Peter Bentley

Christies Scotland Ltd (Mr Gordon Foster)

A C Cooper Ltd, Maddox Street, London (Photography)

Mr George Dalgleish, National Museums of Scotland, Edinburgh

Mr Kirkpatrick Dobie

Rev William Dunphy

Mr Eric Galloway

Mr Martin Gubbins

Ms Helen Kemp, NMS Publishing, Edinburgh

Mr Ian Kinnear

Mr J I R Martin

Mr Iain Marr (Iain Marr Antiques, Beauly, Inverness-shire)

Ms Fiona Morrison (Tomnahurich Burial Ground)

Mr William Morrison Snr

Mr William Morrison Jnr (Watchmaker & Jeweller at Finkelstein, Inverness)

Mr Hugh Naughten

Mr Keith G Peterkin

Phillips Auctioneers Edinburgh (Mr Trevor Kyle) & London (Mr Michael Prevezer)

Ms Estelle Quick

Rev I R Ramsden

Mr C Richards (John O'Groats Journal)

Rev Arthur Sinclair

Mr Nicholas R Shaw (Great Grooms Antique Centre, Billingshurst, West Sussex)

Mr Ewen Weatherspoon (Photography)

Mr Robert Wilson

Finally, a very special thank you to Mrs Gail Roe who very patiently helped with the research and checking.

Inverness from the South c1860

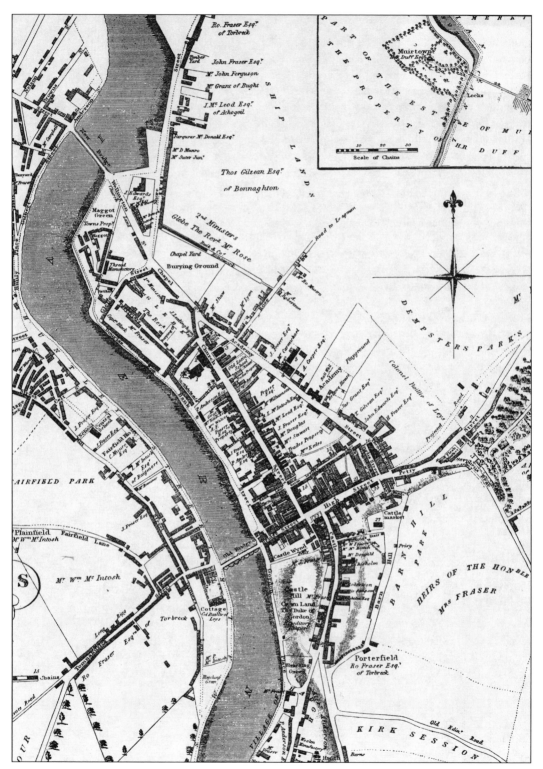

Map of Inverness 1821 survey by John Wood, Edinburgh.

CHAPTER ONE

INVERNESS

Inverness, capital of the Highlands, was a royal burgh from ancient times. David I (c1130) constituted it 'one of the six chief places of the kingdom where the King's Justiciar held his court. It was at the same time made a royal burgh and the seat of a sheriff whose authority extended over all the North of Scotland, and was thus one of the earliest free towns in the kingdom.' Unfortunately, the Town records were destroyed by fire in 1556 and consequently its early goldsmiths' names are lost to us.

In 1676 disquiet amongst the inhabitants, unhappy with the existing Magistrates and Councillors and having no power to remove them, caused a Committee of the Convention of Royal Burghs of Scotland to meet in Inverness 'for taking notice of and Rectifying the Differences betwixt the said Magistrates of the said Burgh and others'.

A new Sett was constituted which allowed the formation of six Incorporated Trades 'Providing that each one of the Incorporations underwritten Consist of Seven freemen Burgesses Hammermen Wrights Shoemakers Taylors Skinners and Weavers'. (It also gave them some rights to police their own trades.)

Three silversmiths from about this period are mentioned in *Inverness Silversmiths* by Margaret MacDougall, but no confirmation of their existence has been found.

At the turn of the eighteenth century it was customary for freemen burgesses to choose between becoming merchants (in which case they could belong to the Guildry, which allowed them to put themselves forward for membership of the Council), or to stay with their trade and Incorporation. It seems that in order to induce silversmiths to come to Inverness it had become accepted that they would be granted Guildry membership although they were in fact tradesmen. Robert Elphinston, the first Inverness silversmith for whom a mark is known, was given his freedom and made a Burgess and Guild Brother 'gratis' but still retained membership of the Hammermen's Incorporation.

In 1708 the ambiguous status of silversmiths was finally resolved. George Leith, who had been trading as a merchant, decided to work at his old trade as a silversmith.

Two other silversmiths, William McLean and Simon McKenzie, knowing this, went with other members of the Hammermen's Incorporation to his workshop and took some silver spoons away. Being brought before the Town Council, the Hammermen were fined and had their burgess tickets taken from them. They agreed to appear before a higher court and another Committee of the Royal Burghs was called. They upheld the men's interpretation of the old rules of Sett, as they stood, and their fines and burgess tickets were returned to them; however, an amendment was made to the Act of Sett. Copies of the Act of Sett and the amendment to the Sett can be read in the Appendix.

Under the new ruling all burgesses had to decide whether to continue in their trade or become guild brethren. The Sett also stipulated that there should always be two silversmiths in the Burgh and that they should admit anyone competent in his craft on such terms as the magistrates should think fit to maintain the status quo. It was also constituted that the visitor (or overseer) of any trade was not lawfully entitled to remove any work or working tools from anyone without first applying to a magistrate.

Over the years several silversmiths took the opportunity to sever their connection with the craft to become guild brothers, notably William McLean, Robert Innes and, later, Robert Naughten; William McLean, in fact, eventually became Provost of Inverness.

By the second quarter of the nineteenth century, the power of the guildry was waning and the hold of the Incorporations over their members was less rigid. The 1846 Act which abolished trade privileges only enforced what was already in progress.

The early Inverness silversmiths Robert Elphinston, William McLean, Simon McKenzie and Robert Innes produced, between them, some magnificent items of silver including communion cups, quaichs and thistle cups. Robert Elphinston is known to have made a number of distinctive miniature thistle cups, three of which are illustrated in G E P How's *Notes on Antique Silver*.

It is surprising to discover the complex essay requirements made of the Inverness silversmiths in the first half of the eighteenth century. Evidence of this is found in the *Hammermen Minute Book* dated 12 January 1727, when Collin McKenzie was asked to make 'a Sword hilt in silver' and 'A raised decanter in Silver and a Chiny fashioned Teapot also in Silver'. John Baillie, in September 1735, was asked to pass the same exhaustive test and several of the items bearing his marks which still exist in museums and private collections are testament to his ability.

The essay pieces were usually items for which an order had already been placed with the Master silversmith. The pieces would be made under the supervision of essay masters, chosen by the Incorporation, and had to be completed within a given time. On some occasions, especially during the winter months, extra time was given for the completion of essays, due to the short hours of daylight.

A number of pieces of domestic silver, such as teapots, waiters, sauce boats and quaichs were made during the eighteenth century but much of the work from this period was flatware. As the century drew to a close, some items of silverware were being bought-in from other towns such as Edinburgh, Sheffield, Birmingham and London.

During the last quarter of the century, betrothal brooches began to be made in increasing numbers; these became generally known as Luckenbooth brooches after the Luckenbooths, or locked booths, in Edinburgh, where many were made. A great variety of single and double heart designs, usually in silver, but occasionally in gold, were produced and the National Museums of Scotland has a simple gold example by Alexander Stewart of Inverness, made around 1800. Ian Finlay remarked, in *Scottish Gold and Silver Work* that there was a type of heart brooch which 'must especially be associated with Inverness'. He continued, 'Its peculiar features are (1) the crown, which is conventionalised into a device rather like a pair of spectacles; (2) the odd, angular projections on the heart itself; (3) a leaf ornament like a fleur-de-lys upside down, at the lower extremity; and (4) a small, chevron-like bar sometimes present within the lower part of the heart.'

In 1729 Katherine Duff, Lady Drunmuire, gifted the six Incorporated Trades and Masons of Inverness the ground for the Trades to build a meeting hall. This building has long been demolished; however in School Lane the stone plaque from the original building has been set, high up, on the side wall of a house (right).

Stone plaque in School Lane commemorating the gifting of land to the Incorporated Trades

The earliest commercial directory which covers the Town, *Pigot's 1821-22 & 23*, recorded the population of Inverness as about 10,000. It stated:

> The County Town of Inverness-shire is situated 156 miles North of Edinbro' and 115½ N.W. of Aberdeen. It is a Royal Burgh of great antiquity, having received its first charter from Malcolm Canmore[1]. The Town is handsome, and consists of four principal streets viz. Church-street, East, or Petty-street, Castle-street and Bridge-street: there are some other smaller streets and lanes branching off from the main streets, all of which are kept well paved, lighted, and very clean. – Inverness is the capital of the very extensive district of the North Highlands of Scotland, and from the great air of importance and even elegance of its appearance, added to the respectability of its inhabitants, is justly entitled to the distinction of a capital. The Town is beautifully situated on the banks of the River Ness, the South side being by far the most considerable, and where the principal business is transacted. That part on the West side of the River is termed the Merkinch. Muckle Green, &c. is united by a neat stone bridge of seven arches, leading from Bridge-street, and some distance above that, nearer to the Moray Frith, an extensive wooden bridge is lately erected, which also crosses the Ness: immediately above this bridge are the Quays, which are commodious and well constructed, and will admit of vessels of 200 tons to unload along side of them. The Harbour is very safe and spacious; and vessels of 500 tons may ride in safety in the Frith. Not a mile from the Town; nearly opposite to the Quay in the West side, towards the Ferry, a small new Quay has lately been built, which admits of a great draught of water. Oliver

Cromwell's Fort, now called the Citadel, is also contiguous to the Quays on the South side, the remains of which may be visibly traced... The environs of Inverness are extremely romantic and well cultivated: the River Ness forms a grand object in the picturesque beauty of the surrounding scenery. Near the Town, on the west side, is Tom-na-heurich, the hill of fairies, a beautiful insulated hill, covered with trees; and Culloden Moor, so fatal to the hopes of the Stuart family, lies a short distance S. E. of Inverness. About 18 miles to the West is the tremendous water fall, called the fall of Foyers, which is generally considered the most grand, magnificent and highest fall in the world, and far surpasses that celebrated cascade of Niagara in North America: the height of one part of the fall of Foyers, in one continued stream, being 207 feet, that of Niagara being only 140 feet.

A survey by Lt Dawson of the Royal Engineers was made in 1832; he had this to say about Inverness:

INVERNESS is the County Town of the large Shire of that name, and also generally regarded as the Capital of the Northern Highlands. The Town is compact, and the streets regular, with large and well-provided shops; and it contains a great number of wealthy and respectable inhabitants. Many handsome Villas are also erected in the neighbourhood. There are Manufactures of Woollen Goods, Hemp and Leather; and at the Fairs, Sheep and Wool to a great amount are disposed of. The Harbour of Inverness is good, and frequented by a number of Vessels of considerable tonnage. Intercourse by Steam has been established with Aberdeen and Edinburgh, and also with the Western Coast, through the Caledonian Canal; and Smacks sail regularly to London, conveying both goods and passengers. The Caledonian Canal has not hitherto added much to the commerce of the District, but beneficial effects may be expected to result from that great work. The Town has been recently lighted with

gas, and well supplied with water; and the Academy is considered one of the best in Scotland. Inverness is a very thriving place, and likely to increase.... The population of the burgh was 12,264 in the 1821 census and 14,324 in the 1831 census according to this report, of which nearly 10,000 belonged to the town of Inverness. The municipal government was vested in a provost, four bailies, a dean of guild, treasurer, and fourteen councillors, in all twenty-one. Travel in these times, between major centres, was by ship and Inverness boasted links by steam-ship and sailing vessels between Inverness and London, Inverness and Leith, Inverness and Aberdeen, and Inverness and Glasgow.

In the nineteenth century the Highlands became popularised by the visits of Queen Victoria and her husband Prince Albert, and, with the advent of steam locomotion tourism flourished. This led to an interest in all things 'Celtic', from which Inverness benefited, and the number of silversmiths and jewellers in the town rose dramatically to cope with the demand for Highland jewellery and accoutrements such as plaid brooches, buckles, sporran-mounts, dirks, sgian dubhs, kilt-pins, doublet buttons, dress snuff horns and powder horns. Inverness Museum and Art Gallery has a fine representative collection of these items.

Silver is tested, assayed, to ascertain the standard of the metal. The marks stamped on the article, after the assay, are the guarantee that the standard has been reached, as laid down by Acts of Parliament. The various Acts, amply dealt with in *Jackson's Silver & Gold Marks*, which applied to the marking of silver, appear to have been completely ignored by the Inverness silversmiths, which can only be due to their remoteness from the empowered authority in Edinburgh. Inverness silver marks are those of the maker (usually his initials) and of the town (usually INS); the

Inverness Halfpenny Trade Token showing the cornucopia. J I R Martin

The old Town crest carved into the stone of the front of the Town House.

Cover of an Inverness Bible with the Town Coat of Arms. J I R Martin

size and shape of punch may vary during a silversmith's working life. There is no statutory letter to date the piece as on Edinburgh and Glasgow silver. A few 'date' letters have been noted on Inverness silver, but only the T on the Forres communion cup by Simon McKenzie, later discussed, appears confirmed. The prevalence of names beginning with 'Mc' led to some early makers using an M, conjoined with the first letter of the surname following 'Mc', for example conjoined MK for McKenzie. From the first known marks, the contraction INS was adopted as the town-mark, (later INVS or INV[ss] are found). Two elements of the Burgh's arms are often present; one of the supporters, a dromedary (sometimes a Bactrian) camel[2]; and from the crest, a cornucopia[3] or horn of plenty. Robert Anderson seems to have been the first to have used the camel; in the nineteenth century the cornucopia was adopted by Jameson and Naughten and later Robert Naughten working alone. In addition Robert Naughten, John McRae and Thomas Stewart, amongst others, occasionally used a thistle.

The arms of six of the Incorporated Trades of Inverness are depicted in the East Windows of the Town House, one of which is that of the Hammermen's Incorporation.

While working on this book we have spent a great deal of time photographing marks and pieces of silver; we have found considerable numbers of toddy ladles and, of course, spoons but few forks and no knives. A variety of larger items of hollow-ware have been found in private collections and museums, and photographs of these appear in the book.

The present list of goldsmiths has been compiled from the *Inverness Hammermen Minute Book*, the Town and Burgh records, various ecclesiastical records, census returns, trade and post office directories, and newspapers.

Miss Margaret MacDougall was curator of the Inverness Museum from 1952 until her death in 1960; during her long association with the Museum, which included many years prior to her position as curator, she researched the gold and silversmiths of Inverness. Her notes, now in the possession of the Highland Council Archives, were the basis of her booklet *Inverness Silversmiths*, published by the Inverness Museum and Art Gallery. Her work has also been used as the source material for other publications. Her notes were studied as part of the research for this book and the dates given by her for the three earliest recorded silversmiths were noted. The authors' comments are as follows:

JAMES INNES

Miss MacDougall stated that James Innes, 'Silversmith in Inverness', was admitted freeman burgess and member of the Merchants Guild on 17 April 1663. No entry was recorded for that specific date but two entries were found in the Burgh Court Book for a John Innes; the second, dated 16 April 1663, recorded his admission as a burgess and Guild brother; however, neither entry gives his trade as gold or silversmith. He was, in fact, noted as a 'glasinwricht [glazier] burges of Invernes'.

JOHN BAYNE

Miss MacDougall stated that John Bayne was mentioned in an action for debt before the Magistrates of Inverness described as a 'silversmith in Inverness'; he was being sued for payment of a consignment of 'broken silver and for tobacco'. The suggested date given was c1668. The authors have been unable to confirm this.

ALEXANDER FRASER

Miss MacDougall stated that Alexander Fraser, 'Silversmith in Inverness', was admitted to his burghal freedom and membership of the guildry on 26 June 1676. Both the *Town Council Minute Book* and the *Burgh Court Records* do contain entries for Alexander Fraser's freedom on this date; however, in neither entry is his occupation stated as gold or silversmith. In fact, he was not a craftsman; the *Town Council Minute Book* recorded him as a 'cremar [one who sold goods from a pack or stall] at ye croce [cross] called Jonsone'.

Miss MacDougall may have had access to other contemporary material, now lost; the *Hammermen Minute Book*, dating from 1690, is now missing but a microfilm copy was commissioned by her and this is in the care of the Inverness Museum and Art Gallery. They have allowed us to view this film to aid our research. The *Minute Book* was obviously in poor condition in places when the film was made and this, added to the quality of film processing in the 1950s, has made the reading of several pages almost impossible. It seems that some pages may have been missing or perhaps not filmed; whatever the reason, some entries quoted by Miss MacDougall cannot be confirmed.

The Inverness Gold and Silversmiths with their Dates as Known:

[1] Robert Elphinston	c1654-c1720 Deacon. Moved to Forres.
[1] Simon McKenzie	c1678-1759
John Glennie	1680-82 From Aberdeen. Moved to Orkney.
George Leith	c1680-c1716 Possibly from Banff.
William McLean	c1683-1766 Became Provost.
[1] Robert Innes	c1688-c1725
Collin McKenzie	c1698-c1740
[1] William Livingston	c1700-57 Worked in Edinburgh, Elgin, Inverness & Glasgow. Returned to Edinburgh.
John Munro	1702 ?
[1] John Baillie	c1703-53 Deacon.
Alexander Mackintosh	1716
[1,2] Robert Anderson	c1733-92 Boxmaster.
[1] Thomas Borthwick	1750-c1794 Moved to Montrose.
[1,2] Charles Jameson	c1754-1829 Robert Naughten became his partner in 1813. Worked Church St.
Alexander McPherson	c1762-89
[1,2] Alexander Stewart	c1766-c1845 Worked East St. Boxmaster in Inverness. Moved to Tain in 1812.
[1,2] Donald Fraser	c1780-c1829 Worked Church St (1807). East St (1821). Boxmaster.
[1] Thomas Stewart	1784-1856 Worked in Elgin. Became bankrupt in 1827 and moved to Inverness. Worked 14 Petty St.
[1,2] Robert Naughten	1786-1857 Born in Forres. Worked Church Street.
[1,2] Alexander McLeod	c1786 -1870 Worked 1 High St, 99 Church St, 40 Bridge St. Deacon. Became bankrupt 1857.
[1,2] John Anderson	c1791-c1818 Worked East St.
[1] Alexander MacRae	1794-1856 Worked Castle St, 13 Bridge St.
[.2] Charles Crotchie	c1796-1858 Bridge St, 25 High St, 94 Church St.
[1] William Munro	c1800-c1842 Worked East St.
John McLeod	c1801-72 Jeweller. King St, 29 Church St, 82 Castle St.
James Jack	c1803-c1839 Jeweller/silversmith.
[1,2] John McRae	c1804-72 Worked 11 High St. Moved to Pollokshaws.
[1,2] William Mason	1808-70. 13 High St, 1 High St. Became bankrupt in 1868.
[1] Donald MacKenzie	c1809-c1851 Lived Castle St, Chapel Street.
Angus MacLeod	c1810-c1845 Lived High St, Castle Street, Huntly St. Moved to Elgin c1841.
Alexander Falkner (Falconer)	c1810-37 Jeweller.
James Pearson	c1812-c1852 Came from Perth. Apprenticed to Charles Murray. Lived 12 Chapel St.
[2] Richard Lockwood Stewart	1812-87 Worked 14 Petty St. Moved to Dundee.
[1,2] Jameson & Naughten	1813-c1820. Worked Church Street.

[1] Example of mark illustrated.
[2] Advertisement illustrated.

[1,2]	Daniel Ferguson	1814-92 Worked in Nairn, 74 High St. Moved to Inverness in 1862, worked 4 Inglis St, 33 Union St.
[2]	John Pratt	c1820-1901 From Aberdeen. Worked 11 High St.
[1,2]	Robert Naughten junior	1830-99 Worked 14 Church St.
	William Grant	Died 1832. Jeweller.
[1,2]	James Ferguson	1834-1910 Worked 15/17 Bridge St. See Ferguson Brothers (1866-80), James Ferguson & Son (1880-89), Ferguson Brothers (1889-c1906).
	William Ferguson	1836-98 See Ferguson Brothers (1866-80), Ferguson & MacBean.
[1,2]	Alexander Dallas	1838-1906 Worked 30 Church St, 77 Church St.
[1,2]	Peter George Wilson	1843-1925 From Keith, Banffshire. Worked 8 Union St, 44 High St.
[2]	Donald Sabiston	1840-72 Jeweller.
	James MacBean	c1847-1905 See Ferguson & MacBean. 41 Union St.
[1,2]	Arthur Medlock	1852-1930 Worked 6 Bridge St. See Medlock & Craik. James Roberts Craik Succeeded to business 1913.
[2]	Duncan MacRae	c1858-92 Watchmaker/jeweller, 15 Church St.
[2]	John Ferguson	1858-c1900 Son of Daniel Ferguson. 40 Castle St.
[1]	Charles Doherty	1859-c1912 From Edinburgh. Worked Millburn Rd, 16 Union St, 24 Union Street.
[2]	Harold Chisholm	1862 58 Academy St.
[1,2]	William R. Christie	1863-c1916 1 Queensgate.
[2]	Alexander William Fraser	1863-1945 From Grantown-on-Spey. See Fraser, Ferguson & MacBean 41 Union St.
[1,2]	Ferguson Brothers	1866-80 Corner of (41) Union St, (James and William) (Opposite Caledonian Hotel).
[1,2]	Donald MacRae	c1866-c1929. Eastgate.
	William Fraser	c1869-c1883. Gold & silversmith & jeweller. 1 High St. Became bankrupt 1875.
	William Robb	1873-74. Worked in Inverness as a jeweller journeyman. Lived 7 Celt St, directory recorded him as silversmith. 7 Crown St, jeweller journeyman. Later moved to Ballater.
	James Roberts Craik	1874-1948. See Medlock & Craik.
[2]	John A. MacPherson	1867-1926 18 Bridge St, 3 Castle St, 17 Bridge St, 61 Castle St, 56 Castle St.
[1,2]	William Buchanan Taylor	1876-1942 Worked 10 Bridge St, 27 Church St, 25/27 Church St.
[1,2]	Ferguson & MacBean	1880-1906 41 Union St, (William Ferguson & James MacBean).
[1,2]	James Ferguson & Son	1880-89
[2]	MacKenzie Bros	1881-c1890 17 Lombard St, 22 Union St.
[2]	Ferguson Bros	1889-c1906
	Alexander Fraser	1892
[2]	John MacKenzie	1884-1900
	MacKenzie & Co	1903-c1910 11 Lombard St.
[1,2]	Fraser, Ferguson & MacBean	1906-45 41 Union St.
[1,2]	Medlock & Craik	1913-92 6 Bridge St, 33 Bridge St, 20 Queensgate.

EXTRACTED FROM THE
INVERNESS HAMMERMEN MINUTE BOOK:

Master	*Apprentice*	*Date*
Robert Elphinston	Simon McKenzie[1]	2 Feb 1693
	William McLean[1]	10 Nov 1696
Simon McKenzie	Colin Mackenzie	3 Oct 1712
William McLean	Robert Innes[1]	Nov 1708
John Baillie	Robert Baillie	28 Aug 1740
	Lachlan Baillie	28 Aug 1740
	Collin MacKenzie[2]	8 Nov 1742
	Robert Anderson[1]	21 Nov 1754
Robert Anderson	John Grant[3]	22 Dec 1760
	Hector McLean	10 Feb 1772
Alexander Stewart[4]	James Forbes	28 May 1800
	Thomas McGuirman[5]	27 Sep 1805
	Hugh Macintosh	18 Jun 1809
	Alexr McRea (sic)[1]	22 Apr 1812
	Andrew Clark	22 Jul 1812
Charles Jameson	Donald Fraser[1]	19 Oct 1801
	Hugh Reid	27 Sep 1805
	Charles Fowler[6]	27 Sep 1805
	Robert Naughty[7]	15 Oct 1809
Jameson & Naughten[7]	John Fraser Reid	11 Oct 1815
	John Ross	11 Oct 1815
Donald Fraser	John McGregor	15 Oct 1809
	John Anderson[1]	23 Oct 1811
	Charles McGrigor	22 Apr 1812
	Alexr Williamson	28 Oct 1818
	John Jack	1 Nov 1820
Robert Naughten	John McLeod[1]	5 Aug 1823
	James Jack[1]	5 Aug 1823
	William Mason[1]	c1842
	George Macpherson[8]	1840
Alexander McLeod	Alexander Falkner[1]	4 May 1830
	James McKiligan	4 May 1830
	James McLeod	23 Jul 1858
John McRae	John McKenzie	4 Feb 1833

[1] Worked in Inverness.
[2] Noted in Inverness Burgh Treasurer's Account's Book, in 1783, as silversmith/goldsmith at 2nd Exchange.
[3] Moved to Tain in 1812.
[4] This entry and date taken from indenture.
[5] Worked in Elgin as Thomas Stewart, then returned to Inverness.
[6] Worked in Elgin and moved to Aberdeen as a dentist and cupper in 1823.
[7] Worked for Jameson, then as a partner; later, on his own account.
[8] This entry taken from Inverness Burgh Treasurer's Accounts Book.

CHAPTER TWO

INVERNESS CRAFTSMEN OF THE SEVENTEENTH AND EIGHTEENTH CENTURIES

ROBERT ELPHINSTON c1654–c1720

SIMON MCKENZIE c1678–1759

JOHN GLENNIE 1680–82

GEORGE LEITH c1680–c1716

WILLIAM MCLEAN c1683–1766

ROBERT INNES c1688–c1725

COLLIN MCKENZIE c1698–c1740

WILLIAM LIVINGSTON c1700–57

JOHN MUNRO 1702

JOHN BAILLIE c1703–53

ALEXANDER MACKINTOSH 1716

ROBERT ANDERSON c1733–92

THOMAS BORTHWICK 1750–c1794

CHARLES JAMESON c1754–1829

ALEXANDER MCPHERSON c1762–89

ROBERT ELPHINSTON c1654-c1720

The earliest Inverness silversmith for whom a maker's mark is confirmed is Robert Elphinston. Only a few pieces of his silver survive and two of them (opposite), can be seen in the Inverness Museum and Art Gallery. No record of his birth or baptism has been found; we are also unable to say where and to whom he was apprenticed. However, in the *Goldsmiths of Aberdeen 1450-1850* by I E James and the *Roll of Apprentices, Burgh of Aberdeen 1622-1699* by Frances McDonnell, it is recorded that a William Elphinstoun/Elphinstone, lawful son of Robert in Govell, was registered as an apprentice to William Scott[4], goldsmith, on 15 September 1668. William's baptism was dated 29 March 1653. It is also known that a Robert was baptised in Old Goval, Aberdeen, on 4 April 1654, the son of William Elphingstone and Jeane Kemptie; but no documentary evidence has been found to make a positive link between this Robert and the silversmith in Inverness.

The first record of Robert Elphinston in Inverness is to be found in the *Town Council Minute Book* dated 27 September 1686; it reads, 'That day counsell voted unanimously to grant to Robert Elphingstoun Goldsmith his freedom Burgeship and gild brother of this burgh gratis Thereupon act.'

On 11 November 1687 the *Town Council Minute Book* recorded a case brought before the Council by Jeane Cuming, 'a child', daughter of the Minister of Edinkillie. She was protesting against the 'scandalous report' made by William Niven, Professor of the 'Musick School', that he had married her on 'Halloweven last'. Robert Elphinston, goldsmith in Inverness, was called and bore witness to the clandestine marriage ceremony but stated that William Niven 'did not lie with her that night'.

On or about this date, a letter was sent to thirteen provincial goldsmiths throughout Scotland, warning them to maintain the standard of their gold and silver work. A draft of the letter, undated, from the Incorporation of Edinburgh Goldsmiths is to be found in the back of their minute book of that period. One of the thirteen was 'Robert Elphingstoun in Inverness Goldsmith'.

Robert Elphinston 'Silver Smith & Burger' appeared in the *Inverness Parish Register* for 18 August 1689, when he was a witness to the baptism of Robert, son of Robert Neilson, merchant. Throughout the period 1689-1702 he was often called upon in this capacity.

In 1690 the *Inverness Hammermen Minute Book* recorded the first entry pertaining to Robert Elphinston. Though the entry is in poor condition the following was noted: 'Robert Elphinston goldsmith maister of the said trade.' Other entries were as follows: '22 Sept 1691. ... Georg Leith saidler Robert Elphinston Goldsmith wer admited Maisters[5].'; '2nd febry [1693] Robert Elphinstone The said day entred his prentice Symone McKinzie to the goldsmith tread, Begining his Tym from febry last by past the year of god Jyvj[6] nyntie two years and hes pad his entrie being four pounds Scots.'; 'Sept 26 1693. The sd day Johne Clark diemited his Change of deconrie in favors of Robert Elphinston Goldsmith being that chosen deacon to the Hamern trade And ... his Accompts And Left in the box in money and Ane hundred and twentie pounds fourteine shillings ten penies scots money ...'.

The Inverness Marriage Register was destroyed by fire in 1707, consequently we do not have Robert's marriage date. The Inverness Kirk Session Book, dated 16 February 1692, stated: 'Also Compeared Mariel McLalan & Confest her fall with

Thistle cup by Robert Elphinston (H 4.1 cm W 5.1 cm).
Inverness Museum and Art Gallery. Ewen Weatherspoon

Communion cup by Robert Elphinston (H 21.5 cm W 13 cm).
Inverness Museum and Art Gallery. Ewen Weatherspoon

Robert Elphinstonn Goldsmith'; Robert was compeared on 22 March and 'payed his penalty ... eight pound Scotts'. It appears, however, that later that year or early the next Robert married Kathrin Keiloch, as the *Inverness Parish Register* listed the baptism of his first recorded child: 'August 4th 1693 That day Robert Elphinstone Silver Smith and burges in Inverness and his Spouse Kathrin Keiloch had a childe baptised named ... wittnesses.' No name for the child was scribed.

The *Inverness Town Council Minute Book* noted on 9 October 1693 that Robert Elphinston was made constable for Castle Street. This might indicate that his business was in Castle Street. Other entries were as follows:

> [26 November 1693] 'That Day also the Crafts and trades of this burgh after mentioned gave in to the Councill Conform to the Demand of Sett the Lists or Leets following, ... viz be the smiths & hammermen John Clark Robert Elphinston George Leith, ... Leet may be Choosen visitor to oversee their ascribd trades for the ensueing year viz Michaelmasse Jajvis & nyntie three years to Michaelmasse & nyntie four years ... and appointed the said Robert Elphingstown as visitor or over-seer[7] of the Smiths & hamermen ...'; [16 April 1694] 'The Magistrats and Councill Conveened annent the Towns affairs ... appoint Hugh Robertson Late provost James McLean Dean of gild Donald Grant mert John Fraser mert ... Robert Elph-ingstown ... to be stentmasters for proportioning the sd stent.'; [25 September 1694] 'appointed the said Robert Elphingstown as visitor or overseer to the Smith & Hamermen.'

On 8 August 1694 the Inverness Kirk Session Book recorded 'Robert Elphin-stone, goldsmith' among a list approved by the Committee of General Assembly for the North to be made Elders of the congregation.

The *Hammermen Minute Book* dated 4 October 1695 recorded that Robert Elphinston was their Deacon. The *Inverness Parish Register* detailed Simon McKen-zie as a witness to a baptism, on 12 June 1695: 'David Dunbar prentice to Thomas Killgowr Watchmaker in Inverness hade a childe baptised gotten in furnicat'n wit Margret Comper named Janet wittnesses Thomas ... Servitor to provost Dick John hepburn Mr Gunner Simone McKenzie Servitor to Robert Elphinston Gold Smith Donald Beaton Servitor to Hugh Robertson late provost.'

The same *Parish Register* dated 16 July 1695 recorded that 'Robert Elphinstonne Goldsmith and burges of this burgh and his spouse Kathrin Keiloch hade a childe baptised named ...'. The child's name was again not given.

In the *Town Council Minutes* dated 24 September 1695 Robert Elphinston was elected as visitor or overseer for the 'smith & Hamermen'; and on 20 July 1696 was mentioned with regard to the imposition of three months 'Cess[8]'.

A Disposition, held by the Highland Regional Archives, dated 21 October 1696, stated that Robert bought from Elizabeth Cuthbert, his mother-in-law (with the approval of her husband, William Keiloch, merchant), 'a burgage Land with houses biggings yeard kiln ... on the east syde of the Kirk Street'.

The *Hammermen Minute Book* dated 10 November 1696 recorded that: 'The sd day Robert Elphinstone late deacon hes Payed his prentise his entrie money, and hes (entered) it himselfe foure pounds ... money as payment to Johne Monro our Clark for his bygone fies his prentise was William McLean.'

The *Town Council Minutes* dated 4 January 1697 noted: 'The Counsell Conveened annent the towns affairs The magistrats and Counsell appoints ane new list to be mad of the Inhabitants burgess who shall keep the keys of the Inner tolburth weekly viz,' (there followed a list of 46 names including Robert Elphinston).

The *Inverness Parish Register* recorded on 25 April 1697: 'Robert Elphinstone goldsmith burges & his spouse Kathrin Keiloch hade a childe baptised be Mr Andrew Foulis minister of Killmarnock named [Isobell] wittnesses James McLean late baillie James Keiloch ship carpenter burges James porteous Tailor burges & Master Charles McLean town Clerk.' On 28 June 1698 Robert and Kathrin had another child baptised, named James.

The *Inverness Town Council Minute Book* dated 9 May 1698 recorded that 'Robert Elphingstown' was one of the stentmasters and on 22 September 1702 Robert was again elected visitor or overseer of the Smiths and Hammermen.

The *Hammermen Minute Book* dated 3 November 1702 noted that Robert Elphinston, Deacon of the Hammermen, nominated Robert Low, armourer, as boxmaster.

The *Inverness Parish Register* of 10 November 1702 recorded 'upon the, 4th of November 1702, Ther was a childe born to Robert Elphinstonn goldsmith burges procreat betwixt him & Kathrin Keiloch his Spouse baptised upon the <u>tenth</u> day of the said moneth by mr James Buchan min att Zeatland named Robert godfayrs Robert Rose Portioner of ... Robert Robertson of ... Robert Monro mer't Robert Low armourer burges & Robert Millar Copersmith burges and Robert Innes glazier burges'.

The last noted entry for Robert Elphinston, in Inverness, was in the *Hammermen Minute Book* on 26 May 1703, when he was recorded as the Deacon. Between May 1703 and October 1706 it appears that Robert moved to Forres and settled there as a goldsmith, the earliest known in that Royal Burgh.

The *Forres Parish Register* recorded on 20 June 1706 the baptism of two of Robert's children: 'James & Elizabeth the children of Robert Elphinston Gold Smith in Forres & Katherine Keiloch, were born, and bapt: the 25, witnesses Mr James Gordon Min[r] at Kinloss & Mr James McKenzie Scholmr.'

A Forres Court Process detailed a 'complaint' by David Short and Agnas Cuming, his spouse, against Robert Elphinston, goldsmith, in February 1709.

The *Forres Town Council Minutes*, dated 30 April 1709, noted that a fine of ten pounds Scots was imposed on Robert Elphinston, goldsmith in Forres, for non-appearance before the Magistrates, and for him to appear on 10 May.

The *Forres Parish Register* recorded on 20 December 1710 the baptism of another child: 'Anna daur to Robert Elphinston Goldsmith in Forres & Katherine Keilock was baptised witnesses John Brodie Late provest, & Alexr Nielson litster in Forres.'

The *Register of Sasines*[9] contains an entry dated 2 May 1711 recording that Robert Elphinston was owed the sum of two hundred and twenty pounds Scots money by Mr Patrick Tulloch and took in lieu of payment 1½ arbers of arable burgage land 'from the highway that leads from Forres towards Kinloss'.

Forres Archives hold a document, dated 6 December 1711, which described Robert Elphinston as in possession of an Inland Bill for 'Twenty pounds three Shillings four pennies Scots money' owed to him by Samuel Tulloch. Having discovered that Tulloch was unable to repay him, Robert brought an action against Tulloch which was brought before the 'Nottar Publick' and other witnesses.

Inverness Museum and Art Gallery

Throughout this period, mention was made on many occasions in the *Forres Town Council Minutes* of a 'Robert Elphinston of Coldmyre', but as yet we are unable to prove a connection with the goldsmith.

Elphinston's marks are found on a set of six spoons and a small thistle cup, which are held in a private collection, as well as on the Episcopal Church of Fortrose communion cup, which is now in the Inverness Museum and Art Gallery (p13). His mark was 'R E, INS', and a 'date letter' (above).

SIMON MCKENZIE C1678–1759

Simon McKenzie was probably born in Inverness around 1678; however, the first entry for him is in the *Inverness Hammermen Incorporation Minute Book*, in 1693: '2ⁿᵈ febry Robert Elphinstone The said day entred his prentice Symone McKinzie to the goldsmith tread, Begining his Tym from febry last by past the year of god Jyvj nyntie two years and hes pad his entrie being four pounds Scots.'

The *Inverness Parish Register* noted him as a witness at a baptism on 12 June 1695 (see page 14). The marriage register for this period, as previously mentioned, was destroyed by fire in April 1707 and no other record of Simon McKenzie's marriage has survived; however, it appears likely that it occurred shortly before this date. His first recorded child appears in the *Inverness Parish Register* on 26 February 1708: 'Simon mackenzie gooldsmith & his spouse Jean Grame hade ane child baptized named Cristan godfayrs Colline Grame of drynie Capt John McIntosh Robert Ross elder baillie and Robert Ross younger baillie.' On 8 June 1708 the *Parish Register* recorded the burial of 'a child to Simon Mackenzie Goldsmith burges in this Burgh called Christan.' Later in that same month the *Hammermen Minute Book* detailed the following: '17 of June 1708. That day Simon Mack Kenzie Goldsmith entred freeman receaved the oath in Comon form has given his bond for his Composition which was payed the 9ᵗʰ of No.ʳ 1708.' In August 1708 McKenzie was involved in the 'Silver Spoon' controversy (see page 21).

His second child was recorded in the *Parish Register*, on 27 January 1709: 'Simon McKenzie Goold Smith and his Spous Jean Graham hade ane Child baptized named William godfayrs William Earle Seaforth, William Duff late provost William McLeane Goold Smith & William Hoame mert.'

The *Inverness Parish Register* detailed Simon McKenzie, goldsmith, as a witness at baptisms on numerous occasions: 2 May 1709 to Christian, daughter of Alexander McKenzie 'appothecarie burges'; 11 May 1709, Anna, daughter of George McKenzie 'marchend in Inverness'; 23 Sep 1709, Marjorie, daughter of George Anderson; 24 March 1713, Simon, son of Thomas Fraser, 'brewer burges of Inverness';

8 April 1714, Janet, daughter of Donald Morison, Taylor in Inverness and 9 July 1714, Margaret, daughter of David Ross, merchant in Inverness.

Another child was baptised in February 1710. 'Symon McKenzie Goldsmith in Inverness & Jane Grahame his Spous hade a child called Alexr baptised by Mr Hector McKenzie Alexr McKenzie of Balnaduthie (Balnaduthac) Alexr McKenzie apothecarie Alexr Stewart Mert Alexr McKenzie of Applecross wits.'

The death of his wife was recorded in the *Inverness Parish Register* on 14 April 1710, 'Departed Jean Graham spouse to Simon Mackenzie Goldsmith burges in this Burgh.' Her gravestone was located in the Chapel Yard Burying Ground but it is badly eroded. Another child was buried, on 22 September 1710; it was Alexander, who had been baptised earlier that year.

Later in the year Simon was noted again in the *Hammermen Minute Book* 'Nober 1st 1710 Decon Denoon gott 6£ scots to pay the Generall box for Simon McKenzie and John Cambell freedom to the Mortcloth.'

The *Inverness Town Council Minutes* recorded on 28 September 1711: 'That Day The Magistrats and Councill Have given and granted Licence and Attollerance to Simon McKenzie Gold Smith with his wife children and Servants to pass and repass the Stone bridge[10] of this Burgh free from payeing of toll money therat in all tyme here after for payment of Eight pounds Scotts money ...'

The *Hammermen Minute Book* noted Simon McKenzie next on 3 October 1712:

'Simon McKenzie for his prentis
Colin Mackenzie is to pay   04-0-0
and ...... for his Jurniman
James Gutrie one half crown   01-10-0'

The *Town Council Minutes* dated 19 April 1714 recorded:

That Day John Bayne Burrow officer has found Simon Mackenzie Goldsmith and Burges of Invernes as Caur for his fidelitie in the station as one of the officers of this Burgh And binds and enacts himself his heirs Successors and exers as Caurs for the said John Bayne his fidelitie, care, diligence obedience and punctuall attendance in the forsd station, And that he and his forsds shall relieve the Magistrats of this Burgh and their Successors in place and office of all cost skaith & damnadge that they may anyways Sustain throw the sd John Bayne his infidelity & remissness in the said office and the sd John Bayne enacts himself for his Cautioners relieff qron Act.

Simon McKenzie's signature appeared under this minute.

The *Inverness Parish Register* recorded the contracted date, 22 April 1715, for the second marriage of 'Simon MKenzie Goldsmith in Inverness & Sibylla Geddes[11] there.' There was no marriage date entered in the register.

On 13 July 1715 there was a blank space in the Baptismal Register after the recording of 'Simon McKenzie goldsmith' only. This probably related to the baptism

Communion cups by Simon McKenzie. Christie's, Glasgow

of his son, a second Alexander, who was buried in February 1717. On 3 July 1716 another child was baptised: 'Simon Mackenzie Goold Smith & his spous Sibela Geddes hade ane Child Baptd by Mr Hector McKenzie Caled /Christan/ Allexr Stuart Bailie & Donald McKenzie of Culroy witt.'

The deaths of two of Simon's children were noted in the *Inverness Parish Register* in 1717; the first was Alexander, on 11 February, followed four months later by Christan on 6 June. During the next five years the *Parish Register* detailed the baptisms of a further four children of Simon McKenzie and Sibylla: Anable, on 12 February 1718; two un-named[12], on 27 September 1720, and an un-named child[13] on 30 November 1722. Three of the above died in infancy; Kenneth, on 9 February 1721; Kathrine, on 11 January 1722 and another Alexander on 9 August 1726. It would appear that only two of Simon's nine children survived childhood: William and Anable.

Tumbler cup by Simon McKenzie
(H 4.2 cm W 5.4 cm)
Inverness Museum and Art Gallery. Ewen
Weatherspoon

The *Inverness Parish Register* recorded on 6 April 1754 the death of Simon's second wife: 'Sibilla Geddes spouse to Simon Mackenzie Goldsmith Burges.'

The *Inverness Town Council Minutes* for 18 September 1758 recorded:

> That Day there being a petition presented to the saids Magistrats & Council by Robert Anderson Goldsmith in the said Burgh representing his having Servd his Brother in law the deceast John Baillie Goldsmith in the said Burgh, his haveing acquird a further knowledge in the said business, & that there is non of his business in this Burgh therefore creaving to be admitted Burges & Freeman to the Hammermen Incorporation of this Burgh, They the saids Magistrats & Council created received & admitted the said Robert Anderson Burges & Freeman to the said Incorporation of Hammermen gratis qron Act.

Inverness Museum and Art Gallery

This proved that Simon McKenzie had ceased work as a goldsmith and, indeed, the following year the *Parish Register* recorded, on 31 October 1759, his death with the entry 'Simon Mackenzie Goldsmith Burges'.

He was the maker of a number of quaichs, thistle cups and spoons. His marks were 'MK conjoined INS', often followed by a 'date letter'. The 'N' of 'INS' is sometimes found reversed (see bottom right). The Forres communion cups, which were donated in 1643 by John Nicolson, a native of Forres, carry the letter 'T', which corresponds with the Edinburgh date letter for 1723-24, and 1724 was the year that the cups were refashioned. They bear the marks of Simon McKenzie.

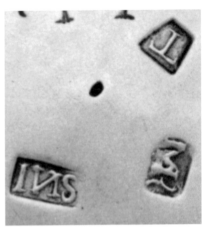

N R Shaw

JOHN GLENNIE (GLENNY) 1680–82

An entry in the *Presbytery of Inverness Minute Book*, dated 29 September 1680, reads: 'That day John Glennie Goldsmith in Inverness being referred from that Session to this dyet citted, not compering is to be sumoned to the next meitting'. Between this date and 4 October 1682 mention was frequently made of this goldsmith, described as a 'fugitive from the discipline of Aberdeen[14]'. On 12 January 1681 he did 'compear' and asked if 'they would desist from further proceeding aga'st him & he would give all satisfac'n to ye discipline of the Church', and would 'procure a testimonie from Aberdein'; however, on 9 February 1681 he was told to 'repair thither & satisfie the disciplin of the Church'. By 1 March 1682 arrangements were made for him to 'repare to Aberdeen & report a testimony thence ...'. On 22 March he agreed 'to make adress' to the presbytery and to 'obey the Ordinance'. Eventually, on 30 August 1682, the following minute stated: 'That day John Glenny Goldsmith in Inverness fugitive from the disciplin of Aberdeen haveing given so many dissapointments, and that there Came a letter to ours hands from Mr Patrick Sibbald one of the Ministers of that town, declareing his Continued Contamarie, & earnestly desireing he may be processed we remitt him to the Session of Inverness to enter in process against him'. On 4 October 1682: 'That day the Minister of Inverness declared that John Glenny Goldsmith there who was formerly under process is now fugitive to Orknay, and whither to insist in ye process against him is referred to the Synod for advice'.

The *Kirk Session Minutes* for St Nicholas, Aberdeen, recorded on 29 December 1679: 'Elspet Sheppard being formerlie delate to have fallen in fornica'n ne with John Glennie to be cited to the next day'. Despite continually being called to account, on 3 May 1680 the minute included 'John Barbar to Inverness anent John Glennie.' On 27 September of that year a missive was reported from the Ministers of Inverness 'anent John Glennie' returning to Aberdeen. The last entry in these Kirk Session records was dated 2 October 1682 when it was 'Reported that John Glennie is gone from Inverness to Orknay to reside there.'

No further reference to John Glennie has, as yet, been found. There is no mark known for this goldsmith.

GEORGE LEITH c1680–c1716

There is some doubt as to the origin of George Leith, goldsmith or merchant, in Inverness. A George Leith was apprenticed to George Walker, goldsmith, in Aberdeen, and Dr I E James, in *The Goldsmiths of Aberdeen, 1450–1850* noted that he was in the recorded accounts for 1693–94. This may have been the craftsman who worked in Banff[15] from 1700 to 1702; his name is noted in *Jackson's Silver & Gold Marks* for the same years. Of course, it is entirely possible that he moved to Inverness around 1703.

In Inverness there were many references to a George Leith, saddler, in the *Hammermen Minute Book* in the late seventeenth and early eighteenth centuries, and the following entry, on 13 August 1703, may be significant: 'That Day George Leith sone to George Leith saidler in the sd burgh has entered prentise to his sd Fraser And hes payed foretie shillings scots at hes enteir to the box.' Margaret

MacDougall, in her notes for *Inverness Silversmiths* considered this to refer to the silversmith, but the wording must cause some doubt.

There was no marriage recorded for George Leith in Banff, and the marriage records for Inverness have not survived for that period; however, the *Inverness Parish Register* detailed, on 10 February 1708, the baptism of a daughter: 'George Leith goold Smith in Invernes & his Spows Dorothia Mcpherson hade ane child baptized named (Anna) godfayrs Will Hoome Donald McCay vintiners John Neilson dyer & John Mcpherson mr of musick in Inverness'. Again, on 17 June 1709, 'George Lieth Goldsmith in Inverness & Dorothea Mcphersone his spous hade a child baptised by Mr Hector McKenzie called John who was born upon the first current John Mcphersone Musician John Baillie John Mackay Mert John Mcbain writter wits'.

In 1708 George Leith, by then acting as a merchant, decided to manufacture a set of silver spoons for a customer. However, members of the Hammermen's Craft felt that he should have renounced his guildry membership before taking up his old trade as a silversmith. Two silversmiths in the town, Simon McKenzie and William McLean, together with James Porteous, taylor (Trade's Deacon), and Walter Denoon, shoemaker (Trade's Officer), went to Leith's workshop and confiscated the spoons. The two silversmiths were fined and lost their burgess tickets; however, it forced a clarification of the Burgh Sett; the amendment was confirmed on 13 October 1709. The Magistrates returned the burgess tickets later that year (see details of the amendment to the Act of Sett). Nothing further has been discovered of George Leith while in Inverness.

On 14 June 1716 a baptism was registered in the *Kirkwall and St Ola, Orkney, Parish Register*: 'Margaret Leith Lawfull daughter to George Leith Silver Smith and Dorothea McPhersone was baptized by Mr Ker Witnesses Robert Barkie of Tankernes and Margaret Sinclair his Lady with Margaret Leith.' No further record of George Leith has been found.

WILLIAM MCLEAN c1683–1766

The first record of William McLean is of his apprenticeship to Robert Elphinston, in the *Inverness Hammermen Minute Book* on 10 November 1696: 'The sd day Robert Elphinstone late deacon hes Payed his prentise his entrie money, and hes (entered) it himselfe foure pounds ... money as payment to Johne Monro our Clark for his bygone fies his prentise was William McLean.' William McLean was recorded in the *Hammermen Minute Book* on 2 May 1705, and, on 5 October 1705[16] an entry stated 'That day Robert Miller Copersmith was entred Decon for the Corporation and hes chosen Will. McLean Goldsmith for boxmaster and on of the Counsel ...'

The *Inverness Town Council Minutes* of 23 September 1707 detailed 'That Day The Trades & Craftsmen aftermen'd gave in to the Councill ... or lists following ... viz be the Hammermen Robert Miller Coppersmith Wm McLean Goldsmith and Ro't Low Armourer ...'. (Robert Miller was elected as 'visitor or overseer to the hammermen'.)

While there was no record of William McLean's marriage, the baptism of a child was noted in the *Inverness Parish Register* on 19 December 1707: 'William McLeane

Gold Smith in Invernes & his Spows Isobell Inglish hade ane child baptd by Mr Wm Stuart on of the minesters of Invs named (Margrat) godfayrs James McLeane Leat baillie allexr McLeane marchand Wm makintosh marchand & Thomas fraser mard.' Margrat may not have been their first born child as there was a son, John, recorded as the 'Eldest lawfull son to the said William McLean' (see *Town Council Minutes*, 16 June 1740).

In August 1708 William McLean was involved in the 'Silver Spoon' controversy (see previous page).

The *Hammermen Minute Book* recorded in November 1708 that 'Robert Innes prentise to William McLean Goldsmith pay 4£ scots as his entrie.'

The *Inverness Parish Register*, 21 June 1709, recorded 'William Macklean Gold Smith and Isobel Inglish his spous hade a child baptised by Mr Robert Baillie called Magdalen Mr Robert Baillie Minr of Inverness Alexr Patersone Apothecary Thomas Kilgour watchmaker John Fraser wits.'

The *Inverness Town Council Minutes* of 20 September 1709 noted that William McLean was on the Leet for election as Deacon of the Hammermen; he was not elected.

The *Inverness Parish Register* dated 9 May 1710 recorded the death of one of his daughters: 'Departed a child to William McLeane Goldsmith burges in this burgh called Magdalene'. During the next five years the *Parish Register* detailed the baptisms of a further five children to William McLean and Isobel: William, on 3 September 1710; Alexander, on 25 September 1711, whose death was noted on 6 January 1712; Robert, on 7 July 1713, and Barbara and Isobell on 10 May 1715.

The *Inverness Kirk Session Minute Book* recorded, on 5 August 1712: 'Ordered that the Communion Cups be given to the Goldsmith in order to be reformed & made more fashionable.' On 16 September, an entry revealed the name of the Goldsmith: 'Ordered that Wm. Mclean[17] Goldsmith his accompts for translating the silver Cups[18] & making them larger & more fashionable be payed by the Church treasurer.'

The *Inverness Town Council Minutes* recorded that at a meeting held on 2 April 1714 'William McLeane Goldsmith in Inverness' acted as a 'Cautioner' and had signed the minutes accordingly.

The *Hammermen Minute Book* noted on 22 May 1714 'That day Receivd from Willam McLean Goldsmith in Inverness the sum of seven pound scots for ane Lock being Rodrick Fraser his say pise.'

The death of William's wife was noted in the *Parish Register* on 30 May 1715: 'Departed Isobel Inglish spouse to William McLeane Goldsmith burges in this Burgh.'

The *Inverness Parish Register* dated 9 March 1716 recorded his second marriage: 'Compeared William Mcleane Gold Smith & produced a testimence of his Contract of Marriage with Kathrin Lowe at Abdn Married there.' The *St Nicholas Parish Register, Aberdeen*, records their marriage on 3 March 1716: 'William McKlain merchant in Inverness, and Katherine Low Relict of Thomas Kilgour being contracted and Cautioner for the man John Deans Baillie and for the woman James Morrison Baillie payed two pound money presant'. Thomas Kilgour, watchmaker, had been a witness to the baptism of Magdalen, daughter to William McLean, in 1709, and further investigation showed that Thomas had married Katherine Low in Aberdeen, in 1701, according to the *Old Machar Parish Register*:

> August 2[d] Saturday. Comp[d] Thomas Kilgour Watchmaker in Inverness & Katherin
> Low[19] lawfl Daughter to Robt Low mercht in old Aberdeen & Contracted Marriage
> according to order They did not consign pledges Mr George Fraser Sub princl of the
> Kings Colledge Caunr for the man, Robt Low forsd for the woman they were Thrice
> proclaimed & maried here August eleventh Javij & on years being Munday at eight a
> cloke at night in Robt Lows house forsd'. The *Inverness Parish Register* recorded the
> death of 'Thomas Killgour watchmaker Burges in this Burgh' on 5 October 1710.

The *Inverness Town Council Minutes* recorded on 25 September 1716: 'That Day
The Magistrats and Councill Have Nominat and appointed the persons to be
Constables of the Burgh for the ensueing year … viz … John Fraser elder mert &
William McLeane Goldsmith …' Over the following years McLean appears on
numerous occasions, notably on 3 December 1716 'That Day the Shope and Cellar
yrto belonging under the Town house … William McLeane mert is to be rouped

*Coconut cup by
William McLean.*
National Museums of
Scotland

from the term of Whitsunday ... for the space of three years after the sd term to William McLeane mert who offered most for the same for the Sum of Thirttie Nyne pounds Scots money payable to the Thes'r of his ...'. (William McLean merchant's signature was the same as William McLean goldsmith's for 2 April 1714). On 18 August 1718:

> The Magistrats and Councill considering That there is one moneth and one halfs Cess[20] payable to His Majestie by act of parlia't of Great Brittain upon the twenty fourth day of September ensueing, Therfor and for the more speedy & effectual method of paying the sd Cess They have Nominate the persons following as Stentmasters to proportion the sd Cess upon the Inhabitants of Town & Territory who are lyable in payment of Cess viz ... William McLeane ...'

On 23 September 1718:

> That Day The provost Baillies & councllers being conveen'd within the new Session house of this burgh conform to ... and choose the persons following to rule as Magistrats for the ensueing year viz Mr Alexr Fraser provost, James Mackintosh, James Thomson, James Dunbar, William McLean, Baillies.

On 24 September 1723: 'That Day the Saids Magistrats & Councill Conformd to the said Ancient and Laudable Customs Did elect Nominate and Choose William McLean Merchant & Late Baillie of Inverness as Dean of Guild thereof for the said Ensueing year viz' from Michelmass Jajvijs[21] and Twenty three to Michelmass Jajvijs and twenty four years.' William McLean appears in the *Town Council Minutes* until 25 September 1727.

The *Inverness Parish Register* recorded the death of his wife, on 4 January 1732: 'Katharine Low spouse to William McLean Late Baillie of this Burgh.'

William's name reappears in the *Town Council Minutes*, on 20 September 1736, as 'one of the New Councillers late Baillie'. On 26 September 1737 he was elected 'counciller late Baillie', and on 27 September as a 'New Magistrate, Baillie'.

The *Town Council Minutes* for 26 September 1738 recorded:

> That Day the saids Magistrats and Town Council being Conveend, according to the antient and laudible Custome and priviledge of this Burgh for Electing and Chooseing of Magistrats to Rule and Govern this Burgh and affairs thereof for the ensuing year viz' from Michaelmass Jajvijs and therty eight till Michaelmass Jajvijs and therty nine Did in prosecution of that antient and laudible Custome & priviledge and conform to the powers lodg'd in them by the rights of the Town annent chooseing A Sheriff and Corroner within themselves / after Prayers and supplication to Almighty God for a blessing on the work by Mr Alexander Fraser one of the Ministers of the Burgh Elect and choose the persons following to Rule a Magistrats for the said ensueing year viz' William McLean Esq' Provost Sherriff & Corroner.

The *Town Council Minutes* for 16 June 1740 noted:

> That Day the saids Magistrats & Council Did Creat receive & admitt Mr John McLean Merch' at London Eldest lawfull son to the said William McLean Esq' Provost (he being occasionally here) Burges Freeman and Guild Brother of this Burgh, And appoint the Magistrats to deliver an extract thereof to him, And likewise that they render him the hearty thanks of this Council in name of the Community for the Signal & notable good offices, which he hase been in use of doing to the young men, who go recommended from this town to London, whither Merchts or Mechanicks in procureing

them, upon his recommendation & credite proper service, whereby they improve in their Severall occupations, & become usefull to themselves & Society qron Act.

On 8 January 1749 the signature of William McLean, Provost, was identical to the earlier one for William McLean, Goldsmith, albeit a little more unsteady. He was Provost between 1738-41 and again between 1747-50.

The last entry found for William McLean in the *Town Council Minutes* was 9 September 1766 when he was chosen as a member of Dean of Guild Council. By this date McLean was a very old man and it was not surprising to find the record of his death in the *Inverness Parish Register* on 12 October 1766, 'Departed William McLean late Provost & Burgher of Inverness.'

William McLean's marks were 'ML, INS' usually with a date-letter. The ML was conjoined with a pellet below. The coconut cup on page 23 is in the National Museums of Scotland.

Will. MacKleane Provost

ROBERT INNES c1688-c1725

The first noted reference to Robert Innes is in the *Inverness Hammermen Incorporation Minute Book*. It is dated November[22] 1708 and reads: 'Robert Innes prentise to William McLean Goldsmith pay 4£ Scots as his entrie.'

By 1716 it would appear that Robert Innes had begun to associate with the Guildry, as on 6 September, the *Inverness Town Council Minute Book* recorded: 'That Day Robert Innes goldsmith was Created received and admitted Burgess and Gild-brother of this Burgh of Inverness gratis qron Act.' Additionally, on 23 September 1717, the *Town Council Minute Book* detailed: 'The Councill conveened anent the Towns affairs & ... and choosing new Councillours ... made choise of the persons following ... Robert Innes Goldsmith.'

It has been suggested that Robert Innes took an apprentice in 1717 by the name of Hugh Ross, for a period of five years, who might have become the silversmith of that name in Tain, but the authors have been unable to substantiate this.

The *Inverness Town Council Minutes* also recorded, on 30 September 1717: 'That Day The Magistrats and Councill Have Given and Granted licence & attollerance to Robert Innes Goldsmith with his familie & Servants to pass & repass the Stone bridge of this Burgh free from paying of toll yrat in all tyme hereafter And that for payt of Eight pounds Scots money to Thomas Alves Thesaurer qron Act.'

The *Inverness Parish Register* noted on 24 January 1718: 'Robert Innes Goldsmith & Janet Maxwell' were contracted to marry, and they were duly married on 28 February. The *Parish Register* also detailed the baptism of four children, born to 'Robert Innes Goldsmith in Inverness', and his wife, Janet Maxwell: Mary, on 24 July 1719; Robert, on 3 December 1720 (one of the witnesses was Robert Innes, Provost of Elgin); James, on 28 July 1722 (one of the witnesses was James Innes, Provost of Elgin); the last was Jean, baptised on 3 July 1724.

Quaich by RI (unascribed).
Private collection. Ewen
Weatherspoon

*Hanoverian rat-tailed spoon by
Robert Innes.* Christie's, Glasgow

*Thistle cup by Robert Innes
(H 4.5 cms W 5.1 cms).*
Inverness Museum and Art Gallery.
Ewen Weatherspoon

The *Town Council Minute Book* for 21 September 1719 recorded that Robert Innes was again chosen as a 'Counciller' for the year. On this occasion his occupation is given as goldsmith and merchant.

The *Inverness Parish Register* recorded on 6 May 1722: 'Departed a child to Robert Innes Goldsmith burges called Robert.' It was probably a misinterpretation of this record which lead Margaret MacDougall, in *Inverness Silversmiths*, to state that Robert Innes, goldsmith, died in 1722, when it was in fact his son who died in that year. No record of Robert Innes' death has been found in Inverness.

His marks were, 'R I, INS, A', which are illustrated on a rat-tailed tablespoon (left) and a thistle cup (left). The mark on the quaich (left) is 'R I' only. It has been suggested that this may be another mark of Robert Innes, but this is not proven.

Inverness Museum and Art Gallery

COLLIN MCKENZIE C1698–C1740

The *Inverness Hammermen Incorporation Minute Book* dated 3 October 1712 recorded: 'Simon McKenzie for his prentis & Colin Mackenzie is to pay – 04-0-0 ...'

The *Inverness Town Council Minute Book* recorded an entry on 2 October 1721:

> That Day Collin Mackenzie Goldsmith Lawfull son to George Mackenzie of Gruneard was created received & admitted Burges freeman & Guild brother of this burgh gratis as the provosts burges from Michelmass Jayvijs and Twenty one to Michelmass Jayvijs & Twenty two years Wherean act.

The *Hammermen Minute Book* dated 12 January 1727 gave a further entry for Collin McKenzie:

> That Day Collin M'Kenzie Goldsmith was admitted freeman to the hammermen incorportn and has payd his Composition And is to Make ane Essey which is a Sword hilt in Silver, The Essey Masters are Donald Fraser and Andrew Dnoon and Mr. Whitehall as Oversman, And he is also oblidged to Make as an oy' part of his Essey A raised decanter in Silver and a Chiny fashioned Teapot also in Silver.

Collin McKenzie was last noted in the *Hammermen Minute Book* dated 2 September 1740 when his name appeared in a list of members of the Incorporation.

WILLIAM LIVINGSTON C1700–C1757

William Livingston was born in the County of Down in Ireland, the son of Mr John Livingston, according to *The Register of Edinburgh Apprentices* compiled by the Scottish Record Society from the City archives. The entry, dated 10 March

1714, notes that William was apprenticed to James Tait, goldsmith burgess in Edinburgh. The *Incorporation of Edinburgh Goldsmiths Apprentice Records* recorded that on 2 February 1714 James Tait paid £9 Scots to the Boxmaster and 6 shillings Scots to the Deacon. A note inserted in the margin stated that the apprenticeship was discharged on 2 February 1721.

The Kirk Session records of Colinton dated 6 June 1724 recorded that at Oxgangs, William Livingston, goldsmith in Edinburgh, and his wife Anne Tait[23] were brought before the committee of the Kirk Session because a report had been received regarding the couple, Anne 'being with child'. Fortunately, the couple were able to produce a certificate of their marriage, which had taken place on 5 October 1723 in Edinburgh. The minister was a 'chaplain to one of his Majesties men of war'.

The *Elgin Parish Register* contains a baptism, on 1 October 1724, which fits well with the fact that Anne Livingston was 'with child' in June of that year when she was called before the Kirk Session of Colinton. The child was called Adam, surprisingly not named after the paternal grandfather, John. Their next child was James[24], baptised on 7 January 1726 and the third, baptised on 13 January 1727, was named Robert, after Anne's father. The fourth, baptised on 1 August 1729, was named Euphania, after James Tait's wife. The last child born in Elgin was baptised on 17 August 1731, and named Christian. On each occasion William was recorded as a goldsmith in Elgin.

An Instrument of Sasine, registered at Elgin on 23 May 1726, recorded WILLIAM LIVINGSTOUN, goldsmith in Elgin, as a witness concerning 'the rood of Burrow bigged land with house and biggings built or to be Builded theron lying within the burgh of Elgin'.

Rev Thomas Burn's *Old Scottish Communion Plate* stated, under Elgin: 'WILLIAM LIVINGSTON (1729), late apprentice to James Tait, gave in his assay as a gold and silver smith, and the same being found good and sufficient work he was admitted.' It is clear that William had been working in Elgin before he was admitted to the freedom of the craft. In the 1989 revised edition of *Jackson's Silver & Gold Marks* there is an entry under Elgin with William Livingston's mark; this differs from the one illustrated in that it consists of the individual capitals 'w L'. *Jackson's* gives an 'earliest mention' date of 1726 for William Livingston in Elgin, but from the baptismal register we know now that he was working there in 1724. There must also be some doubt as to the entry for James Tait, in Elgin, in 1720.

In *Old Scottish Communion Plate* reference is made to communion cups found in the parishes of Boharm and Rothes[25]. The Boharm beaker is perfectly plain and bears the inscription 'These cups were gifted to the parish of Dundurkass by Margaret and Christian Lesslies of Akenwall 1728.' The companion to this cup is in possession of the Kirk-Session of Rothes, to which parish, along with Boharm, the parish of Dundurcas was added when suppressed in the year 1788. Both cups bear the contracted Town-mark 'ELG', the maker's initials of William Livingston, in Elgin about this date, and the letter 'O'.

The Dundorcas Kirk Session records for the year 1728 contain an entry concerning the gifting of money by Margaret Leslie 'for buying Communion Cups to the Session of Dundorcas'. Further entries regarding the details of payments by the executor of her estate led to the final payment of eighty five pounds Scots money. On Tuesday 25 June 1728, when the bequest had been paid to them: 'The

National Museums of Scotland

Session in regaird that the forsaid money was now given up for buying of Communion Cups thought fitt that on of our number should goo in to Elgin to the gold smith yr, and cause make them and it was agreed upon that Mr Robert Dalrymple should goo'.

The goldsmith was not named, but it would appear that there was no choice, there being only one goldsmith in Elgin at that time capable of carrying out the work, William Livingston.

On 4 August 1728 the cups were presented to the session by Mr. Robert Dalrymple, 'having this inscription upon them THESE CUPPS WERE GIVEN TO THE KIRK SESSION OF DUNDORCAS BY MARGARET AND CHRISTIAN LESLIES DAUGHTERS OF THE FAMILY OF AIKENWAY. according to the will of the deceast Margaret Leslie, with which cups the Session was very well pleased both as to the workmanship and biggness'. The cups are actually engraved 'THESE CUPS WERE GIFTED TO THE PARISH OF DUNDURKASS BY MARGARET AND CHRISTIAN LESSLIES OF AKENWALL 1728.' The Session decided to take 'four pounds 8 shillings scots money' out of the box (collection money) in order to pay the remainder 'of the making of the Cups'. The Kirk Session records have no further mention of the communion cups or the goldsmith.

The *Inverness Town Council Minute Book* dated 9 September 1728 revealed: 'That day the Sds Magistrats & Councill Created received and admitted William Livingstone Goldsmith Burges & Freeman to the Hammerman Craft gratis in consideration of the paucity of Goldsmiths in the Burgh.' This implies that William Livingstone worked in Inverness; however, as two of his children were born in Elgin after that date, it seems he took the burgess-ship and freedom to allow him to trade in Inverness.

The next mention of William Livingston and Anna Tait is in the *Glasgow Parish Register*, when a daughter called Mary was born on 13 March and baptised on 7 April 1734. There was no occupation given for William nor the witnesses, one of whom was called John Bilssand. *Jacksons' Silver & Gold Marks* lists under Glasgow an entry in 1717 for a goldsmith called Johan Gotleiff-Bilsinds, and another in 1735 for John Bilsing; possibly his son. If, as appears likely, Johan was of European extraction, it is plausible that the spelling of his name would have been very approximate, and that Johan or John could be the same person as the witness above.

The next baptism found was in Edinburgh in the year 1741. This time there was no doubt that the father, William, was a goldsmith. The child, called Henry, was born on 30 September and the witnesses were John Wallace, surgeon, and George Forbes, goldsmith. It is possible that William was working as a journeyman for George Forbes; however, we do know that Henry was apprenticed, on 3 February 1757, to George Forbes[26]. Henry Livingston's apprenticeship was transferred to James Campbell on 6 March 1759 following George Forbes' death.

*The Boharm and
Rothes Communion
cups by William
Livingston 1728.*
Courtesy of the Parishes

*The marks on the
Communion cups by
William Livingston.*

Sometime before 1747 Anne Tait died and William married for a second time. The occasion was recorded in the *Edinburgh Parish Register* for 29 November 1747; his new wife was Isobel Davidson, widow of David Yeaman. On 6 January 1751, in Glasgow, a baptism was recorded for Janet, daughter of William Livingston and Isobel Davidson; the witnesses were James Glen and John Belsing (see p29). Both witnesses were known to be goldsmiths so it is certain this is our William Livingston, now working in Glasgow. A further birth was recorded in Edinburgh on 13 May 1753, Grizell; the witnesses were James Gillsland and Edward Lothian, both master goldsmiths, and William is once again described as a journeyman goldsmith.

The last birth date so far located is 7 January 1756, for a son named Edward[27]. William was listed as a goldsmith and the two witnesses were Edward Lothian, goldsmith, and Patrick Robertson, who was also of the same guild. Edward was probably named after Edward Lothian; William may have been a journeyman to Lothian and Robertson, who by that date were in partnership and two of the best goldsmiths working in Edinburgh.

In the *Minute Book of the Edinburgh Goldsmith Incorporation* it is noted that William Livingston first asked for help from the Trade on 12 August 1755; he stated that he was 'reduced by sickness' and in 'great Want' and that he had been a journeyman goldsmith 'in this Place' for forty years[28]. The Incorporation paid him £1 sterling and in November granted him a further £1. On 25 May and 15 September of 1756 similar grants were made. The last petition was made by William on 24 May 1757, and once again £1 was paid.

In *The Roll of Edinburgh Burgesses* published by the Scottish Record Society, the following entry appears: 'Livingston Wm. Goldsmith B., as p. to James Taitt, Goldsmith B. (to Mar 1744) 12 Jan 1757.' As a Burgess, William Livingston, and especially his family in this particular case, would have been entitled to the extra privileges that burgess-ship brought.

A further search of the *Incorporation Minute Books* revealed 'Petition of Isobel Davidson Relict of William Levingstone Goldsmith & Burgess of Edinr now deceast craving that the Incorporatn. would prefer Janet Levingstone Daughter of the said Willm. Levingstone to a presentation in the Trades Maiden Hospital[29].' From this petition, dated 4 December 1759, we learn that William was dead. A further petition from Janet on 10 February 1761 requested £20 Scots money for entry to the hospital.

William Livingston did not leave a will and no burial record in Edinburgh has been found.

The illustrated marks of William Livingston are on a spoon held by the National Museums of Scotland and the Communion Cups of the parishes of Boharm and Rothes which bear the contracted mark 'ELG' with William Livingston's initials and the letter 'O' (opposite).

JOHN MUNRO 1702

Margaret MacDougall's notes for *Inverness Silversmiths* state that on 5 August 1702 John Munro was admitted to the Hammermen's Craft and was the late apprentice of William McLean. However, as she states that William McLean was also admitted to the craft on this date there appears to be a discrepancy. The *Inverness Hammermen*

Minute Book is missing, and the microfilm copy cannot confirm any of these details.

Jackson's Silver & Gold Marks, third edition, illustrated marks which they considered may belong to John Munro. They are 'M, INS, cornucopia'.

JOHN BAILLIE c1703–53

The first noted entry[30] for John Baillie, goldsmith, is in the Inverness *Hammermen Minute Book*:

> Invernes thirteenth Day of September one thousand Seven hundred and thirty five years. That Day John Baillie Goldsmith in the sd Burrow was admitted freeman to the Hammer mens Incorporation and has payed his Composition and is to make an Essay which is a Sword hilt of Silver a Silver tea pot of a China fashion and likeways a raised Decanter in Silver; The Essey Masters are Donald Fraser present Deacon of the Above Incorporation William Pringle late Deacon of the samen Incorporation and Charles McCulloch Gunsmith in the sd Burrow oversman.

In 1735 an entry in the *Inverness Burgh Treasurer's Accounts Book* recorded a payment of £15-16-0 Scots to John Baillie for a silver box to hold the Burgess Ticket, on the award of a Burgess-ship of Inverness to General Oglethorpe.

The *Inverness Parish Register* recorded the marriage of John Baillie on 3 September 1737 with the entry 'John Baillie Goldsmith & Mrs Janet Anderson[31]'. The *Inverness Parish Register* recorded the baptisms of their nine children: Elizabeth[32], December 1738; Mary, 5 May 1741; John, 24 April 1743; James, 1 August 1744; Katharine, 4 April 1746; Alexander, 8 July 1747; Janet, 26 May 1749; Jean, 9 September 1750, and Elizabeth, 29 August 1752. John Baillie was recorded as a goldsmith on all occasions, except at the baptism of John, in 1743, when he was styled silversmith.

The *Inverness Parish Register* recorded on 4 April 1739 the death of his daughter Elizabeth: 'Bettie Baillie a child of John Baillie Goldsmith Burges'.

The *Hammermen Minute Book*, dated 1739, listed among a number of bills due to the Incorporation one for John Baillie, for 18s 4d. In the same *Minute Book*, for 28 August 1740, the following was recorded, 'Likewise Robert & Lachlan Baillies payed eight pound Scots money as there apprentice dues haveing served prentice to John Baillie Goldsmith.'

The *Burgh Treasurer's Accounts Book* contains an entry under 'Public Works & Reparations', dated 1740, for the payment of £24-4-0 Scots to John Baillie, silversmith, for engraving the Town's Arms on their two drums.

The *Inverness Town Council Minutes* dated 17 September 1744 record:

> That Day the saids Magistrats & Council ... the election of the Deacons of the six incorporat Trades ... Viz. For the Hammermen William McDonald Armourer Lachlan Dallas Peutherer & John Baillie Goldsmith ... which Leets being considered by the S'ds Magistrats & Town Council, They made choise of & nominated & Appointed ... The said John Baillie Deacon of the Hammermen.'

The following week the *Inverness Town Council Minutes* contained the following:

> 'Att Inverness the twenty fourth day of September Jajvijs & fourty Four years ... That Day the said Senior Baillie William McIntosh Reported that in obedience to the Act

of Council of the Seventeenth Currt., he did conveen the Deacons of the Six Incorporated trades, And that in his presence John Baillie Deacon of the Hammermen was
by his the said Baillies Supernumerary voice Elected Deacon Conveener of the said
Incorporated trades of this Burgh for the ensueing year...' The fact that John Baillie
was elected Deacon Convenor was noted in the *Hammermen Minute Book*, 26 October
1744.

On 30 October 1745 the *Burgh Treasurer's Accounts Book* detailed that 'John Baillie
Goldsmith & Vintner' was paid £118-19-0 and £4-0-0 for provisions at 'Intertain-
ments' given by the Council.

The *Town Council Minutes* recorded, at a meeting held on 16 September 1745,
that John Baillie again stood for election on the Trades' Leet but he was not chosen.
He was not on the Leet for the following year, but in 1749 the *Town Council Minutes*
recorded: 'At Inverness the eighteenth day of September Jajvijs & fourty nine years
... Election of the Deacons of the six Incorporate Trades ... Viz. For the Hammermen Lachlan Dallas Peutherer John Baillie Goldsmith Daniel Denoon Peutherer
...' (the latter was elected).

The *Inverness Parish Register* noted, on 28 June 1750, the death of 'Katharine
Baillie a child of John Baillie Goldsmith Burges'.

The *Parish Register* recorded the burial of John Baillie with this modest entry on
19 May 1753: 'John Baillie Goldsmith Burges'. *The Friars Churchyard, Inverness,
Monumental Inscriptions Index*, held by Inverness Library, contains the following:
'Jean[33], daughter of the late Mr. John BAILLIE, gold smith and wife of Alexander
SIMPSON died March 5th 1786 aged 35 yrs.' Also, 'John Baillie, gold smith, who died
18th day of May 1757 aged 50 yrs[34].'

*Milk jug by John
Baillie (H 12 cms).*
Inverness Museum and
Art Gallery. Ewen
Weatherspoon

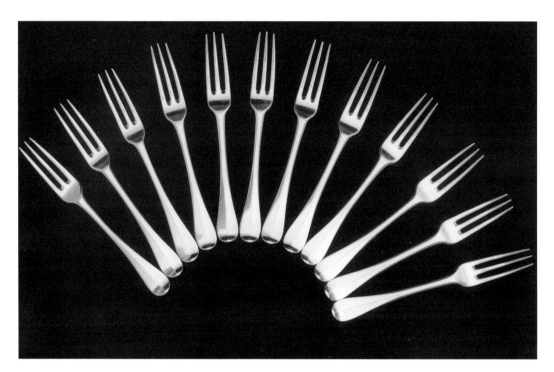

Three-pronged forks by John Baillie.
Private collection. Ewen Weatherspoon

The *Hammermen Minute Book* revealed, on 21 November 1754, one last piece of information regarding John Baillie: 'Of said date Robt. Anderson Goldsmith haveing payed Six shillings & Eightpence Sterling as his apprentice dues haveing Served prentice with John Baillie Goldsmith.'

There were only four known apprentices to John Baillie: Robert & Lachlan Baillie (recorded paying apprentice dues on 28 August 1740); Collin MacKenzie, from 2 August 1741 for 5 years (indenture registered 8 November 1742); Robert Anderson (recorded paying apprentice dues on 21 November 1754).

In John Baillie's testament, inventory and confirmation, his wife, Janet Anderson[35], was recorded as the 'widow of the deceast John Baillie Goldsmith in Inverness'. In the confirmation the names of two of Janet's brothers were given as cautioners: Ludovick Anderson, square wright, and Robert Anderson, goldsmith, both in Inverness. John and Janet's eldest lawful son, John Baillie, was a witness to the confirmation.

John Baillie's signature appears (below) as recorded on Collin MacKenzie's apprenticeship indenture.

Baillie made quaichs with the typical hatched lines which almost invariably decorated the lugs. Additionally, there is a fine pair of beer mugs made by him in a private collection.

His marks were 'I B, INS, .X'. However, other marks 'I B, F B, fleur-de-lys' have been attributed to him, but there are doubts as to whether they are his marks.

INDENTURE BETWEEN JOHN BAILLIE AND COLLIN MACKENZIE - 1742

This Indenture made and entered into betwixt John Baillie Goldsmith in Inverness on the one part and Collin Mackenzie Son to Alexander Mackenzie of Lentran with the Special advice and Consent of his said father, and he as takeing burden on him for his said Son on the other part Binds and obliges the saids parties in manner following. That is to Say the said Collin Mackenzie with advice and Consent foresaid hereby Becomes apprentice and Servant to the said John Baillie in his Art and vocation of the Goldsmith Trade, And all other his lawfull Commands. And that for the space of five years Compleat from and after the said Collins Entry which is hereby Declared to have Commenced the second day of August last by past. During which space of five years the said Collin Mackenzie as principall and with and for him the said Alexander Mackenzie of Lentran as Cautioner Bind and oblige them Conjunctly and Severally their heirs Executors & Successors, That he the said Collin Mackenzie Shall be ane honest faithfull and obedient apprentice and Servant and shall punctually attend his said masters service and nowayes absent himself therefrom without his leave first asked and obtained under the penalty of Six Shillings Eight pennies Scots money or two Days Service for each days absence, And sicklike that he shall not play at Cards Dyce nor any other immoderate Games, neither haunt or frequent Taverns nor the Company of idle Leud and debauched people. That he shall not Committ fornication Nor Contract in Matrmony during the space foresaid under the penalty of Serving two years longer than the said Space of five years. And finally that he shall be such ane apprentice, as that his said Master shall sustain no Damnadge through his default under the penalty of Redressing all such Damnadges. Likeas the said Alexander Mackenzie of Lentran has engaged to content & pay to the said John Baillie in name of apprentice fee for his Said Son the Sum of Five hundred merks scots money whereof he has instantly delivered him the Sum of Twenty pounds Sterling, and the Remainder being Seven pounds fifteen Shillings Six pence and two thirds of a penny Sterling he obliges him and his heirs thankfully to Content & pay to the said John Baillie his heirs or Assigneys in full of the said apprentice for precisely at and upon the Second day of August next One thousand Seven hundred and fourty three years. With failzie and annual rent according to Law. And in Like manner the said Alexander Mackenzie binds and obliges him and his foresaids to uphold the said Collin Mackenzie his son During the Space foresaid in all Cloths & habutriaments of body Requisite as also to free and Relieve the said John Baillie from payment of all publick burdens due to His Majestie or to the Town and Trades of Inverness on account of the foresd Apprentice. For the which Causes and on the other part the said John Baillie binds and obliges him sufficiently to teach and Instruct the said Collin Mackenzie his apprentice in his foresaid Art & Vocation of the Goldsmith trade, and to conceall no part thereof from him So far as he is skilled in himself & the apprentice Has a Capacity to conceive. And to mantain him at Bedd board and washing during the Space foresaid Suitable to ane apprentice of his Station. And both parties oblige them to perform the premises hine inde under the penalty of one hundred merks Scots money by and attour performance. And they Consent to the Registration hereof in the Books of Councill and Session or others competent that all Executorrals need- full may pass thereupon in form as effeirs and thereto They Constitute.

Their prors^d & In witnes whereof thir presents {written on this & the preceeding page of Stampd paper by Nathanael McIntosh Writer in Inverness } are Subscribed by them as follows. Vist by the said Alexander Mackenzie of Lentran att Arcan the twenty Seventh day of September Jajvijs and fourty two years before these witnesses Alexander Simpson Tenent & William Junor Glover both in Arcan and by the said John Baillie and Collin Mackenzie att Inverness the twenty Eighth day of September & year last as mentioned before these witnesses William MacIntosh Senior Merchant & late Baillie of Inverness William Fraser Town Clerk of the said Burgh & the sd Nathanael McIntosh. (All the above signed).

Att INVERNESS the eighth day of November Jajvijs fourty two years. That Day the within Indenture was recorded in the Register Appointed for recording of Inden- tures within the Burgh of INVERNESS By me Willm Fraser.

(Around 1740   Merk = 13s-4d scots   Merk = 1s-1⅓d sterling   Scottish £ = ½₂ of £sterling)

ALEXANDER MACKINTOSH 1716

The following entry appears in the *Inverness Parish Registers*:

30th October 1716.

McCoulloch.   Charles Mc Coulloch Gunn Smith & his
               spous Janet Mackintosh had ane Child Bap^'d
               by M^r. Robert Baillie Caled Marjorie, Alex^r
               Wright: William dirk Carpenter & Alex^r
               Mackintosh Goold Smith witt.

While Alexander Mackintosh was recorded as a goldsmith, he was probably a journeyman. No evidence has so far come to light that he was a master goldsmith, and there is no known record of a mark for him.

ROBERT ANDERSON c1733-92

Robert Anderson was probably born about 1733, the son of James Anderson of Knocknagiele and his wife Elizabeth Gordon. He was apprenticed to his brother-in-law, John Baillie, from about 1747; the apprenticeship was registered, after its completion, on 21 November 1754, eighteen months after the death of his master.

He was admitted a freeman and of his craft on 23 April 1755; the *Inverness Hammermen Minute Book* recorded: 'That Day Robert Anderson was admitted freeman as Goldsmith and gave in his Esay which was aproven of, and likewise gave his Note for his Composition &c to the trade, and the Same was atested by ... Robt Smith. Dea'. N. B. The Esay was the piece of work that goes Comonly in this place.' On 28 October 1755, 'At Michalmas last Alex^r Squair Chosen Deacon, ... Key Masters James Fraser Robt Anderson & Dan'l Denoon ... The following bills are delivered the present boxmaster ... Bill Robt Anderson £3.' On 3 December 1755

'Then Robert Anderson payed in part of his bill to the trade two pound Sterling and the Same was lodged in the box - Alexr Squair Deacon.'

The *Inverness Burgh Treasurer's Accounts Book* noted on 27 September 1756 the payment of £10-16-0. to Robert Anderson, goldsmith, 'for engraving the Towns Arms on two Blasons for the Towns Carriers'.

The *Inverness Town Council Minutes* for 18 September 1758 recorded:

That Day there being a petition presented to the Saids Magistrats & Council by Robert Anderson Goldsmith in the Said Burgh representing his having Servd his Brother in law the deceast John Baillie Goldsmith in the Said Burgh, his haveing acquird a further knowledge in the Said business, & that there is non of his business in this Burgh therefore creaving to be admitted Burges & Freeman to the Hammermen Incorporation of this Burgh, They the Said Magistrats & Council created received & admitted the Said Robert Anderson Burges & Freeman to the said Incorporation of Hammermen gratis qron Act.

The *Minute Book of the Hammermen Incorporation* recorded in December 1758, that 'At Michalmas last John Grant Copper Smith was (elected) Deacon Robt Anderson boxmaster ...' On 15 December 1759, 'At Michalms Last John Grant was Chosen Deacon Robt Anderson Boxmaster ...' The same day he was recorded as having given in the Boxmaster's account 'which was aproven of'. On 20 December 1760 he was noted as acting as 'oversman[36]'. On the same day, 'At Michalemass

Wine funnel stand by Robert Anderson.
Private collection.
Ewen Weatherspoon

Robert Anderson

Aberdeen Journal 26 November 1792

last John Grant Coppersmith was Ellected Deacon and of this date Robert Anderson Gold Smith was by the meeting Reelected Boxmaster.' On the 22 December 1760 'Robert Anderson Silversmith paid nine Shills & two pence Sterling as the aprentice dues of his aprentice John Grant and the dues of his Jurneman John Campabell.' On 22 December 1761 'At Michelmas last John Grant Coppersmith was Reelected Deacon for the Inshewing year And of this date Robert Anderson Goldsmith was Reelected boxmaster the key masters Continued as Formerly the Councile of Trade as the Former year.'

Robert Anderson was also a Freemason and a member of No 6 St John's Old Kilwinning Lodge, Inverness. *Freemasonry in Inverness* by Alexander Ross, states that Robert Anderson was appointed as a Junior Warden in 1759, Senior Warden in 1761 and Master in 1763. He was also recorded as Master for the years 1775 to 1777, and 1779 and 1780.

The *Inverness Parish Register* recorded his marriage, in the year 1766: 'Robert Anderson Goldsmith and Lilias McKinnon February 22'.

He continued to take an active part in the affairs of his craft and was again noted as an 'oversman' in the *Hammermen Minute Book* on 1 October 1766. On 10 October 1767 it recorded 'John mDonald Watchmaker ... Admitted to his assey which is an Eight day Clock the Sayz masters are Robert Anderson Goldsmith Daniel Dunoon Peuterer & John Grant Coppersmith as oversman...' On 11 February 1768 it mentioned: 'The Council of Trade Robt Smith Sadler Robt Anderson Silversmith Daniel Dunoon Peuterer & James Fraser Blacksmith', and he appeared as a member of the Trade's Council on numerous occasions over the next twenty years. On 10

February 1772 the *Hammermen Minute Book* recorded: 'Received six shillings & eight pence from Robert Anderson Goldsmith as the Apprentice dues of Hector McLean.'

The *Inverness Parish Register* for 19 June 1788 noted the death of his wife: 'Departed Liliash McInvin Spouse to Robert Anderson Gold Smith in this Burgh.' His death was recorded in the *Parish Register* on 12 November 1792, 'Dep:Robert Anderson Gooldsmith.'

The *Aberdeen Journal* of 26 November 1792 carried a notice to creditors (opposite).

As well as hollow-ware, Robert Anderson also produced both Hanoverian and Old English pattern flatware. His marks were 'R A, CAMEL, INS', or 'R A, CAMEL, C' which were always boldly punched.

THOMAS BORTHWICK 1750–C1794

Thomas Borthwick was born on 3 June 1750, in Leith. He was baptised on 14 June and his parents were recorded as Joseph Borthwick, a ship master, and Marion Evanson. Joseph and Marion had been married in Edinburgh on 10 October 1742. Joseph was described as a portioner[37], in Logtoun, parish of Dalkeith, 'now in S.W.' parish of Edinburgh; his wife, Marion, was the relict of Edward Chalmers, ship master in Leith. Joseph was described as a merchant at the birth of his first two children, twins, in 1743; a shipmaster at the baptism of an un-named child in 1745; a mariner in 1757, and finally a wine cooper in 1766.

Thomas Borthwick was apprenticed to the Edinburgh goldsmith Robert Clark. The *Apprentice Book of the Goldsmiths of Edinburgh* recorded his entry on 20 December 1766:

> Compeared Robert Clark Goldsmith in Edinr & produced Indentures dated the 19th & 20th Decr Currt past betwixt him and Thomas Borthwick Son of Joseph Borthwick Wine Cooper in Leith and desired that an Abstract thereof might be recorded in the Trades Books which the Trade thought reasonable Therefore the preceeding Abstract of said Indentures is hereby recorded in terms of the Acts of the Trade thereanent he having paid Thirty Shillings to the poor of the Trade & six pence to the Magdalen Chappel.

To prove conclusively that Thomas Borthwick, goldsmith apprentice in Edinburgh and later silversmith in Inverness, was the son of Joseph Borthwick, portioner, merchant, ship master and mariner, a link had to be established. This was achieved by a search of the *Particular Registers of Sasines for Edinburgh*; a sasine dated 29 April 1786 provided the information:

> Said Thomas Waterstene having and holding a disposition and assignation of the date mentioned in the precept of Sasine after inserted made and granted by Joseph Borthwick portioner of Dalkeith and Thomas Borthwick merchant in Inverness his Son whereby for the Causes therein mentioned They disponed to and in favours of the Said Thomas Waterston his heirs and assigneys All and haill that tenement of land houses and others with the Yard and Croft of land adjacent there to of old pertaining to umquhile Robert Yool lying in the town of Lugtoun...

Additionally, an earlier sasine, dated 7 January 1780, recorded,

In presence of me Notary publick and witnesses subscribing compeared personally Robert Skinner wright in Leith as attorney for and in name of Thomas and Johanna Borthwicks children of Joseph Borthwick Portioner of Lugton and Marion Evanson relict of Edward Charlmers Shipmaster in Leith now spouse of the said Joseph Borthwick...

These documents prove conclusively the parentage of Thomas Borthwick.

The *Inverness Town Council Records* for 2 November 1772 detail a petition by Thomas Borthwick:

Thomas Bothwick Jeweler & Goldsmiths petition.
    That Day there was a petition preferrd by Thomas Bothwick Jeweler & Goldsmith at Edinr. Humbly Shewing that their Petitioner servd for many years at Edinr. & learnd the said trade & business & thereafter went to London where he servd As A Journy man to be further instructed in the sad business That their Petitioner was informd, that for many years past, there was only one person of the forsaid Craft to serve the Town & Country notwithstanding that by the Act of Sett & constitution of this Burgh there should be at least two of each Incorporation therein for serveing the Town & Country, which induced their Petitioner to come north to sett up his forsaid business under the protection & countinance of their Honours. Therefor craveing it would please their Honours to consider the premises & to creat receive & admitt their Petitioner Burges & freeman to the Hammermen Incorpora" of this Burgh As the petition signd by him

Luckenbooth by Thomas Borthwick.
Private collection

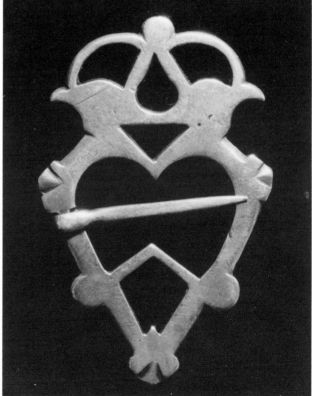

bears, & there haveing ben given a Certificat by John[38] Clark Jeweler & gold Smith at
Edinr with whom he servd of his sufficiency in the forsaid trade & of his moral Char-
acter, They therefor creat receive & admitt the said Thomas Bothwick Burges &
freeman to the said Hammermen Incorporation gratis qron Act.

The *Inverness Burgh Treasurer's Accounts Book* record that Thomas Borthwick was
in possession of the '5th Shop' in the 'Town House' and that the rental due from
Whitsunday 1777 was £4-6s-od, similarly for 1778.

There was no record in Inverness of a marriage for Thomas Borthwick; however,
the following was noted in the *Inverness Parish Register*: 'Thomas Borthwick, Goldsmith, begotten in fornication, Isable, 10 December 1786, from Katherine Fraser.'

The *Town Council Minutes*, dated 27 July 1789, record that the Tollbooth Steeple
had been pulled down and that a number of inhabitants had previously come
forward to subscribe towards the pulling down and rebuilding of the said Steeple.
The list, dated 29 April 1789, contains the name of Thomas Borthwick, who
subscribed two guineas.

The *Particular and General Registers of Inhibitions*, held by the Scottish Record
Office, provided evidence that Thomas Borthwick had run into financial difficulties whilst in Inverness. An Inhibition at Inverness, dated 7 July 1792, recorded that
an intended action had been raised against 'John McPherson Thomas Borthwick
& William Welsh in Invs all as Partners under the firm of McPherson Welsh & Co
late Merchants there ...' It continued 'that they ought & Should be decerned and
ordained by decreet of the Lords of our Council & Session to make payment to the
Pursuers of the sum of Sixty Six Pounds eleven Shillings Sterling ...' The pursuers
of this debt were John T Younge & Sons[39], Merchants in Sheffield. There was a
further Inhibition, dated 18 March 1793, followed by a Petition, dated 6 March
1794, brought by Hodgson & Nicolson, Merchants in Birmingham, against John
McPherson & Co, Merchants in Inverness, whose partners, John McPherson and
Thomas Borthwick, were being pursued for goods supplied between July 1790 and
October 1791 totalling £364-6-7½d. Although £30 had been paid on 4 June 1792
and £100 on 29 April 1793, the petition stated 'That the said John McPherson &
Co. are under diligence by Horning and Caption for debt and have fled or
absconded for their personal safety as will be instructed by a variety of diligences at
the instance of Sundry Creditors of the Bankrupts who are now utterly insolvent.'
It continued, 'May it therefore please your Lordships to grant warrant for citing the
said John McPherson & Company and John Macpherson Merchant in Inverness
and Thomas Borthwick late Merchant there now at Montrose the individual partners in that concern ...' From this we now know that Thomas Borthwick moved
from Inverness to Montrose sometime between July 1792 and March 1794. No
further evidence has been found of Thomas Borthwick after this date.

During his time in Inverness there was no record of his name in the *Hammermen Incorporation Minute Book*. His marks were 'T B, CAMEL, INS'.

CHARLES JAMESON C1754-1829

Charles Jameson was born about 1754, but no record of his birth or baptism has been found; we have found no trace of an apprenticeship.

The *Inverness Town Council Minutes* dated 27 February 1797 stated on his admission as a Freeman Burgess of the Hammermen Incorporation that, 'Thereafter Charles Jameson Silver Smith in Inverness was upon his Petition received and admitted Freeman Burgess of the Hammermen Incorporation in terms of the Act of Sett there having been no other Exercising that Craft in Town when he came to it and the Burgess oath was admintstred to him.' This would indicate a date prior to the admission of Alexander Stewart to his craft freedom on 10 May 1796, but perhaps after the death of Robert Anderson in 1792, assuming of course, that Robert Anderson had worked right up to his death. The *Inverness Journal* of 27 August 1813 records, however, that Charles Jameson 'Takes this opportunity of returning his most grateful thanks to his friends and the public for the many favours conferred on him in the way of his business last twenty-seven years.' This implies that Charles Jameson had been in business as a silversmith in Inverness from around 1786, and would have overlapped with Robert Anderson, who died in 1792, and Thomas Borthwick, who was still in Inverness in 1792. It is possible, of course, that Robert Anderson had not worked at his trade for some time and we know that Thomas Borthwick had for many years been a merchant. It is interesting to note that the Phillips of Edinburgh auction catalogue of 20 February 1987 listed a soup ladle (lot 203), with the following marks: 'C J, four London hallmarks for 1787[40], INS'.

Charles Jameson was a Freemason and a member of the St John's Old Kilwinning Lodge, according to *Freemasonry in Inverness* by Alexander Ross. Charles Jameson was recorded only once, when he was Treasurer in 1794. This was a post that would have been entrusted to an honest and proven member, implying that he had been a Mason for some time but not necessarily in Inverness.

In the *Inverness Parish Register* we found that a Charles Jameson, merchant, married Katherine Inglis on 17 August 1789[41]. They had at least five children: Ketherecon, born 14 August 1790; Hugh, baptised 5 October 1791; William, baptised 26 January 1793; Charles, born 4 November 1795, and George Inglis, born 24 November 1801. However, this was not the gold and silversmith.

A further search of the *Inverness Parish Register* located the children of Charles Jameson, silversmith, and his wife Jean Denoon. They were: Elizabeth[42], baptised 28 May 1795; Mary Inglis[43], baptised 3 November 1796; David Denoon[44], baptised 13 June 1799; William, baptised 8 July 1802; Hugh, born 4 October 1804, and Catherine Inglis[45], born 3 November 1805. No record was found of the marriage of Charles Jameson and Jean Denoon. There appears to have been a seventh child as the *Parish Register* recorded, on 21 June 1798, the following burial: 'Dep a Child of Mr Jamison Goldsmith'. No baptism has been found for this child in Inverness, and the three children born prior to this date lived into adulthood. Jean's father was the Rev David Denoon and her mother Mary Inglis of Kingsmills; they married on 30 November 1761 and were both from important local families. Jean was the fourth and last child, born in Killearnan on 15 June 1766; her mother died the following year, on 30 April 1767. There was obviously a family connection between the two Charles Jamesons as the names of their children indicates, and further research may prove that they were, in fact, cousins.

The *Inverness Hammermen Minute Book* recorded that Charles Jameson, goldsmith, petitioned and was admitted into the Hammermen's Incorporation on 12 June 1800, after paying the sum of £3-10s.

The *Town Council Minutes* recorded at a meeting of 10 August 1801, that 'Mr. Charles Jameson, Silver Smith, was one of the Stent[46] Masters for the Craftsmen'.

The death of another child, in 1803, was noted in the *Inverness Parish Register*: 'March 29 Dep a Child of Charles Jamison Goldsmith.' This child was almost certainly William, who had been baptised the previous year.

The next occasion Jamseon was noted in the *Hammermen Minute Book* was in connection with a bill for £20 on 26 June 1806.

The *Town Council Minutes* dated 25 September 1809 reported: 'The Clerk produced a List made up by him of the Members of the different Incorporations who have been admitted to the freedom of the Town since the year one thousand seven hundred and seventy three and which List was given to the Deacon Convener to be communicated to the different Incorporations that such of their Members as are not Burgesses may furthwith apply to the Town Council in the usual manner ...' Under Hammermen, Charles Jameson, silversmith, was recorded, with the date, 27 February 1797. His name was also repeated on the list dated 22 September 1812.

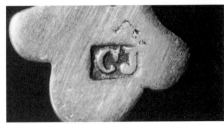

Luckenbooth by Charles Jameson. Private collection

43

Quaich by Charles Jameson.
Private collection.
Ewen Weatherspoon

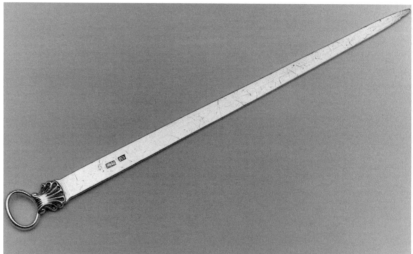

Meat skewer by Charles Jameson.
Private collection. Ewen Weatherspoon

Cream scoop by Charles Jameson.
Private collection.
Ewen Weatherspoon

FRIDAY, AUGUST 27, 1813.

CHARLES JAMESON,
GOLDSMITH AND JEWELLER,
CHURCH-STREET, INVERNESS,

TAKES this opportunity of returning his moſt grateful thanks to his friends and the public for the many favours conferred on him in the way of his buſineſs laſt twenty-feven years. He now begs leave to intimate that he has admitted as a Partner ROBERT NAUGHTEN, a Young Man thoroughly qualified to carry on the trade in all its branches. His known abilities have already convinced C. Jameſon's Cuſtomers that their orders in time coming will be executed with promptitude and diſpatch. C. J. has further to intimate that the buſineſs from this date will be carried on under the firm of JAMESON and NAUGHTEN. Orders directed under the firm of the Company, or to either of the Partners, will meet due attention. Thoſe who are pleaſed to favour the Company with their commands may rely on having their work done in a workman-like manner, and on the ſhorteſt notice.

Coats of Arms, Creſts, &c. engraved in the neateſt ſtyle. Higheſt price given for Old Gold and Silver.

There were only four known apprentices trained by Charles Jameson: Donald Fraser, registered 19 October 1801, who became a goldsmith in his own right in Inverness; Hugh Reid, 27 September 1805; Charles Fowler (Foular), 27 September 1805, who became a goldsmith in Elgin, and Robert Naughty (Naughten), 15 October 1809, who became his Master's partner in 1813. An advertisement in the *Inverness Journal* of 27 August 1813 recorded the partnership of Jameson and Naughten, with a business address in Church Street. Under the partnership there were two known apprentices: John Fraser Reid and John Ross, both registered on 11 October 1815.

The *Town Council Minutes*, dated 21 April 1817, following a letter from Lord Sidmouth dated 27 January 1817, Whitehall, London, referring to the strengthening of Civil Power, recorded 'Special Constables were accordingly appointed ...' Charles Jameson, merchant, and Charles Jameson, goldsmith, were among those nominated.

The last occasion Charles Jameson was noted in the *Hammermen Minute Book* was at a meeting of 16 November 1819, when his name and that of Robert Naughten appeared after the minutes. *Pigot's Directory* 1821-22 & 23 recorded Robert Naughten working alone as a jeweller, in Church Street, Inverness.

Pair of Salts by Jameson and Naughten.
Christie's, Glasgow

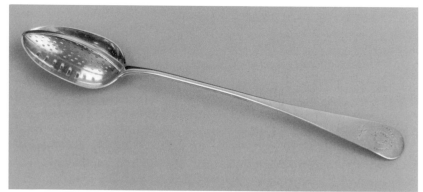

Straining spoon by Charles Jameson.
Private collection.
Ewen Weatherspoon

Wine funnel by Charles Jameson.
Private collection.
A C Cooper, London

46

The *Inverness Courier* of 13 July 1876 carried an advertisement for Robert Naughten's business having been 'ESTABLISHED SIXTY YEARS'. This would broadly tie in with the partnership between Charles Jameson and Robert Naughten, which commenced in August 1813. However, it might also indicate that 1816 was the year in which Robert Naughten parted from Charles Jameson.

The *Inverness Courier* of 29 April 1829, reported his death thus, 'Here, on the 8th instant, Mr Charles Jameson, late Goldsmith, aged 74.' He was interred in the Chapel Yard Burying Ground, Inverness; the inscription on his headstone, transcribed at a later date, read as follows: 'Charles JAMESON late goldsmith, Inverness, died 8th April 1829; and his spouse Jean JAMESON died 10 May 1838; also their granddaughter Catherine J. Smith, youngest daughter of Mr James Smith, bookseller, Inverness who died 9th Dec 1857 aged 20 years.'

His marks were usually 'C J, J, INS, CAMEL', but not all of the last three marks were used on every piece he made; often the 'J' is struck sideways. The wine funnel (opposite) has the marks 'C J, J' only. His 'C J' mark has been seen with or without a pellet.

ALEXANDER McPHERSON c1762-89

In the *Inverness Parish Register*, dated 30 July 1785, an entry states 'Alex' McPherson Goldsmith & his Spouse Marg' M'Don' had a child baptized by M' George Watson called Anable / Hugh M'Intosh Cooper & Robert Steel Coper Smith W'.' The baptism of another child to Alexander and Margaret was recorded in the *Parish Register* on 27 June 1787; her name was Katherine.

The *Hammermen Incorporation Minute Book*, dated 17 March 1788, contains an entry: 'Upon a Petition present by Alex' McPherson Silver Smith to the Corporation praying he might be admitted a member The meeting after Considering his Petition upon his giving his Bill for Three pounds and paying 10/- for the Morth Cloth he was accordingly sworn in a Member of said Incorporation.' No record of birth or baptism has been found in Inverness for Alexander McPherson.

A further entry in the *Parish Register*, dated 8 September 1789, details: 'Alex' McPherson Gold Smith deases'd and his Spous Margt McDonald had there Child Book'd to be Call'd Alex' [47].'

The *Parish Register* recorded on 28 April 1789, the death of Alexander McPherson; it simply read: 'Dep Alexr McPherson Silver Smith.' He was buried in the Chapel Yard Burying Ground, Inverness, and the inscription on his gravestone read as follows: 'Alexander MACPHERSON, silversmith of Inverness died 28 April 1789 aged 27 yrs: his spouse Margaret McDONALD; and their children'.

Margaret MacDougall, in her notes for *Inverness Silversmiths*, states that she had seen the marks 'AMP, INS' on brooches and a few spoons, but that his work was rather scarce. The authors have not seen this mark during their research.

CHAPTER THREE

INVERNESS CRAFTSMEN OF THE NINETEENTH CENTURY

DONALD FRASER c1780–c1829

THOMAS STEWART (Thomas McGuirman) 1784–1856

ROBERT NAUGHTEN 1786–1857

ALEXANDER MCLEOD c1786–1870

JOHN ANDERSON c1791–c1818

ALEXANDER MACRAE 1794–1856

CHARLES CROTCHIE c1796–1858

WILLIAM MUNRO c1800–c1842

JOHN MACRAE c1804–1872

WILLIAM MASON 1808–1870

DONALD MACKENZIE c1809–c1851

ANGUS MCLEOD c1810–c1845

JAMES PEARSON c1812–c1852

RICHARD LOCKWOOD STEWART 1812–87

JOHN FARLAHA LEITH PRATT c1820–1901

ROBERT NAUGHTEN junior 1830–99

JAMES FERGUSON 1834–1910

WILLIAM FERGUSON 1836–98

ALEXANDER DALLAS 1838–1906

PETER GEORGE WILSON 1843–1925

JAMES MACBEAN c1847–1905

ARTHUR MEDLOCK 1852–1930

WILLIAM REID CHRISTIE 1863–c1916

ALEXANDER WILLIAM FRASER 1863–1945

DONALD MACRAE c1866–c1929

JAMES ROBERTS CRAIK 1874–1948

WILLIAM BUCHANAN TAYLOR 1876–1942

CHARLES DOHERTY 1859–c1912

Brooch 'essay piece' by Donald Fraser.
Inverness Museum and Art Gallery

Spirit bottle labels by Donald Fraser.
Private collection. A C Cooper Ltd, London

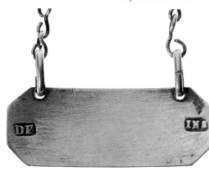

DONALD FRASER c1780–c1829

Donald Fraser was born about 1780 but nothing is known of his early years. He was, however, known to have been apprenticed to Charles Jameson from about 1794, his indenture registered on 19 October 1801. What is thought to be part of his essay, a brooch illustrated here, is now displayed in the Inverness Museum; it is in the shape of a cross, engraved and mounted with five orange quartz stones.

It would appear that Donald Fraser was one of Charles Jameson's first apprentices and Donald probably stayed with his Master as a journeyman for further two or three years, prior to opening his own business in about 1804.

The *Inverness Hammermen Minute Book* recorded on 7 September 1804: 'At a full Meeting of this date the Pettions of Donald Fraser Silversmith & John McDonald Saddler was presented to the meeting which unamiously agreed to admit theme as members of the Corporation on their paying the Sum of three Pounds ten Shillings each ...' Donald Fraser, now recorded as a goldsmith, was appointed one of the Key-keepers in 1805 or 1806 (page missing).

His first business advertisement[48] was in the Inverness Journal of 4 September 1807:

SILVER–PLATE, JEWELLERY, &c DONALD FRASER, GOLDSMITH, takes the liberty of acquainting his Friends and the Public, that he has just returned from his annual visit to the principle manufacturing towns in Britain, where he has selected, in addition to his former Stock, a very superior assortment of the most fashionable Silver-plate and Jewellery articles now made use of in the highest circles; and which he can with confidence recommend, being of the very best finish. D. F. has also selected (of the newest articles) an extensive assortment of Cutlery, Japanned, and miscellaneous goods, with a neat collection of the finest Toys for children, which will be found of the best manufacture, besides being considerably lower than the usual prices. The highest prices given for old Silver, Church-street Inverness, Septr. 1807.

The *Inverness Town Council Minutes* of 22 September 1807 report: 'Thereafter the said Magistrates and Council did and hereby do nominate and appoint the persons following as Constables of this Burgh ...' One of the persons named was Donald Fraser, silversmith, Church Street.

The *Inverness Journal* of 9 July 1813 carried an advertisement for his shop (below). The *Inverness Town Council Minutes* of 19 August 1816 record:

> That Day a petition was presented for Donald Fraser Gold Smith in Inverness for being admitted a Burgess of the Hammermen and which petition being considered by the Magistrates and Council they received and admitted the said Donald Fraser freeman Burgess of the Hammermen Incorporation of the said Burgh upon payment of one pound thirteen shillings and four pence Str to John Simpson Treasurer of the said Burgh to be a charge against him in his treasury accounts declaring that the admission of Mr Fraser as a Burgess of the Incorporation shall not entitle him to infringe upon the privilege of the Guildry.

It is interesting to note that the Town Council were still endeavouring to enforce old restrictions of trade, despite the general loosening of trade barriers at the time. The *Town Council Minutes* for 15 September 1817 noted: 'The Committee also Report that the admission Dues of Donald Fraser Goldsmith ... Hammermen Corporation of £1 . 13s . 4^d ...'

The *Hammermen Minute Book* recorded on 29 January 1818 that Donald Fraser had been appointed Boxmaster: 'At a meeting of this date Boxmas Master Accot. was examined & found Correct at the same time they Elected Donald Fraser Gold

NEW GOLDSMITH AND JEWELLERY SHOP.
D. FRASER begs leave to return his moſt grateful thanks to his friends and the public in general for the very liberal ſupport which he has experienced ſince his commencement in buſineſs, and that he has lately removed to the new corner Shop in Church Street, which he has got elegantly fitted up and furniſhed with a choice aſſortment of Goods, entirely new and faſhionable, conſiſting of Silver Plate, beſt Plated Sheffield Goods, with Silver edges, a great variety of Jewellery and Trinkets, new patterns of Cutlery and Japanned Goods; plain and hunting Watches, by the firſt Makers; which will be exchanged if not approved of; beſt London Paraſols and Umbrellas; with numberleſs other articles.—all of which he has ſelected from the Makers' hands when in London and the different manufacturing towns.
N. B. The higheſt price given for old Silver.
Inverneſs, 8th July, 1813.

Inverness Journal 9 July 1813

Smith to be there Boxmaster and was delivered him the Sum of three Pounds to accot. for, With Ten Pounds to be lodged in the Bank.' His signature was appended under the record of the following meeting, on 21 April 1818.

The *Town Council Minutes* for 14 September 1818 record that Donald Fraser, silversmith, was one of the three nominated Hammermen at a meeting called for the election of their Deacon, but he was not chosen.

The *Inverness Journal* of 26 March 1819 carried an advertisement for:

D. FRASER, GOLDSMITH, Having Subset that part of his Shop, fronting Church Street, will expose to Public Sale, on Tuesday the 30th instant, for Ready Money, his whole Stock of GOODS, consisting of a variety of CUTLERY, CABINET, JAPAN, and MISCELLA-NEOUS ARTICLES, of the best quality, well worthy the attention of persons furnishing houses.

Later that same year, in the *Inverness Journal* of 1 October 1819, he advertised:

WANTED AN APPRENTICE, TO THE GOLDSMITH BUSINESS, apply to Donald Fraser.

The next record of his business was in *Pigot's Directory* 1821-22 & 23, when he was noted as working in East Street as a jeweller.

The *Inverness Journal* of 16 April 1824 advertised that a large tenement of houses, within the Atheneum, 'situated at the top of Church Street, and on the east side thereof, with SHOPS and CELLARS of the same', would be sold by Public Roup, 'on Thursday the 13th of May next, at 3 o'clock afternoon.' It continued, 'This Property is immediately opposite the Exchange, and occupies the most central situation in the Town of Inverness. It consists of five Shops, and four separate Dwelling Houses above the same, including the Athenaeum, as is at present Let to respectable Tenants.' The property fronted the two principal streets in the town, these were Church Street and, probably, East Street. One of the shops was occupied by Mr Donald Fraser, Goldsmith; his shop had its front on Church Street. A similar advertisement appeared in the *Inverness Courier* of 22 April 1824.

In *Pigot's Directory* 1825 Fraser was listed under 'jewellers and silversmiths', in East Street.

Donald Fraser, goldsmith, was noted on four occasions in the Inverness Small Debt Books: 5 February 1827, being pursued by John McDonald, mariner in Inverness; 4 January 1828, being pursued by the Gas & Water Company, Inverness, for non-payment of gas light, and, on 27 March 1828, by John Grant, spirit dealer in Inverness. Additionally, he was recorded as the pursuer in a complaint, dated 11 March 1828, against a Lieutenant Urquhart, Rs Militia, who had not paid a bill for 6s 6d; however, this was later withdrawn.

No record of death or burial has been found for Donald Fraser; he is not listed in *Pigot's Directory* 1837 for Inverness. It is possible that he moved away, but we would have expected to find an advertisement or some other record of the business closing. The *Inverness Journal*, of 20 November 1829, carried on the front page a 'NOTICE': 'THE DWELLING HOUSE and PREMISES, belonging to the Heirs of the deceased Donald Fraser, Smith, East Street, Inverness, are for Sale, by Private

Bargain. They will be pointed out by J. Mackenzie, Merchant, Tomnahurich Street.' It is possible that this referred to Donald Fraser, goldsmith, but it is not proven.

While working in Inverness as a goldsmith he trained five known apprentices: John McGregor, registered 15 October 1809; John Anderson, 23 October 1811, who was to become a silversmith in his own right in Inverness; Charles McGrigor, 22 April 1812; Alexander Williamson, 28 October 1818, and John Jack, 1 November 1820.

Inverness Courier
22 April 1824

HOUSES AND SHOPS FOR SALE,
IN INVERNESS.

To be Sold by Public Roup, within the Athereum, Inverness, on Thursday the 13th of May next, at 3 o'clock afternoon,

ALL and WHOLE that large tenement of HOUSES, lately built by Mr GEDDES, Vintner, situated at the top of Church Street, and on the east side thereof, with the SHOPS and CELLARS of the same, and ground right and property thereof, which, tenement comprehends the sites of three separate tenements of Houses, as more particularly described in the Rights and Infeftments thereof.

This property is immediately opposite the Exchange, and occupies the most central situation in the town of Inverness. It consists of five Shops, and four separate Dwelling Houses above the same. including the Athenæum, and is at present let to respectable tenants. It comprehends an extensive front of property towards the two principal streets in the town, and may be turned to good account by a judicious Purchaser.

If not disposed of in one, it will be divided into two separate Lots,

LOT FIRST, to consist of the division of the building fronting the Exchange. and to comprehend the Shops and Cellars occupied by Bailie SMITH, and Mr FRASER, Tertius, with the Athenæum and Billiard Room, and Lodging of two flats and Garrets, occupied by Mr CANT.

LOT 2d., to consist of that part of the building fronting the Church Street, and to comprehend the Shops occupied by Mr DONALD FRASER, Goldsmith, Mr M'DONALD, Watchmaker, and Mr MITCHELL, Druggist, and the three Lodgings immediately above the same.

The Articles and conditions of sale may be seen, and any other information obtained on application to Mr THOMSON. Accountant.

Inverness, 13th April, 1824.

His Inverness marks were 'D F, INS', 'D F, INS I', 'D F over INS', and 'D F, INS, S, S'. Some items marked with 'D F' have been confused with Daniel Ferguson's punch; however, Fraser's punches are clearly different.

There was a silversmith who used a 'D F' punch, about 1820, on silver with the 'WICK' town mark; it has been suggested that this may have been Donald Fraser, although the 'D F' punch is slightly different from the one known to have been used by him while in Inverness.

DONALD FRASER AND THE ISLE OF SKYE VOLUNTEERS

Alexander Nicolson, in *History of Skye*, states that a volunteer regiment was raised to defend the Isle of Skye from the French. It was formed in 1798 and, having been disbanded after the Peace of Amiens in 1802, was reformed in 1803 when the French once again threatened Britain. The regiment was finally demobilised in 1814.

Silver shoulder badge 'Isle of Sky Volunteers' by Donald Fraser c1806 (10 cm x 8 cm).
Private collection

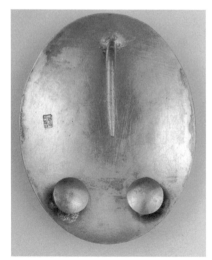

The Isle of Skye Volunteers were divided into two battalions, Northern and Southern; each battalion was divided into five companies. The Northern battalion was commanded by Lieutenant Colonel Alexander MacDonald of Lyndale, Isle of Skye, and the Southern battalion by Lieutenant Colonel James MacLeod of Raasay.

A silver shoulder badge worn by Officers of this regiment is illustrated opposite. The reverse of the badge, marked with the initials 'D F over INS', is the maker's mark of Donald Fraser.

THOMAS STEWART (THOMAS McGUIRMAN) 1784-1856

Thomas McGuirman[49] was born on a farm near Inverness, and baptised on 12 September 1784; the son of Donald McGuirman[50], a farmer, and Elspat (Elizabeth) Kerr. The *Inverness Parish Register* records the baptism of at least ten children born to Donald and Elspat, of which Thomas was the eldest.

Nothing further is known about Thomas McGuirman until the *Inverness Hammermen Minute Book* records the completion of his apprenticeship to Alexander Stewart on 27 September 1805[51]. At about this point Thomas appears to have changed his surname to that of his Master[52], the reason for which remains a puzzle.

It was not uncommon for Highland silversmiths to travel south to further their knowledge of the trade and this must have been what Thomas Stewart did, as his marriage was recorded on 26 February 1812 at St Martin in the Fields, London. Thomas married Mary, daughter of Richard Lockwood, a London jeweller, and his wife Mary Turner. Mary, who was the middle child of five, was born on 17 March 1792 and baptised on 10 April 1792 in the parish of St James, Clerkenwell[53], London. It is possible that Thomas served his time in London as a journeyman to Richard Lockwood.

It is known from London directories that Richard Lockwood was a goldsmith; in 1805 he was recorded as such, at 8 Clerkenwell Green, and as a goldsmith and undertaker, in 1808, at the same address.

The *Inverness Journal*, of 14 August 1812, carried an advertisement for Thomas Stewart which informed 'the Gentry of Moray-shire, and the Public in general, that he has commenced business in Elgin, and entered into that Shop in the corner of Batchin's Lane, where he manufactures and sells all kinds of Plate, Silversmiths Goods, and Jewellery of every description, on the most reasonable terms.' It concluded 'An Apprentice wanted.' Beneath this advertisement was another: 'Mrs Stewart begs leave to inform the Ladies of the County of Moray that she has commenced business in Elgin as a Fancy Dress and Pelisse Maker.' Mary Stewart was listed in the 1841 census as a Bonnet Maker and in the 1851 census as a Dressmaker. Thomas Stewart was admitted a Guild Brother of the Burgh of Elgin in 1813. The entry from the *Merchant Guild Minute Book*, dated 19 February 1813, reads: 'Said Day the Court Received Created and admitted Thomas Stewart Gold and Silversmith in Elgin a Guild Brother of this Burgh for which he paid the Collector Eight pounds Sterling and declared him entitled to all the privelages and immunities thereto belonging'.

His shop was in the High Street, listed in *Pigot's Directory* 1821-22 & 23 as a silversmith and 1825 under Jewellers. The *Elgin Courant & Courier* of 16 November 1827 advertised 'SALE OF JEWELLERY, HOUSEHOLD FURNITURE, &c FOR THE BEHOOF

Silver beaker by Thomas Stewart marked Elgin. Phillips, Edinburgh

Tablespoons by Thomas Stewart marked Inverness with Elgin Cathedral punch. Private collection. Ewen Weatherspoon

OF CREDITORS.' It continued: 'There will be sold by PUBLIC ROUP, at Elgin, on Friday, the 23d day of November current, the WHOLE STOCK OF JEWELLERY, SHOP GOODS, GLASS CASES, and a large assortment of WORK TOOLS, which lately belonged to THOMAS STEWART Jeweller in Elgin, and now to the Trustee on his Estate, for behoof of his Creditors.' The advertisement went on 'And there will also be sold at Elgin, on Friday, the 30th day of November current, the WHOLE HOUSEHOLD FURNITURE which likewise belonged to the said THOMAS STEWART, consisting of BEDSTEADS and CURTAINS, FEATHER BEDS, BLANKETS, CARPETS, MAHOGANY CHAIRS, a CHEST OF DRAWERS, an EIGHT DAY CLOCK, MIRRORS, and a variety of PRINTS, with KITCHEN FURNITURE and other articles too numerous to mention. The Roup to begin at 11 o'clock forenoon, on these respective days, and to continue till all be sold off.' From this it is clear that Thomas Stewart had become bankrupt[54]. The *Inverness Courier* of 4 June 1828 recorded a notice to creditors (opposite). A similar advertisement appeared in the *Aberdeen Journal* of 4 June 1828.

While in Elgin Thomas Stewart and his wife, Mary, had seven known children: Richard Lockwood, born 9 November 1812; Elizabeth[55], died 15 September 1815, aged 1 year; Mary Elizabeth, baptised 21 June 1816; Donald McGuirman, born 16 January 1819; Isabella Sarah Ann Martha, born 20 February 1823; Martha Johanna Lockwood, born 25 October 1824, and

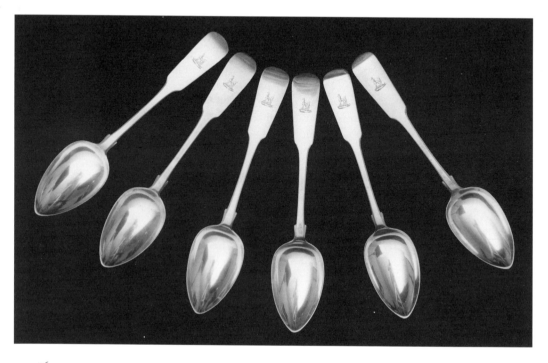

Inverness Courier 4 June 1828

NOTICE

TO THE CREDITORS OF THE THREE
FOLLOWING ESTATES.

IT is hereby requested that the respective Creditors of THOMAS STEWART, Jeweller in Elgin, of DAVID M·KENZIE, late Merchant in Elgin, and of DONALD and ROBERT BAIN, late Fish Curers in Burghead, who have not already done so, shall lodge their Claims with Oaths of Verity thereto, with WILLIAM GRANT, Accountant in Elgin, on or before the 20th day of June current ; Certifying to those who fail to do so, that they shall receive no share of the respective Trust Funds realized. Schemes of Division will be exhibited at the Office of the said WILLIAM GRANT, to the respective Creditors from the 20th to the 30th current, and he will be prepared to pay the Dividends any time after the last mentioned date.

Elgin, 2d June, 1828.

Inverness toddy ladle by Thomas Stewart.
Private collection. Ewen Weatherspoon

Ann Margaret, born 1 October 1826. Thomas and his family moved from Elgin to Inverness sometime between November 1827 and 26 February 1829, the date the *Inverness Parish Register* recorded the baptism of his next child Wilhelmina McRae[56] Stewart. Another child, George, was born in Inverness about 1832, but no record of his baptism has been found.

Thomas appeared to have worked as a journeyman until 1835, when an entry of 4 February in the *Inverness Hammermen Minute Book* noted: 'Thomas Stewart Jeweller was admitted as a member upon paying free apprentice dues the sum of five pounds Sterling which was likewisd lodged in the Box and he likewisd produced the stamp.'

He was recorded at 14 Petty Street in *Pigot's Directory* 1837 under 'Jewellers – Working'.

The 1841 Inverness census listed Thomas Stewart, aged 55, a jeweller, living in Petty Street with his wife Mary, aged 45, a bonnet maker; also recorded were his children: Richard, aged 28, a jeweller; Mary, aged 25, a straw bonnet maker; Donald, aged 22, a painter; Isabella, aged 18; Martha, aged 16; Ann, aged 14; Williamina, aged 12, and George, aged 9 years. The household was completed by a servant, Mary Ross.

The 1851 Inverness census, for 15 Petty Street, recorded Thomas Stewart, aged 66, a working jeweller, with his wife, Mary, aged 59, a dressmaker, and their children: Mary, aged 34, a dressmaker; Martha, aged 26, a milliner; Ann, aged 24, a dressmaker; and George, aged 19, a carpenter.

Stewart was recorded at 14 Petty Street in *Slater's Directory* 1852 under 'Jewellers and Silversmiths'.

Thomas Stewart died on 3 March 1856, aged 72, at 15 Petty Street, and was buried in Inverness Churchyard. His death was registered by his son Richard.

Mary Stewart, a widow, aged 70, was still listed at 15 Petty Street in the 1861 census with her unmarried daughter, Mary, aged 43 years. She died on 21 October 1863, aged 71, at 57 King Street, Inverness. The informant was her son George.

The inscription on the family gravestone in the Old High Church Yard, Inverness, read as follows:

> THIS STONE Was placed here in Memory of DONALD MᶜGUIRMAN Farmer in the Barnhill of Inverness who departed this life, 6ᵗʰ day of November 1822, Aged 73 Years and his Spouse, ELIZABETH KERR who departed this life, the 4ᵗʰ day of February 1821, Aged 62 Years, And their Children MARTHA, SIMON and JOHN who died in Childhood Also of their son THOMAS STEWART Late Jeweller Inverness Who departed this life on the 3ʳᵈ March 1856. Aged 72 years. And of his Wife MARY LOCKWOOD Who died 21st Octʳ 1863 Aged 71 years.

Thomas Stewart's silver marks from Elgin and Inverness are illuatrated above: 'T S, EL^N', 'ST GILES, T S, EL^N, CATHEDRAL', 'T S, THISTLE, INS' and 'T S, INS, THISTLE,

CATHEDRAL'. He used a large and a small 'T S' punch. One striking point about these marks is that they are large, very clear and always symmetrically arranged. His signature is reproduced above.

ROBERT NAUGHTEN (NAUGHTY) 1786-1857

Robert Naughty[57] was born on 6 April 1786 at Cottehall in Forres, the son of Thomas Naughty[58], a miller, and Elspet Clunis; Thomas and Elspet had a previous son called Robert, born on 17 March 1779 at Mills of Forres. Thomas Naughty and Elspet Clunas were married at Dyke, Elgin-shire, on 11 June 1778; they had at least three sons and five daughters.

There was some confusion, over which Robert was the silversmith, as the age of Robert Naughten, as taken from contemporary records, varied wildly. The son who was born in 1786 was recorded in the *Parish Register* as Robert Davidson Naughty[59], after the Findhorn merchant Robert Davidson. It was unlikely that the family would have had two sons who survived named Robert; therefore we believe that the first, born in 1779, died in infancy.

Nothing is known of Robert's early life until he was apprenticed to Charles Jameson, in Inverness, around 1802. We do know that his family moved from Forres to Inverness sometime between July 1792 and June 1794, as their last known daughter was baptised in Inverness at the latter date. Two advertisements in the *Inverness Journal*, of 1 July and 9 September 1814, refer to 'BARLEY MILL, NEAR MIDMILLS, INVERNESS', concluding 'Orders received by Thomas Naughten, at the Mill.' Robert's mother, 'Elisabeth Clunas Spouse of Thomas Naughtin', died on 9 June 1814 according to the *Inverness Parish Register*.

The *Inverness Hammermen Minute Book* recorded, on 15 October 1809, the registration of the apprenticeship of Robert Naughty to Charles Jameson; an entry fee 'dues' of 6s 8d was paid to the Boxmaster. Following his apprenticeship Robert Naughten continued as a journeyman to Charles Jameson.

The *Inverness Journal* of 27 August 1813 carried an advertisement:

CHARLES JAMESON, GOLDSMITH AND JEWELLER, CHURCH-STREET, INVERNESS, Takes this opportunity of returning his most grateful thanks to his friends and the public for the many favours conferred on him in the way of his business last twenty-seven years. He now begs leave to intimate that he has admitted as a Partner ROBERT NAUGHTEN, a Young Man thoroughly qualified to carry on the trade in all its branches. His known abilities have already convinced C. Jameson's Customers that their orders in time coming will be executed with promptitude and dispatch. C.J. has further to intimate that the business from this date will be carried on under the firm of JAMESON and NAUGHTEN. Orders directed under the firm of the Company, or to either of the Partners, will meet due attention. Those who are pleased to favour the Company with their commands may rely on having their work done in a workman-like manner, and on the shortest notice. Coats of Arms, Crests, &c. engraved in the neatest style. Highest price given for Old Gold and Silver.

While working for Charles Jameson, Naughten's fellow apprentices were Donald Fraser (registered 19 October 1801 - though he was probably a journeyman when Robert started his apprenticeship); Hugh Reid (27 September 1805), and Charles Fowler (27 September 1805 who became a successful goldsmith in Elgin before changing his trade to that of a dentist, in Elgin and Aberdeen, in 1824). During the partnership the company took two further apprentices, John Fraser Reid and John Ross (both registered on 11 October 1815).

It was not until 1814 that Naughten was admitted into the Hammermen's Incorporation, as the *Minute Book* recorded:

> Inverness 29th July 1814. At a meeting of this date theire was Collected Five Pounds Sixteen Shilling Sterling as payt of Quarter pence & entrey money the Pettitions of <u>Robert Naughten</u> Silver Smith here & Simon Munro Blacksmith was receivd and enterd as Members of this Incorparation where the Above Five Pounds Sixteen Shilling was given in to the Box Master to Account. Alexʳ Dallas.

The *Inverness Town Council Minutes* dated 21 April 1817 record that 'Robert Naughton, Goldsmith' was appointed a Special Constable along with Charles Jameson (see page 45).

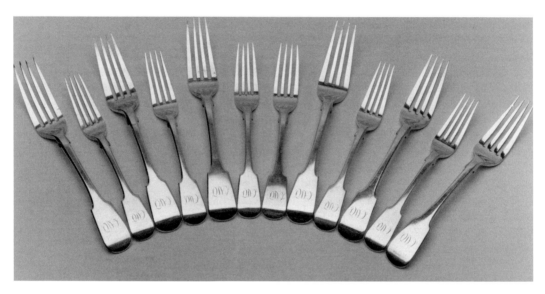

Table and dessert forks by Jameson and Naughten.
Private collection. Ewen Weatherspoon

Quaich by Jameson and Naughten.
Private collection. Ewen Weatherspoon

The *Inverness Parish Register*, 1818, makes the following reference to Robert: 'Robert Naughten Jeweler And Catherin McKenzie[60] had A child in Fornication Born the 20th And Baptized this date (24th February 1818) by the Rev^d Mr Alexander Rose named Sarah.' Catherine later married John Bruce, from Dunnet, on 17 February 1825, in the parish of Loth. Sarah married Suther Sutherland, draper and grocer, from Portgower, Loth, and died aged 68[61] on 9 July 1888.

Shortly afterwards, there is an intriguing entry in the *Parish Register*, recording a marriage ceremony on 15 July 1820 in Inverness: 'Naughten: Mr. Robert Naughten Jeweler and Miss_____ Alves[62].'

The partnership with Jameson was severed sometime between 1816[63] and 1820; why is not known as Charles Jameson did not die until 1829. *Pigot's Directory* 1821-22 & 23 listed Robert Naughten, working alone, as a jeweller in Church Street and in 1825 as a jeweller and silversmith in Church Street. During this period Naughten had three apprentices recorded in the *Hammermen Minute Book*: John McLeod (registered 5 Aug 1823) who became a master jeweller in Inverness, James Jack

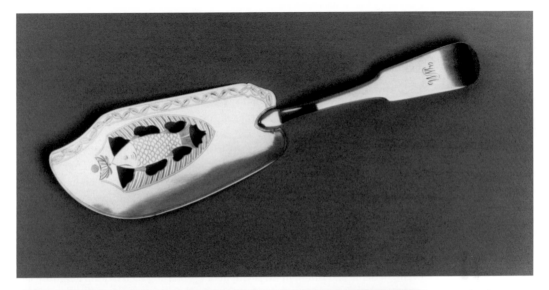

Fish slice by Jameson and Naughten.
Private collection.
Ewen Weatherspoon

Snuff box by Jameson and Naughten.
Private collection.
Ewen Weatherspoon

Vinaigrette by Robert Naughten.
Private collection.
Ewen Weatherspoon

(5 Aug 1823), and William Mason who also became a jeweller in Inverness, with a shop at 13 High Street, by 1837.

The *Inverness Town Council Minutes* of 19 May 1823 stated: 'The Dean of Guild reported to the Meeting that so far back as the month of February last the officer of Court had called upon a number of persons carrying on business as shopkeepers within Town & not admitted to the freedom of the Town or Guildry-but that hitherto they decline to come forward.' The list included 'Robert Naughton, Jeweller'. The *Minutes* dated 13 September 1824 reported: 'A Petition was presented for Robert Naughton Merchant Jeweller in Inverness for being admitted a Freeman Burgess and Guild Brother of the said Burgh, and which Petition was remitted to the Dean of Guild and his Council to settle for the freedom of the Guildry and report.' The *Minutes* for 20 September 1824 state: 'The Dean of Guild reported that Robert Naughten Merchant Jeweller settled with the Guildry for his freedom and he was appointed to attend at next Council in order to be admitted and to pay the dues to the Town.' Finally, the *Minutes* dated 18 October 1824 record: 'That day ... Robert Naughton Jeweller & Silversmith (together with others) in terms of former Minutes attended the Council this day. - The Burgess Oath was read in their presence and they were accordingly admitted & received Freemen Burgesses & Guild Brethren of the said Burgh upon payment of £5 Sterling each to John Ferguson late

Quaich by Robert Naughten.
Private collection.
Ewen Weatherspoon

Treasurer ... inserted in each of the Burgess Tickets Viz – Declaring that the Burgess by his acceptance of his privileges becomes solemnly bound to every civil duty incumbent on a true & faithful Burgess of the Burgh into which he is admitted.'

Robert Naughten married his second wife on 26 May 1829, in Inverness; the *Parish Register* records: 'Robert Naughten Jeweller Church Street and Sarah G. Nicholson by the Revd. Mr. Campbell Croy.' Sarah Greenslade Nicholson was born around 1800, in England, the daughter of Thomas Nicholson, an Adjutant, and Mary Greenslade.

The *Inverness Courier* of 3 November 1830 carried an article headed 'NORTH-ERN INSTITUTION'; it described the fifth anniversary meeting of the 'society' held within the Museum, and listed all the donations received during the late recess, which included: 'A Pair of large Brown Eagles, shot last summer', 'Large Slab of petrified Wood, from Van Dieman's Land' and a 'Land Turtle, from Gibraltar, (alive)'. Among the office-bearers of the Institution nominated by the Meeting for the ensuing year was 'Curator of Museum – Mr Naughten, Jeweller'.

The *Inverness Journal and Northern Advertiser* of 14 September 1832 reported under the heading 'BOARD OF HEALTH. SUBSCRIPTIONS FOR SUPPLYING THE NEEDY WITH FOOD AND CLOTHES UNDER THE DIRECTION OF THE BOARD'; included was a list of subscribers, one of which was Mr Robert Naughten – £2-2s.

Pigot's Directory 1837 listed Robert Naughten as a jeweller and silversmith, and, highland accoutrement maker, at 14 Church Street.

The *Inverness Courier* of 27 November 1839 carried an advertisement for his shop.

The *Inverness Burgh Record of Indentures Book, 1836-1846* recorded two further apprentices indentured to Robert Naughten: George MacPherson, for 6 years from 26 December 1833 and James Urquhart, for 7 years from 20 October 1840. The *Inverness Burgh Treasurer's Accounts Book* detailed for the year ending 30 September 1840 the payment of £5-0-0. for recording the indenture between Robert Naughten and George Macpherson.

Robert Naughten was a Freemason of St John's Old Kilwinning Lodge (*Freemasonry in Inverness* by Alexander Ross). He was a Junior Warden in 1830, and a Senior Warden from 1846 to 1855.

The Book of Country Work and Registrations of the Incorporation of Edinburgh Goldsmiths recorded that Robert Naughten sent for assay eight parcels of silver, weighing in total 572 ounces, between 12 April 1839 and 7 August 1840.

FOR SALE.

HANDSOME GOLD WATCH, maker's name– "BARBANDS, London" Duplex escapement, with four jewels,

Rich GOLD WATCH CHAIN, with KEY,

Two SEALS—one Cornelian—the other Topaz, with the Fraser's Arms engraved thereon, and set in gold,

Two massive GOLD RINGS,

For Sale, either together or separately, for behoof of the legatees of a gentleman deceased. The articles may be seen, and offers received at the shop of Mr Naughten, Jeweller, Inverness.

Inverness, 25th October 1839.

Inverness Courier
27 November 1839

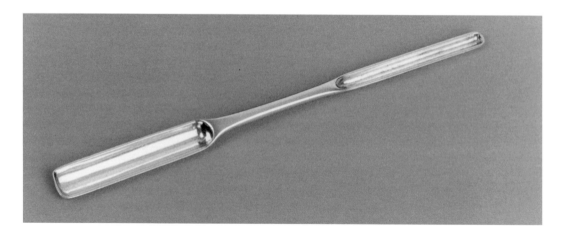

Marrow scoop by
Robert Naughten.
Private collection.
Ewen Weatherspoon

The 1841 Inverness census listed Robert, aged 50, a jeweller, living in Church Street with his family; Sarah, his wife, aged 40; Robert, aged 11; Frederick, aged 6; Thomas, aged 4; Elizabeth, aged 9, and Mary, aged 1 year. There were also two servants in the household.

Robert Naughten and Sarah had six known children, all born in Inverness: Robert, born 23 May 1830; Greenslade, 11 June 1832 (possibly died in infancy); Elizabeth Sutherland, 26 April 1834; Frederick, 9 August 1836; Thomas William, 28 September 1838, and Mary, 13 April 1840. Mary died in 1856; Robert Naughten junior erected a headstone in the Chapel Yard: 'ERECTED by ROBERT NAUGHTEN in memory of his beloved sister MARY who died 15 June 1856, aged 16 years'

The last mention of Robert Naughten in the *Hammermen Minute Book* was as follows:

Inverness 12 Dec' 1842. At a meeting of this date Mr. Joseph Willis gunmaker gave in his Bill with Security for Fifteen pounds Sterling - also Mr Angus Cameron gave in his Bill with Security for Fifteen pounds Sterling to the Corporation & Both Bills were lodged in the Box-Mr Alex'... Saddler also produced his Burgess Stamp. Thereafter Mr William Masson Jeweler was called when he produced his Indenture on which it appeared he had not entered Mr Robert Naughten Jeweller service as an apprentice till some time after the date of Mr Naughten resighning his right to this Hammermen Incorporation - on which the meeting came to the unanimous resolution of charging him Twenty pounds Sterling being the ordinary dues of admitting him as a free Member of this Incorporation which he refused to comply with and the meeting therefore resolved to hand the case to Mr Campbell Soliciter for Prosecution. Alexander Mackintosh Interim Chairman.

There was no further record of this dialogue.

The *Inverness Journal* of 12 August 1842 carried an advertisement for Robert Naughten:

Engraving. The Want of a PROFESSED ENGRAVER in Inverness having long been felt, the Subscriber has been induced to engage an experienced hand from the South. The Inhabitants of Inverness and the Northern Counties may now have engraving, in general, done here, in an efficient manner. Coats of Arms, Crests, Mottos, Ciphers, Inscriptions, &c. &c. Specimens of Engravings may be seen at his Shop.

The 1851 Inverness census listed Robert as a jeweller, aged 62[64], born in Morayshire, with his wife, Sarah, aged 50, born in England, living at 15 Church

Street. The children were: Robert, aged 19; Frederick, aged 14, scholar; Thomas, aged 12, scholar; Elizabeth, aged 16, scholar, and Mary, aged 11, scholar. There were also two house servants. *Slater's Directory* 1852 listed him as a jeweller and silversmith working at 14 Church Street.

The *Inverness Courier* of 1 April 1852 offered: 'FOR SALE, SPLENDID LARGE CHINA ORNAMENTS, AND SILVER PLATED ARTICLES, at MR NAUGHTEN'S, JEWELLER, CHURCH STREET. A SUPERB Ornamental Blue and Gold CHINA VASE; and two large CHINA JARS, also Blue and Gold - to correspond, or separately.' This was followed by a list of silver plated items. It continued, 'These were the Property of a Gentleman lately deceased, and will be Sold on reasonable terms.'

Robert Naughten died at 13 Church Street, Inverness, on 18 April 1857, recorded as a jeweller, aged 69; he was buried in the Chapel Yard of Inverness. His gravestone is close to the stone for his daughter, Mary. The inscription is 'ROBERT NAUGHTEN born April 1778[65] died 18th April 1857'. His estate was valued at £2,161-9s-5d. He owned a large amount of property: a flesher's shop, three houses, a stable and coach house, and the Bank Lane Inn which provided a total half yearly rent of £37-2s-6d.

There are three sets of marks associated with Robert Naughten (pages 64-5): 'J & N, INS, long flat cornucopia', which sometimes included a 'G'; 'R N, elongated cornucopia, thistle', and 'R N, short cornucopia, thistle'.

Robert Naughten Goldsmith (signature)

The Inverness 1871 census listed Sarah Naughten as a 71 year old widow, born in Devonshire, living at 1 Hill Terrace with her daughter, Elizabeth, aged 36, and a female servant. Sarah died there on 23 June 1874, aged 74, recorded as the widow of Robert Naughten, master jeweller. Mrs Naughten was listed in the *Inverness Directory* 1866/67 living in Hill Terrace (Barnhill), and also in the *Inverness Directory* 1873/74 at 1 Hill Terrace.

ALEXANDER MCLEOD c1786-1870

Alexander McLeod was born in Kilmuir[66], on the Isle of Skye, around 1786; his parents were Murdoch McLeod, a farmer, and Christina McDonald (the *Parish Registers* for Skye are not available prior to 1800, so his precise date of birth cannot be established). Alexander McLeod was possibly apprenticed in Inverness but no record of an apprenticeship has been found.

The marriage of Alexander McLeod took place in the parish of Ardersier[67] on 7 April 1826. The *Parish Register* recorded: 'This day were legally Married Alexr. McLeod Jeweller from the Isle of Sky-and Jean Falconer daur. of Mr. Hugh Falconer Vintner in Campbeltown[68].' They had six known children: Murdoch was baptised[69] on 29 January 1827; Grace, baptised 26 December 1828; Hugh, baptised[70] 16 August 1830; Christian, baptised 8 August 1831; James, born 25 October 1833, and Alexander, born 29 May 1837; on each occasion the father was recorded as a jeweller in High Street, Inverness. Murdoch and Hugh did not survive infancy and were buried in lair 1602 in the Chapel Yard Burying Ground. The inscription reads: 'Here lies MURDOCH, and HUGH, Infant sons of ALEXR. MCLEOD Jeweller Inverness'. No dates or ages were inscribed.

His wife Jean (Jane) Falconer was born on 12 April 1803 in the parish of Carriden, Linlithgowshire; her father was Hugh Falconer, and her mother Grizel (Grace) Porteous.

The *Inverness Hammermen Minute Book* records that Alexander McLeod petitioned the Incorporation 'craving to be received as a Silversmith' and was admitted on 6 November 1827 on payment of £5 sterling in cash and a bill, at six months for fifteen pounds. At a meeting of 4 November 1828 he paid three pounds sterling as part payment of his outstanding bill. Alexander was admitted a Burgess and Guild Brother on 24 December 1827 and the *Inverness Town Council Minutes* detailed this as follows:

> Alexander McLeod Jeweller James Rose of the Millburn Distillery and Daniel Fraser Haberdasher in Inverness having appeared in terms of former Minutes of Council the old Burgess Oath was read oon in their presence and they were Admitted Burgesses & Guild Brethren of the Burgh of Inverness upon payment of Five Pounds Sterling each to the Chamberlain, But Declaring that this Burgess Act shall have no effect until their Tickets written on the proper Stamps are taken out from the Town Clerk in which Burgess Tickets the usual Clause recommended by the Convention of Royal Burghs is directed to be inserted Whereupon Act.

The *Inverness Journal and Northern Advertiser* of 14 September 1832 reported a list of subscribers to 'INVERNESS BOARD OF HEALTH. SUBSCRIPTION FOR SUPPLYING

left: Wine funnel by Alexander McLeod (H 13.3 cm Dia 9.6 cm). Inverness Museum and Art Gallery. Ewen Weatherspoon

right: Wine funnel by Alexander McLeod. Christie's, Glasgow

THE NEEDY WITH FOOD AND CLOTHES UNDER THE DIRECTION OF THE BOARD', one of whom was 'Mr. Mcleod, Jeweller-10s'.

The *Hammermen Minute Book* recorded on 15 June 1836 that Alexander Macleod Silversmith was at a meeting, 'to bring about a total dissolution of the Corporation' (see page 73).

Pigot's Directory 1837 listed Alexander McLeod as a jeweller and silversmith working at 1 High Street, Inverness.

On at least two occasions Alexander McLeod sent silver for assay in Edinburgh: the King's Duty Book recorded silver from him on 24 March 1838, this consisted of 12 table spoons, 2 gravy spoons and 36 teaspoons - a total of 60 ounces; on 20 August 1838 the consignment was 24 dessert spoons, 6 dessert forks and 12 teaspoons - a total of 45 ounces.

The 1841 Inverness census recorded the family living in Bridge Street: Alexander, a jeweller, aged 50; Jane, his wife, aged 36; Grace, aged 12; Christina, aged 9; James, aged 7, and Alexander, aged 4. Also living with them was John Gunn, an apprentice jeweller, aged 15, who was not born in Inverness-shire.

The *Inverness Advertiser* of 3 July 1849 carried an advertisement for his business at a new address (below). William Mason took over the address at 1 High Street.

The 1851 census showed the family living at 47 High Street: Alexander, aged 63, born Kilmuir; Jane, his wife, aged 46, who was born in Linlithgow; Grace, aged 22; Christina, aged 19; James, a watchmaker, aged 17, and Alexander, aged 13 years. Living with them was Grace Falconer, Alexander's mother-in-law, aged 78, who was born in Moffat, Dumfries-shire.

Slater's Directory 1852 listed Alexander working at 99 Church Street as a jeweller, silversmith, watch and clock maker.

Alexander MacLeod, watchmaker and working jeweller, advertised again in the *Inverness Advertiser* on 17 July 1855 but from a different address, New Building, 40 Bridge Street. He also stated 'an experienced WATCHMAKER wanted immediately'.

The *Inverness Advertiser* of 12 May 1857 under the heading 'SCOTCH BANK-RUPTS' and the subheading 'NOTICE OF CESSIO BONORUM' reported: 'Alexander Macleod, jeweller, Inverness, and presently prisoner in the prison of Inverness - to

Inverness Advertiser 3 July 1849

NOTICE OF REMOVAL.

ALEX. MACLEOD, JEWELLER & WATCHMAKER, Inverness, has REMOVED, from the Corner of High Street, to No. 99 CHURCH STREET, opposite the Caledonian Hotel.

All kinds of Mountings for the Highland Dress, varieties of Silver Highland Brooches, and other Jewellery and Fancy Goods ; Gold and Silver Watches, warranted, are always on hand, and sold for moderate profits ; Watches of all kinds, Jewellery, and Silver Plate, carefully repaired, and orders punctually executed.

A. Macleod has experienced steady workmen, and hopes to be able to give satisfaction to those who will favour him with their patronage.

be examined in the Sheriff's Chambers, Castle of Inverness, 9th June, at twelve o'clock.' No further information has been found concerning this period of imprisonment.

On 23 July 1858 James McLeod, son and apprentice to Alexander McLeod, jeweller, had his apprenticeship entered in the *Hammermen Minute Book*; he would have been aged 24 so this was probably a retrospective recording. On 21 March 1859 it was recorded that he paid 10s 6d as his entry money.

Slater's Directory 1860 detailed Alexander working at 40 Bridge Street as a jeweller, silversmith, watch and clock maker.

The 1861 census listed the family at 10 Shore Street: Alexander McLeod, aged 73, a jeweller; Jane, his wife, aged 56; Grace, aged 30, a teacher; Christina, aged 27, and Alexander, aged 23, a bank clerk.

Alexander had probably retired by 1866 as he was not listed in the *Inverness Directory* 1866/67.

Alexander McLeod's name occurs frequently in the *Inverness Hammermen Minute Book*; he was appointed Deacon on 19 September 1853, on 18 September 1854 and again on 17 September 1855; on each occasion his trade was given as jeweller. He was also recorded as Past Deacon at meetings on 15 September 1856, 21 September 1857, 20 September 1858 and 19 September 1859.

As well as John Gunn (mentioned in the 1841 census) Alexander trained at least three other apprentices: Alexander

Candlestick by Alexander McLeod.
Inverness Museum and Art Gallery

Plaid brooch by Alexander McLeod.
Private collection

Falkner[71], recorded 4 May 1830; James McKiligan, 4 May 1830[72], and James McLeod (his son) 23 July 1858.

Alexander McLeod died on 14 December 1870, aged 84, at Laverock Bank (Drummond Road), Inverness. He was buried in lair 1602 in the Chapel Yard Burying Ground where there is a memorial stone with the inscription:

In Memory OF ALEXANDER MACLEOD, JEWELLER, INVERNESS. DIED 14. DECEMBER 1870. AND HIS WIFE JANE FALCONER. DIED 7. MARCH 1894[73]. ALSO THEIR CHILDREN ALEXANDER, DIED 21. SEPT. 1867 JAMES, DIED 20. JAN. 1876. GRACE, DIED 31. MAY 1881. CHRISTINA, DIED 11. NOV. 1897.

The *Inverness Courier* of 22 December 1870 reported his death: 'At Laverock Bank, Drummond, Inverness, on the 14th inst., Mr ALEXANDER MACLEOD late Jeweller, aged 84.'

His marks were: 'A ML, INS, disc, disc, disc', 'A ML conjoined, INS, A ML conjoined, thistle', 'A ML conjoined, INS, S, S, thistle' and 'A MᶜL, INS, disc, disc, disc'. However, it is possible that one or more of these sets of marks could belong to Angus McLeod.

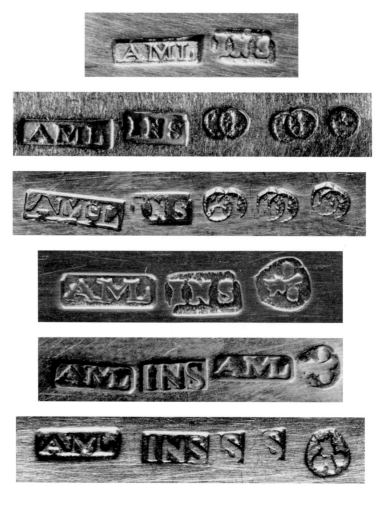

JOHN ANDERSON C1791–C1818

The earliest record that we have for John Anderson is his apprenticeship to Donald Fraser; this is in the *Inverness Hammermen Incorporation Minute Book*, 23 October 1811, when his indenture was registered. Sometime after this date he went to London for experience, as did many of his contemporaries. He moved back to Inverness and was admitted into the Hammermen's Incorporation on the 14 November 1815, when he petitioned, and was 'admitted a Member as a Silver Smith of the Incorporation, and he having satisfied the Incorporation he was received accordingly-at the same time there was delivered to the Box Master the sum of Four Pounds fifteen Shillings to acc"'.

The *Inverness Journal* of 8 December 1815 advertised his new business (below) and in a 'WATCH LOST' advertisement in the *Inverness Journal* of 28 March 1817, he is given as working in East Street, Inverness, as a jeweller. A second 'WATCH LOST' advertisement, in the *Inverness Journal* of 23 May 1817, recorded him in the same street but on this occasion his profession was given as silversmith.

> **JOHN ANDERSON,**
> GOLD AND SILVER-SMITH, FROM LONDON,
> RESPECTFULLY informs the Ladies and Gentle-men of Inverness, and its vicinity, that he has commenced business in the above line, in East Street, (opposite Castle Raat) and he hopes, by his attention, to merit a share of the public patronage. He also flatters himself, that those who may be pleased to favour him with their orders, shall have them executed to their satisfaction, and on the most moderate terms.
> Orders from the country punctually attended to.

Inverness Journal 8 December 1815

There are no apprentices trained by Anderson recorded in the *Hammermen Minute Book*.

The earliest *Pigot's Directory* 1821-22 & 23 does not record his business; therefore it is believed that he had a very short working life in Inverness. There is no mention of him in the *Inverness Parish Registers*, and no record of a burial has been found.

John Anderson's work is rare and difficult to find; it is however, found mainly on fiddle pattern flatware. His marks were 'I A, S, S, INS'; the 'S' in the middle of his marks is the end of the 'INS' punch and has no separate identity of its own.

ALEXANDER MACRAE 1794-1856

Alexander MacRae was born in Inverness and baptised on 30 October 1794; his parents were Murdoch MacRae and Janet Stewart. The *Inverness Parish Register* records Murdoch MacRae as a wheelwright, while Alexander's death certificate gave the occupation of his father as turner.

Alexander McRae was apprenticed to Alexander Stewart, goldsmith in Inverness, and the *Inverness Hammermen Incorporation Minute Book* recorded the registration of his indenture on 22 April 1812. Assuming he was apprenticed around 1808 he appears to have completed his apprenticeship in Tain, following his master's move there in December 1812. He then went to London, sometime after the completion of his apprenticeship, to gain experience in his trade, as did so many of his contemporaries.

Whilst in London Alexander met his future wife and they were married on 6 December 1819 at St Luke's Parish Church, Old Street. Entry No 574 reads: 'Alexander MacRae of this Parish Bachelor and Lydia Davis, of this Parish, Spinster were married in this Church by Banns with Consent of ... this Sixth Day of December in the Year One thousand eight hundred and Nineteen By me, J Rooke, – Minister.' Both Alexander and Lydia signed their names; the witnesses were Dugald MacTavish and Elizabeth Burford. Lydia Davis was born in London around 1792, daughter of John Davis, a merchant, and Lydia Nash. Alexander and Lydia's son Donald was baptised in the Parish of St Botolph, Bishopgate, London, on 20 November 1820. Alexander was recorded as a jeweller of Devonshire Street[74]. He returned to Scotland with his wife and son in about 1822 and lived in Dingwall initially, before commencing his business in Inverness.

Their next child, Sarah, was born in Dingwall around 1823; neither her birth or baptism have been found in the *Dingwall Parish Registers*[75]. Next was Lydia, baptised on 30 August 1825, in Inverness[76], father recorded as Alexander MacRae, jeweller. Their fourth and last known child, Flora, was baptised on 13 June 1827[77], also in Inverness, when Alexander was described as a jeweller, living in Douglas Row (one of the witnesses was James McRea, probably his brother).

The *Inverness Hammermen Minute Book* of 9 October 1823 records that Alexander MacRae, silversmith, was 'Craving delay till next meeting', indicating pressure being exerted by the Hammermen; nevertheless, he was admitted to the Incorporation on 2 November 1824. It seems from this that he probably returned to Inverness in 1823.

The *Inverness Town Council Minutes* of 29 September 1824 recorded: 'The Magistrates and Council appointed the following additional Constables for the ensueing year from this date ... Alex[r]. M[c]Rae, Silver Smith, Douglas Row.'

Pigot's Directory 1825 listed Alexander as a jeweller and silversmith in Castle Street; in the 1837 *Directory* his business had moved to 13 Bridge Street, noted

as a working jeweller, watch and clock maker. He was not found in *Slater's Directory* 1852.

On 15 June 1836 the *Hammermen Minute Book* recorded a meeting called for by a requisition signed by six members, three of which were silversmiths: Alexander MacRae, John MacRae and Alex MacLeod. The meeting minutes were recorded as follows:

> Proposed by Alex. MacRae silversmith and seconded by Alex. MacIntosh, saddler, That it is proper and expedient in consequence of the Bill introduced into Parliament by the Lord Advocate affecting the Royal Burghs of Scotland. That the Members of the Hammermen Incorporation do consider that it is highly proper and judicious to open up the Trade and that no freedom money should be exacted by the Corporation from any new beginners and that to bring about a total dissolution, of the Corporation. It was resolved upon to gather together all the cash belonging to the Corporation, in order to divide the same equally among all the Members entitled to the same and for carrying this to a final conclusion the following were appointed to act as a Committee to carry these objects into effect, and the following are the persons appointed to act on the Committee.

Nine members were listed, two of whom were silversmiths, Alex MacRae and John MacRae. At a further meeting, dated 20 June 1836, convened by the Deacon of the Hammermen Incorporation, the 7th Resolution stated 'That Alex. Macrae be appointed Clerk of the Committee'.

Alex MacRae, silversmith, appears again in the *Hammermen Minute Book* after a meeting held on 8 May 1838.

The 1841 Inverness census listed the family living on the east side of Church Street: Alexander, aged 36, a jeweller born in Inverness-shire; Lydia, aged 36, born in England; Sarah, aged 15; Lydia, aged 13; Flora, aged 11, and Donald, aged 17, a watchmaker's apprentice, born in England.

The 1851 Inverness census recorded Alexander, aged 48, born in Inverness, living at 8 Rose Street with his wife Lydia, aged 59, born in Wapping, London; together with 3 children, Donald, aged 28, a watchmaker born in Bishopsgate, London, Sarah, aged 24, born in Dingwall, and Lydia, aged 22, born in Inverness.

The signature in the *Hammermen Minute Book* for the minutes dated 17 September 1834 was that of Alexander MacRae, Hammermen's Incorporation clerk and jeweller.

In the 1851 census Alexander was described solely as a clerk; at his daughter's marriage and on her death certificate he was described as a writer and then as a mercantile clerk. He probably changed his employment from jeweller to clerk sometime after 1842.

No apprentices were recorded in the *Hammermen Minute Book* as having served time with Alexander MacRae.

Lydia MacRae died on 4 May 1856, aged 64, at 12 Rose Street and was buried in the Chapel Yard. Alexander MacRae died on 20 November 1856, aged 59, also at 12 Rose Street, Inverness; he died of bronchitis and was listed as a widower and jeweller. He was also interred in the Chapel Yard of Inverness. The informant was James MacRae, his brother, who lived at 10 Douglas Row.

Alexander MacRae used the following marks for his silver, 'A M R, HORSE H [incuse], A, A', 'A M R, HORSE, A' and 'A M R, S, S, INS'.

CHARLES CROTCHIE c1796–1858

Charles Crotchie was born in Italy around 1796, but nothing is known of his parents or his actual place of birth. He was first noted in Inverness in 1822 when the *Inverness Journal* of 12 July carried an advertisement for his new shop.

On 25 March and 27 May 1828 Charles Crotchie, jeweller in Inverness, appears in the Small Debt Record Book for the County of Ross pursuing Alexander Munro, carrier in Tain, for the sum of £1-12-9d.

In the *Inverness Journal* of 14 January 1831 Charles Crotchie intimated a change of address for his business to premises on Bridge Street, lately occupied by Mr Simon Fraser, Draper, where he would have for sale, 'Gold and Silver Watches, Jewellery of every description, Silver Plate, Hardware, Cutlery, Mirrors, Barometers, Thermometers, &c. C. C. Having purchased his Stock at the first Markets, with all the advantages that long experience and money command, is enabled to serve Families and Dealers with Goods of superior quality, at such prices as he hopes will ensure him a share of Public patronage. N. B.. Barometers, &c., Repaired.'

The *Inverness Town Council Minutes* dated 24 January 1831 record:

> Thereafter Petitions were presented from the following persons craving to be admitted to the Freedom of the Town and Guildry Vizt Thomas Fraser Draper Bridge Street, Alexander Munro Draper there, Charles Crotchie Jeweller there and John Lillie Grocer Merkinch–which Petitions being considered by the Magistrates and Council They Remit those of Thomas Fraser, Charles Crotchie and John Lillie to the Dean of Guild and his Council to settle for the freedom of the Guildry and report ...

In the *Inverness Courier* of 20 April 1831 Crotchie announced that he was to move his business. On 8 June 1831 the same newspaper reported that the move to 24 High Street had been completed, but to the second shop east of the British Linen Company's Office, not the third.

CHARLES CROTCHIE

RESPECTFULLY begs leave to intimate to the Ladies and Gentlemen of Inverness and its vicinity, and the Public in general, that he has lately opened Shop near the foot of Castle Street, Inverness, where he will always have on hand a large assortment of GOODS, consisting of Looking Glasses, Spy Glasses, Weather Glasses, Thermometers of all sorts, &c. &c. with a variety of other articles too tedious to mention.

N. B. All kinds of Looking Glasses, Spy Glasses, Weather Glasses, Thermometers, and many other articles in the line, Made and Repaired.

Orders from the country punctually attended to on moderate charges.

The *Town Council Minutes* dated 16 May 1831 reported that,'Petitions were also presented for Charles Crotchie and John MacRae Jewellers and Hardware Merchants in Inverness craving to be admitted to the Freedom of the Guildry, which were remitted to the Dean of Guild and his Council in order to fix the dues of their admission ...' The business was a protracted one; the *Minutes* of 5 September stated, 'In absence of the Dean of Guild the Clerk reported that the Dean of Guild and his Council had fixed the dues of admission into the Guildry of the following persons at Twenty pounds sterling each vizt -Alexander White, Charles Crotchie, Charles Playfair and John MacRae -The saids Charles Crotchie, Charles Playfair and John MacRae were directed to pay the ordinary dues to the Town of Five pounds each and afterwards to attend the Council in order to be admitted ...' It was not until 21 May 1832 that, having paid his admission dues, Charles Crotchie was finally admitted a Freeman Burgess and Guild Brother.

The *Inverness Parish Register* recorded on 16 December 1836 that Charles Crotchie, a merchant, of High Street, married Sarah Wells, of Wells Street, Inverness. The marriage is also recorded in St Mary's Catholic Church Register and reported in the *Inverness Journal*, of 23 December 1836: 'At Inverness, by the Rev. Mr Macpherson Mr C. Crotchie, Merchant, Inverness, to Sarah Wells, daughter of the late Mr Jonathan Wells, Founder.' Sarah Wells and her twin sister, Isabel, were born in Inverness and baptised on 23 September 1808; their parents were Jonathan Wells, founder[78], and Mary Muir. The baptisms of Charles and Sarah's children were noted in the St Mary's Catholic Church Register: Charles, born 23 February 1838; Maria, baptized 14 August 1839; John Jonathan, born 17 November 1840; Margaret, born 28 April 1843; Francesca, born 3 January 1845; Charles, born 12 June 1849,

Jewellery and Hardware,
WHOLESALE AND RETAIL.

CHARLES CROTCHIE, in returning thanks to the inhabitants of Inverness and its vicinity, for the very liberal encouragement he has experienced since he commenced Business, begs respectfully to intimate that he has received from the first markets, a large assortment of Gold and Silver Watches, London manufactured, Jewellery of all descriptions; Sheffield Plated Goods, an elegant assortment of Knives and Forks; Fire Irons, &c.

C. C. avails himself of this opportunity to inform his friends, that he intends removing at the term of Whitsunday first, to the third shop East of the British Linen Company's Office, No. 24, High Street, and to assure them that he will offer nothing for Sale but articles of genuine quality, at such prices as he hopes will ensure him of their further support and patronage.

N. B.—Barometers, &c. repaired, and the highest price allowed for old Silver and Gold.

Inverness, 19th April, 1831.

Inverness Courier
20 April 1831

and Sarah Isabella, born 18 March 1850. Unfortunately, their first and second sons died in infancy; a headstone in the Chapel Yard Burying Ground reads:

ERECTED BY CHA⁵. CROTCHIE, Jeweller Inv⁵⁵ And his Spouse SARAH WELES⁷⁹, In Memory of their Children, CHARLES Born 23ʳᵈ Febʸ 1838 Died 14ᵗʰ June 1841 ALSO JOHN JONATHAN Born 17ᵗʰ Novʳ 1840 Died 12ᵗʰ June 1841.

Whilst checking the Catholic Church Register, a baptism was noted of a child named Mary, 'daughter of Charles Crotchie and Isabella Jack born 14 April 1836'; no record of a previous marriage has been found for Charles Crotchie.

Pigot's Directory 1837 recorded Charles Crotchie as a travelling jeweller with premises at 25 High Street, Inverness.

The 1841 Inverness census shows the family living in High Street, on the north side: Charles Crotchie, aged 40, a merchant, not born in Inverness-shire, annotated 'Foreigner'; Sarah, his wife, aged 30; Charles, aged 3; Mary, aged 5; Maria, aged 1, and John, 6 months.

An advertisement in the *Inverness Courier* of 14 April 1841 carried the news that Charles Crotchie was giving up his present line of business.

The *Inverness Journal* of 2 July 1841 was used to announce the removal of all remaining stock to 94 Church Street 'and being in the way of retiring from his present line of business, the whole will be sold off without reserve, and intending purchasers may depend on getting good articles, at greatly reduced prices.'

The new year brought a new occupation for Charles Crotchie. The *Inverness Journal* of 31 January 1845 recorded:

Inverness Courier
14 April 1841

CHARLES CROTCHIE,

IN returning his grateful thanks to his numerous Friends and the Public, for the liberal share of patronage so long bestowed on him, begs leave to intimate, that he is about giving up his present line of business, with a view to which, he now offers his extensive Stock, at such prices as cannot fail to attract the notice of Dealers, and the Public in general. The Stock consists of Jewellery, Watches, Clocks, Cutlery, German Silver and Britannia Metal Goods, Barometers, Thermometers, Spring Glasses, Toilet Glasses, Ladies' and Gentlemen's Dressing Cases, with a great variety of other Articles.

As the whole will be Sold off without reserve, intending Purchasers may depend on getting good Articles, at greatly reduced prices.

C. C. requests that all those indebted to him will please make payment on or before the term of Whitsunday next. Parties having Claims against him, are requested to lodge the same, with as little delay as possible.

No. 24, High Street,
Inverness, 12th April 1841.

Charles Crotchie, MERCHANT, INVERNESS, Begs to intimate to the Nobility and Gentry of this and surrounding Counties, that, in consequence of numerous applications made to him for valuing various kinds of Stock, &c., he has now been induced to take out the License of APPRAISER, VALUATOR, and COMMISSION AGENT; and having a thorough knowledge of the value of all kinds of Merchandise, Household Furniture, as also of Farm Stock and Produce, trusts that, by strict and unremitting attention to all Business entrusted to his charge, he will merit a share of public patronage. C.C.. may state that he has engaged an Auctioneer in whom he has every confidence. N. B..–C. C. has opened the SHOP, NO. 63, PETTY STREET, for a short time, in order to dispose of his extensive Stock of Jewellery, Watches, Clocks, Hardware Goods, Barometers, Mirrors, &c. &.; and as the Stock must be Sold at Greatly Reduced Prices, it will be the interest of those requiring such articles to make an early call.

The 1851 Inverness census records the family living at 1 Cuthberts Close: Charles Crotchie, aged 54, a merchant, born in Italy; Sarah, his wife, aged 44; Maria, 11; Margaret, aged 8; Francis, 6, and Sarah, aged 1 year. There were also two servants living with the family at that address.

Over the next few years Charles Crotchie used the local newspapers to advertise auctions for such diverse items as horses, farm stock, houses, furniture and 'merchandise of every description'. An advertisement in the *Inverness Courier* of 12 March 1857 announced the selling off of the stock.

SELLING OFF, WITHOUT RESERVE, AT No. 7 INGLIS STREET, INVERNESS.

CHARLES CROTCHIE intimates to the inhabitants of Inverness and surrounding country, that he intends to begin on *Monday, the 16th March curt*, to SELL OFF the WHOLE STOCK, consisting of an Elegant Assortment of Superior Gold and Silver WATCHES; Gold and Silver Guards of different patterns; Albert and Fob Chains; JEWELLERY, such as Gold Rings, Ear-Rings, Brooches, Pins, Watch Seals and Keys; Silver Pencil-Cases, ditto Snuff-Boxes, &c., &c., in endless variety of Patterns. Also, CUTLERY; Fenders and Fire-Irons; English and American Eight-day Clocks; Writing Desks; Weather Glasses; Thermometers; Spying-Glasses; Mantelpiece Mirrors and Toilet Glasses of different sizes, of which there is a great quantity; and a variety of other Goods too numerous to mention.

CHARLES CROTCHIE's object in making this Sale is in consequence of his determination to close the Watch and Jewellery department of his business.

Should any party be disposed to purchase the whole Stock of Watches and Jewellery, he will be glad to treat with such party on most liberal terms. In the event of parties not coming forward to take the whole Stock on or before the 16th curt., C. C. will commence to Sell by Private Bargain, on every lawful day, from 9 A.M. till 6 P.M., and at 7 o'clock to Sell by Auction until the whole is cleared off, without reserve.

7 Inglis Street, Inverness, March 9, 1857.

Inverness Courier
12 March 1857

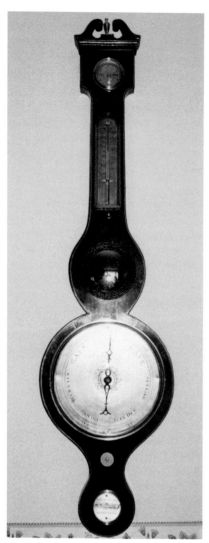

Barometer by Charles Crotchie.
Private Collection

Sarah Crotchie died on 6 May 1857 as the *Inverness Advertiser* of 19 May reported in the deaths column, 'At High Street, Inverness, on the 6th curt., Mrs. Chas. Crotchie, aged 48 years'.

That same year the following announcement appeared in the *Edinburgh Gazette* for 11 December 1857: 'The Estates of CHARLES CROTCHIE, Jeweller and General Merchant, Inglis Street, Inverness, were sequestrated on the 9th day of December 1857.' On 15 December a similar advertisement appeared in the *Inverness Advertiser* with the additional information for his Creditors of a meeting in the Union Hotel on 22 December. The same newspaper of 5 January 1858 stated that Charles Crotchie was 'to be examined in the Sheriff Court-house' on that date. Further meetings of his Creditors were called for on 11 February and 14 April, but while the legal implications of Charles' sequestration carried on, his death was reported in the Inverness Advertiser of 23 March 1858: 'At 26 High Street, on the 16th inst., Mr Charles Crotchie, auctioneer'. His death certificate showed that his date of death was actually 15 March, and that he was aged 62.

On 30 November 1858 the Inverness Advertiser, under the heading, 'Dividend', carried the following statement: 'Charles Crotchie, jeweller and general merchant, Inglis Street, Inverness – Creditors will receive a dividend at the shop of James Fraser, corn merchant, Bank Lane, Inverness, 10th January.'

The last reference to Charles Crotchie's estate was found in the *Edinburgh Gazette* of 14 July 1860, calling 'a meeting of the Creditors on said estate to be held within the Office of Macpherson & MacAndrew, Solicitors, 24, Douglas Row, Inverness, on Monday the 20th August next, at two o'clock afternoon, to consider as to an application to be made by me (James Fraser, Trustee) for my discharge.'

There is no mark known for Charles Crotchie; it appears that his jewellery business was mainly retail, but he may have produced barometers such as the wheel barometer, which bears his name.

WILLIAM MUNRO c1800–c1842

William Munro was born around 1800 but nothing is known of his early years until his marriage in Inverness in 1818. An entry for the 30 April of that year recorded 'William Munro Silversmith And Isabella Stephen'. Only one child was recorded in the *Inverness Parish Registers* for the couple and the baptism took place on 30 July 1829: 'William Munro, Goldsmith High Street and his spouse Isabella Steven had a child baptised by the Revd. Dr. Rose named William'. In the *Parish Registers* there was mention of a William Munro as a witness to

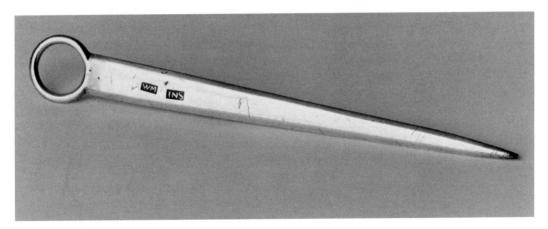

the baptism of Hugh McLeod, the son of Alexander McLeod, the Inverness silversmith who was born on the Isle of Skye; however, it does not state the trade of William Munro.

The 1821-22 & 23 *Pigot's Directory* recorded William Munro working in East Street as a goldsmith. By the 1825 edition he was listed as a jeweller and silversmith with business addresses in Fishmarket Brae and East Street; however, there was no mention of him in *Pigot's Directory* 1837.

The 1841 Inverness census listed William Munro as a journeyman jeweller, aged 40, living in Cummings Close, off High Street; the census stated that he was not born in Inverness-shire. He was living with his wife Isabella, aged 35, and their son William, aged 10, both born in Inverness-shire. As he was listed as a journeyman jeweller in the 1841 census and his business was not found at all in the 1837 *Directory*, it is believed that his business may have failed around 1830, and that he subsequently worked for one of the other Inverness jewellers or silversmiths. No further record of him or his family has been found in Inverness after the 1841 census.

It is possible that one or both of the 'W M, INS' maker's marks seen on Inverness marked silver may belong to William Munro, but they could equally belong to William Mason (see page 82).

Meat Skewer by William Munro or William Mason (14.6 cms).
Inverness Museum and Art Gallery.
Ewen Weatherspoon

JOHN McRAE c1804-72

John McRae was born in Inverness around 1804, the son of John McRae, a master tailor, and Ann McDonald, but neither his birth nor his baptism have been found in the *Inverness Parish Registers* although his parents were married in Inverness on 30 March 1799. No record of his apprenticeship has been found in the *Inverness Hammermen Minute Book*. However, the *Hammermen Minute Book* detailed, on 4 December 1826, John McRae as a 'Silversmith Craving to become a member of the Incorporation.' His petition was received and he was admitted on paying seven pounds sterling.

The *Town Council Minutes* dated 16 May 1831 recorded 'Charles Crotchie and John MacRae, Jewellers and Hardware Merchants in Inverness, craving to be admitted to the Freedom of the Guildry, which were remitted to the Dean of Guild and his Council in order to fix the dues of their admission', but no other evidence has been found to substantiate a possible partnership. The *Town Council Minutes* of 5 September 1831 stated 'In absence of the Dean of Guild the Clerk reported that the Dean of Guild and his Council had fixed the dues of admission into the Guildry of the following persons at Twenty pounds sterling each vizt. Alexander White, Charles Crotchie, Charles Playfair, and John MacRae-The saids Charles Crotchie, Charles Playfair and John MacRae were directed to pay the ordinary dues to the Town of Five pounds each and afterwards to attend the Council in order to be admitted.' However, no evidence has yet been found to indicate that John MacRae did become a Guild Brother.

The *Small Debt Book for the County of Ross* recorded that 'John Macrae, Jeweller Inv[ss]' was the pursuer of a debt against 'Alexander Fraser Tutor Arboll', on 12 March 1832.

Surprisingly, the *Hammermen Minute Book* noted only one apprentice trained by 'John McRae, Silver Smith', namely John MacKenzie, on 4 February 1833, although by this date many of the old strict practices of trade had disappeared.

The *Hammermen Minute Book* recorded on 15 June 1836, 'Jn° Macrae Silversmith' was at a meeting for 'to bring about a total dissolution, of the Corporation' (see page 73).

John McRae was listed in *Pigot's Directory* 1837 as a watch and clock maker at 11 High Street and *Slater's Directory* 1852 recorded him at the same address as a jeweller, silversmith, watch and clock maker.

The 1841 Inverness census listed John MacRae, a jeweller, aged 35, living at 27 Rose Street with Alexander MacRae, a merchant, aged 35, and his wife Mary aged 33.

The *Inverness Parish Register* recorded the marriage of John McRae, a jeweller from Rose Street, to Margaret Milne from High Street, Inverness, on 12 April 1844. Margaret Milne was baptised on 1 February 1825 in Ormiston, East Lothian; her father was John Milne and her mother was Christian Anderson. The St John's Episcopal Chapel Register also records the marriage of John and Margaret.

By the 1851 Inverness census John McRae was living at '3 Site of Old Bridge', an Inverness born jeweller and watchmaker, aged 46 years. His wife was Margaret, aged 26, born in Haddingtonshire[80]; there was a daughter listed called Isabella, aged 11, born in Knockbain[81], Ross-shire, but the *Knockbain Parish Registers* did not reveal whose daughter she was. The other three children were all born in Inverness: John, aged 5, Alexander, aged 3, and Cathine[82], aged 1 year. The children were all recorded in the St John the Evangelist Scottish Episcopal Church Baptismal Register: John, 5 October 1845; Alexander, 24 October 1847, and Christina, born 11 October 1849. There was another child, born on 18 April 1852, named Ann. On all occasions John McRae was recorded as a jeweller.

Soon after the birth of his daughter, Ann, an advertisement in the *Inverness*

Advertiser of 6 July 1852 stated that the partnership between John MacRae and John Pratt was dissolved (below).

Further research showed that a John McRae and Margaret Milne had a child called Jane, born on 8 March 1855, in the parish of Eastwood, Renfrewshire, which lies five miles south-west of Glasgow. The birth certificate recorded that the family lived at 7 King Street, Pollokshaws, that John McRae was a jeweller and clockmaker, aged 50, born in Inverness, his wife, Margaret Milne was aged 30, and that they were married, in Inverness, on 12 April 1844. Additionally, they had had four children, two boys and a girl living, and one girl dead[83]. They had a further six children, three of whom died in infancy, in Pollokshaws: William Finlay and Daniel, twins, born 12 August 1857, although William died 11 June 1866; James Campbell[84], born 27 October 1859; Charles, born 13 March 1862, died 4 December 1863; Mary Ann, born 6 April 1865, died 31 August 1865, and Thomas, born 31 July 1868.

John McRae had therefore moved from Inverness in about 1852 and set up business in Pollokshaws, where he was recorded in the *Slater's Directory* 1860 as a watchmaker, at 62 King Street. Pollokshaws was a manufacturing town and burgh in the parish of Eastwood, situated on the road to Irvine; the prime trade was spinning and weaving. It stands on the old estate of Nether Pollock, from which Pollock or Pollok (the ancient name of the parish of Eastwood), and the word shaw (a grove), the name is derived.

The 1861 Pollokshaws census found the family living at 79 King Street; John, aged 57, a watchmaker, born in Inverness; Margaret, aged 36, born in Pencaitland[85], Fife; Isabella[86], aged 21, a cotton weaver, born in Knockbain, Ross; John, aged 15, an apprentice watchmaker; Alexander, aged 13; Christina, aged 11; Jane, aged 6; William and Daniel, aged 3, and James, aged 1 year; the last four children were born in Pollokshaws.

The 1871 Pollokshaws census found John at 14 King Street, a watchmaker and jeweller, with his wife, Margaret, aged 45, and their children: Christina, aged 21, a draper's assistant; Jane, aged 16, a weaver; James, aged 11, a scholar, and Thomas, aged 2.

John McRae, watchmaker and jeweller, died on 11 August 1872, aged 68, at his home in King Street, of chronic bronchitis; the informant was his son, John.

Inverness Advertiser 6 July 1852

INTIMATION is Hereby Made, that the PARTNERSHIP between the Subscribers, as JEWELLERS and WATCHMAKERS in Inverness, was DISSOLVED upon the second day of June current, 1852, since which time the Business has been carried on solely for behoof of Mr PRATT, who intends to conduct it in future, he trusts, to the satisfaction of his employers.

JOHN MACRAE.
JOHN PRATT.

D. MACLENNAN, *Witness.*
HUGH SQUAIR, *Witness.*
Inverness, 30th June 1852.

John McRae's signature

John McRae's Inverness marks were: 'J.M^CR, INS, THISTLE', 'J.M^CR, INS', 'J M R, INS, running HORSE' or 'J M^CR, INS, BIRD THISTLE'. There are no known marks for him while in Pollokshaws.

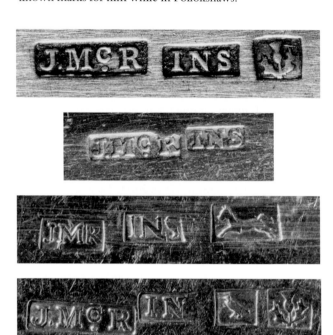

WILLIAM MASON 1808–70

William Mason was born in Inverness and baptised on 17 August 1808. The *Inverness Parish Register* recorded his father as William Masson, a carter, and his mother as Jean Fraser.

It is believed that he was apprenticed from about 1822 to Robert Naughten in Inverness. The only proof of this was recorded in the *Hammermen Minute Book* on 12 December 1842 (opposite).

The *Inverness Parish Register* states that William Mason and May Cameron had a child, Marjory, in fornication on 23 January 1832; William was described as a goldsmith from Green of Muirtown. They were, however, married on 27 December 1832, when they were recorded as both from Merkinch, Inverness. The baptismal register for Stromness, Orkney, recorded the birth of William's wife, Marjory Cameron, on 31 January 1811, the daughter of Lieutenant Allan Cameron of Captain McNiel's Company, 9th Royal Veteran Battalion, and his wife, Ann Purdie. Her death certificate recorded her father's employment as a Lieutenant in the 79th Regiment.

William and May's next child was called Marianne, born 20 October 1833, William described as a silversmith living at Huntly Street. The next recorded child was Jane[87], born on 17 August 1836, the mother given as Marjory Cameron and

William described as a jeweller living at Huntly Street. Their next child was called William, born 28 January 1839[88], the father again described as a jeweller but from Green of Muirton. The next child was Hugh, born 15 April 1841, the son of a jeweller from Huntly Street (this may be the jeweller H C Masson - recorded in William Stephen Ferguson's will of 1875 in Elgin); then Allina, born 13 June 1843, the family at that date living in Queen Street; Margaret, born 8 July 1845, the father a jeweller living in Bridge Street; Jamesina Maria, born 18 April 1847 and twins, James and Ruth, born 15 March 1849, the family still living in Bridge Street. The next child, Grace, was born 29 July 1850, with the family in High Street. Their last child was Janet Amelia Cameron, born 11 May 1853, daughter of a jeweller in High Street.

In *Pigot's Directory* 1837 Mason's business was recorded for the first time at 13 High Street and he was listed as a working jeweller.

William Mason was detailed in the 1841 Inverness census as a jeweller born in Inverness-shire, aged 30, living in Huntly Street with his wife Marjory, aged 25, and their five children: Marjory, aged 9; Maria, aged 7; Jane, aged 5; William, aged 2, and Hugh, aged 2 months; all born in Inverness-shire.

The *Hammermen Minute Book* recorded the following pertaining to William Mason's apprenticeship to Robert Naughten:

> Inverness 12 Dec' 1842. At a meeting of this date Mr. Joseph Willis gunmaker gave in his Bill with Security for Fifteen pounds Sterling-also Mr Angus Cameron gave in his Bill with Security for Fifteen pounds Sterling to the Corporation & Both Bills were lodged in the Box-Mr Alex' ... Saddler also produced his Burgess Stamp. Thereafter Mr William Masson Jeweler, was called when he produced his Indenture on which it appeared he had not entered. Mr Robert Naughten Jeweller service as an apprentice till some time after the date of Mr Naughten resigning his right to this Hammermen Incorporation - on which the meeting came to the unanimous resolution of charging him (William Mason) Twenty pounds Sterling being the ordinary dues of admitting him as a free Member of this Incorporation which he refused to comply with and the meeting therefore resolved to hand the case to Mr Campbell Soliciter for Prosecution. Alexander Mackintosh Interim Chairman.

There was no further record of this proceeding.

The *Inverness Courier* of 12 August 1846 carried an advertisement (below). In the *Inverness Advertiser* of 10 July 1849 Mason stated that he had removed from Bridge

ENGRAVING.

WILLIAM MASON, JEWELLER, most respectfully intimates to his numerous Friends, that he has now engaged an experienced ENGRAVER, whose work may be depended on will give satisfaction.

In this Department W. M. now can execute any orders favoured him, on short notice, in Plain and Ornamental Styles. Crests, Stamps, Name and Door Plates, &c., &c.

17, Bridge Street,
Inverness, 11th August 1846.

Inverness Courier
12 August 1846

Street to 1 High Street, Inverness. This address was previously occupied by Alexander McLeod.

The *Inverness Advertiser* of 4 December 1849 carried the following article:

CAIRNGORMS. — For some years these valuable minerals have been very rarely met with in the lofty mountain where alone they are procured; but the perseverance of some of the searchers would seem to be meeting of late with better success. The great floods, which occurred this year, may have been the means of laying bare the strata where the stones are found most abundant. Eight beautiful specimens were purchased, for a large sum, on Friday, by Mr. Mason, jeweller. They are of different colours, remarkably large, and all will admit of a brilliant polish. In the course of twenty years' experience, Mr. Mason has seen nothing to equal them for largeness of size and beauty. The largest is almost 9 inches in length, and 8½ inches in circumference. As is invariably the case with cairngorms, they are hexagons, with conical points, and protected with a hard crust.

In the 1851 census the family was living at 13 Bridge Street: William, aged 42, a jeweller, his wife, aged 40, together with ten children, two house servants and a nurse.

The *Inverness Courier* of 14 August 1851 carried an advertisement headed 'TO TOURISTS &c. VISITING THE CAPITAL OF THE HIGHLANDS. W. MASON, JEWELLER No. 1 HIGH STREET, begs respectfully to intimate his having on hand at present a choice selection of all the HIGHLAND BROOCHES and PLAID FASTENINGS; also a beautiful collection of CAIRNGORM and Scotch Pebble BRACELETS, &c., and other relics of Scotland.' Other advertisements recorded that he worked in the shop on the corner, 1 High Street, with 106 Church Street next door.

The same newspaper of 2 November 1854 carried a further advertisement (below). In the *Inverness Advertiser* his business was advertised on 19 August 1856 at 1 High Street on the corner of Church Street.

In the 1861 census the family was noted as living at 41 Huntly Street: William, aged 52, a jeweller; Marjory, aged 50; Mary Ann, aged 23, listed as 'attends her Fathers Shop'; William, aged 20, a silver engraver; Hugh, aged 18, a jeweller; then Alina, aged 16; Margaret, aged 14; twins James and Ruth, aged 10; Grace, aged 9, and Janet, aged 7.

The *Nairnshire Telegraph* of 16 July 1862 carried an advertisement (opposite) and the *Inverness Courier* of 15 October 1863 advertised: 'TO TOURISTS AND STRANGERS, &c., W. MASON, JEWELLER, HIGHLAND ORNAMENT MAKER, AND LAPIDARY, NO. 1

Inverness Courier
2 November 1854

WILLIAM MASON,
PRACTICAL JEWELLER, & FONDER OF ANCIENT SCOTCH ORNAMENTS.
SETTER OF SCOTCH PEBBLES, CAIRNGORMS, PEARLS, &c.
1 HIGH STREET,
Corner of Church Street.
Inverness, 15th August 1854.

HIGH STREET (Corner of Church Street), INVERNESS, and NO. 4 GEORGE STREET OBAN, begs respectfully to invite the attention of Ladies and Gentlemen VISITING the HIGHLANDS of SCOTLAND to his varied assortment of PLAID FASTENINGS AND ARMLETS, &c.'

Another advertisement appeared in the *Inverness Courier* of 4 July 1864 and followed a similar vein, except that it added 'W. MASON begs also to intimate that, from the number of Tourists, &c., visiting the picturesque and beautiful little town of OBAN, on their way to STAFFA and IONA, &c., he has been induced to extend a branch of his business there. 4 GEORGE STREET, opposite the Craigaird Hotel, OBAN.' In the 1866/67 *Inverness Directory* he was recorded as living at 41 Huntly Street.

In 1868 he became bankrupt and the *Inverness Advertiser* of 19 June 1868 recorded: 'William Mason, jeweller, Inverness -Creditors meet in the Caledonian Hotel, Inverness, 24th June, at three o'clock.-Stewart & Rule, solicitors, Inverness, agents.'

However, in the same newspaper of 12 February 1869 an advertisement stated that: 'MISS MASON (we presume this was Mary Ann/Marianne) begs respectfully to intimate that she still carries on her Father's business of JEWELLER and HIGHLAND ORNAMENT MAKER at NO. 22 Union Street'.

William's wife, Marjory, died on 10 November 1863, aged 52, at 41 Huntly Street; the informant was her son, Hugh. William Mason died on 4 April 1870, aged

<table>
<tr><td>

TO TOURISTS AND STRANGERS, &c.

WM. MASON, JEWELLER, HIGHLAND ORNAMENT MAKER, and LAPIDARY, No. 1 HIGH STREET *(Corner of Church Street,)* INVERNESS, begs respect-fully to invite the attention of Ladies and Gentle-men, Visiting the HIGHLANDS and its Capital, to his varied assortment of

PLAID FASTENINGS AND ARMLETS, &c.,

including various Ornamental and useful articles peculiar to Scotland, most of which are taken from ORIGINAL DESIGNS, and to the collection of which he has devoted much time for a number of years.

W. M. begs to enumerate a few of the leading articles, which will be found useful as Plaid Fasten-ings, &c., and which can be sent by post to any quarter, only by mentioning the name, viz. :—The Double Heart, the Stuart's Single do., the Flora Macdonald do., the Mary Queen of Scots, the Brooch of Lorn, the Glenlyon do., the Ross-shire Circlet, the Maid of Norway, Bannockburn, Tara, and Hunter-ston Brooches, the Iona Cross, &c.; My Heart's in the Highlands—this latter Brooch, though bearing a fanciful name, is an elegant piece of work; and some very handsome designs in BRACELETS, among them is the handsome

HIGHLAND BRACELET,

so characteristic of the Ancient Trellis and Runic Setting of Scotland. The CAIRNGORM ARMLET, which is set beautifully with Transparent Cairn-gorms of the deepest colour. Scotch Pearls set in Pins and Studs.

CREST BROOCHES *made to order on sending an Im-pression of the Crest or otherwise.*

P.S.—Parties having Cairngorms, Scotch Pebbles or any other Stones, can have them Cut and Polished either for Brooches or Bracelets, or for the Cabinet.
</td></tr>
</table>

Plaid Brooch by William Munro or William Mason.
Inverness Museum and Art Gallery

Nairnshire Telegraph
16 July 1862

61, also at 41 Huntly Street, Inverness. His death was probably hastened by the news of the death of his daughter, Jeanie, who had died in London on 26 March 1870. William's death certificate recorded him as a widowed jeweller who died of 'Cerebral disease with paralysis 2 years'. The informant was James Mason, his son. The paralysis would almost certainly have restricted his working capacity and probably brought about the subsequent sequestration of his estate.

A weathered gravestone was located in the Inverness Church Yard; the inscription, where it can be read, is as follows:

> ... MARJORY CAMERON THE BELOVED WIFE OF WILLIAM MASON JEWELLER INVERNESS DAUGHTER OF THE LATE ... ALLAN CAMERON SCA(MA)DALE ARGYLE-SHIRE WHO DIED 10 NOVEMBER 18 (63). AGED (52) YEARS AND OF THEIR SON WILLIAM WHO DIED (18 JULY 1862) AGED (23) YEARS'.

It is possible that one or both of the 'W M, INS' maker's marks (see pages 79 and 87) seen on Inverness silver may belong to William Mason; but they could equally have been by William Munro (see p78). One further note, a punch mark, 'H M, INV^{SS}', was recorded in Phillips Sale Catalogue of 22 October 1982, lot 202. It is probable that this mark belonged to the Hugh Mason mentioned above; there appear to be no other contenders.

The *Inverness Courier* of 6 January 1870 carried another advertisement for Miss Mason: 'MISS MASON begs most respectfully to intimate that she has REMOVED to that Shop, NO. 1 CHURCH STREET, opposite the Corner Shop, No. 1 High Street, formerly occupied by her father, where she now carries on the Business of JEWELLER and HIGHLAND ORNAMENT MAKER; and from her experience in Designing &c., she trusts that, by devoting her best attention to any Orders with which she may be favoured, to merit the patronage so long bestowed upon her father.'

Marianne Mason was recorded in the 1871 Inverness census living at 74 Church Street; she was the head of the family, aged 33, unmarried and listed as a 'Jewelleress Employing 6 men'. At the same address was her sister, Maggie, aged 24, and her brother, James, aged 21, a jeweller, as well as her married sister Allina Parsons together with her two children, Mary and Allice, born in Oban. The housekeeper was Marianne's unmarried aunt, Margery Parsons, aged 65. A general servant called Catherine Munro, aged 15, completed the household.

After William Mason became bankrupt it appears that William Fraser took over the premises at 1 High Street. The *Inverness Advertiser* of 23 November 1869 carried an advertisement: 'GOLDSMITH, WATCHMAKER, & JEWELLER. WILLIAM FRASER, 1 HIGH STREET, INVERNESS, has a large well-selected Stock, comprising – JEWELLERY OF SUTHERLAND GOLD. CAIRNGORM AND PEBBLE BROOCHES AND BRACELETS. LONDON-MADE JEWELLERY OF CHASE DESIGN. SILVER–ELECTROPLATED GOODS OF BEST QUALITY.'

The 1871 Inverness census recorded William Fraser at 35 High Street, as an unmarried lodger, aged 31; he was a goldsmith, jeweller and watchmaker, born in Kilmorack, Inverness-shire. The *Inverness Directory* 1873/74 gave him as a jeweller working at 1 High Street and living at 35 High Street. He advertised again in the *Inverness Courier* of 19 June 1873 at the same business address.

A further advertisement for this business was in the *Inverness Courier* of 25 February 1876: 'THE GREAT CLEARING SALE OF JEWELLERY, WATCHES, AND CLOCKS,

ELECTROPLATED GOODS, &C., 1 HIGH STREET.' It continued 'The Bankrupt Stock of WILLIAM FRASER, was bought at more than one-third below value, and a lot of first-class Goods have been secured at such low prices as enables the whole to be offered at prices unprecedented in the Capital of the Highlands.' The advertisement was dated 10 May 1875.

DONALD MacKENZIE c1809-c1851

The maker's mark of 'D MK conjoined' (overleaf) is probably that of goldsmith Donald MacKenzie. Donald MacKenzie was born on the Isle of Wight around 1809 and it is postulated that he was the son of a highland soldier stationed in England.

Donald lived in the High Street, Inverness, in March 1830, but by June he had moved to Castle Street, living there till at least 1841; by 1844 he had moved to Chapel Street where he stayed until at least 1851, when his occupation was given as a vintner and grocer in the census of that year. By 1861 the family was back in Castle Street where his wife was recorded as a jeweller's widow.

From the *Inverness Parish Register* we know that Donald MacKenzie, a jeweller in the High Street, married Margaret Macgillivray from Haugh on 2 March 1830. They had a daughter, Janet, born 24 June 1830 and a son, Simon, born 30 January 1832[89]; on both occasions the father was described as a goldsmith in Castle Street. The witnesses to the baptism of Janet were Simon MacKenzie and Alexander MacLeod, possibly Donald's master. The next child, Margaret, was born on 21 May 1834, the father listed as a jeweller in Castle Street, then Mary Chisholm, born 23 June 1836[90], father a goldsmith in Castle Street; Alexander, born 5 March 1839, and Donald, born 9 November 1841[91]; on both occasions the father was described as a jeweller in Castle Street. The next two children were born in Chapel Street: James Goodwin, 2 May 1844, and Donald, 27 July 1846, the father a jeweller in both entries.

It would appear plausible that Donald MacKenzie worked with or for William Munro/William Mason, as there is no record of a business in the name of Donald MacKenzie, and the 'thistle' punch found with the 'D MK' mark is the same as that used by William Munro/William Mason.

In the 1841 Inverness census Donald MacKenzie was listed as a 30 year old journeyman silversmith, born in England. The family was living in Castle Street: Margaret, aged 28; Jess, aged 10; Simon, aged 8; Mary C, aged 5, and Alexander, aged 2; all born in Inverness-shire. Also at that address was James McGillivray, aged 20, a journeyman upholsterer.

In the 1851 Inverness census for 16 Chapel Street, Donald MacKenzie, a vintner and grocer, aged 42, born on the Isle of Wight, was living with his wife, Margaret, aged 41; Simon, aged 18, an apprentice plumber; Mary, aged 14; Alexander, aged 12; James, aged 7, and Donald, aged 4 years.

The 1861 Inverness census for 82 Castle Street recorded Margaret MacKenzie, aged 49, jewellers widow; Simon, aged 28, a plumber; James, aged 16, an engineer, and Donald, aged 14.

There is no record of Donald MacKenzie's death between 1855 and 1861; it is, therefore, assumed that he died between April 1851 and December 1854, prior to the beginning of civil registration in Scotland in 1855. No burial record has been found for him.

The marks on two salt spoons by Donald MacKenzie, but neither are good impressions of his punches. They are depicted because they are the only objects noted by the authors with his maker's mark without 'W M'.

ANGUS MACLEOD c1810–c1845

No record of the apprenticeship of this silversmith has been found in Inverness, but the following was recorded in the register of *Apprentices Bound to the Incorporation of Goldsmiths, Edinburgh*. On 19 August 1825, Angus MacLeod, aged 15, was apprenticed to Andrew Wilkie; the date of expiry was to be 19 August 1832. The discharge of Angus MacLeod was recorded in the *Minute Book of the Goldsmiths' Incorporation* on 9 September 1833: 'There was produced Indenture betwixt Mr Wilkie and Angus Macleod, dated 19 August 1825 and which having expired on 19 August 1832 was discharged by Mr Wilkie on 28 August 1833, and was ordered to be minuted agreeably to the law. Andrew Wilkie Deacon Robert Howden Clerk.' It is possible, though not certain, that this was Angus MacLeod of Inverness and Elgin.

From this indenture and census returns it is believed that Angus MacLeod was born around 1810, but who his parents were and where he was born is unknown.

In the *Inverness Parish Register* Angus MacLeod (sic) was listed as a silversmith in High Street, Inverness, who married Catherine Brown Watson on 28 December 1835. The *Avoch Parish Register* dated 8 January 1836 also recorded details of the marriage and added that she was the daughter of the late Jeremiah Watson and her future residence was to be Inverness. Catherine Brown Watson was born in Inveresk on 4 October 1809, daughter of Jeremiah Watson, private in the Edinburgh Militia, and Anne Aird.

By the birth of Angus MacLeod's first son, Donald, on 11 October 1836, the family lived in Castle Street; their second son, Angus, was born on 24 August 1839, at Huntly Street; on both occasions the father was recorded as a silversmith and one of the witnesses was a William Munro.

The 1841 Inverness census for Huntly Street recorded Angus MacLeod, aged 30, silversmith, Catherine, aged 30, Angus, aged 1, and Ann Watson, aged 60, all born outside Inverness-shire.

Soon after this they moved to Elgin where the *Parish Register* stated that Angus MacLeod, silversmith in Elgin, and Catherine Watson his spouse, had a son, Hugh Watson (MacLeod), born on 28 February and baptised on 2 March 1842. On 19 April 1844 a further son, John, was born and his baptism was recorded in the *Parish Register* on 2 May. On both occasions one of the witnesses was a William Ferguson, whom we believe to be the goldsmith and watchmaker in Elgin (*Provincial Silversmiths of Moray*).

The 1851 Inverness census for 61 Upper Kessock Street noted a Marjory Geddes, aged 63, the widow of an army pensioner, living with her niece and four lodgers; two of the lodgers were Hugh McLeod, aged 9, and John McLeod, aged 7, both described as 'Pauper (Orphan at School)', and born in Forres.

Catherine MacLeod, pauper, died on 17 March 1856 in the Poor House, Inverness, described as a widow, aged 47 years. Her parents were recorded as Jeremiah Watson, a private in the Edinburgh Militia, and Anne Aird. She was buried in the Chapel Yard of Inverness. Despite extensive research in Elgin, Inverness and Forres, no record of the death of Angus MacLeod has been found.

Silver marks which could be attributed to Angus MacLeod are: 'A ML conjoined, INS, THISTLE', 'A ML conjoined, INS, A ML conjoined, THISTLE', and AML, INS, DISC, DISC, DISC'. However, these three sets of marks probably belong to Alexander McLeod (see page 70).

JAMES PEARSON c1812–c1852

James Pearson was born in Perth around 1812, the son of James Pearson, weaver. He was listed in the *Perth Hammermen Incorporation Book*, on 12 June 1827, when he was apprenticed to Charles Murray, goldsmith and jeweller, for 7 years from 16 April 1827; his father was one of his cautioners.

The *Perth Parish Register* recorded the marriage, on 13 July 1838, of James Pearson, jeweller, and Agnes Murie, daughter of the late Thomas Murie, Sergeant Major in the Perthshire Militia, in the East Church Parish. Their first child, Elizabeth Ann, was born in Perth on 28 April 1839, and it appears that James and his family moved to Edinburgh sometime after this as their next child, Agnes, was born there around 1842. We have no further record until the *Inverness Parish Register* details the birth, on 18 April 1850, of a son, James, to James Pearson, jeweller in Chapel Street, and Agnes Murie.

The 1851 Inverness census recorded the family living at 12 Chapel Street: James Pearson, aged 39, a journeyman jeweller, born in Perth; his wife, Agnes Murie, aged 35, born in Perth; Betsy Ann, aged 11, born in Perth; Agnes, aged 9, born in Edinburgh; Margaret, aged 5; Sarah, aged 3, and James, aged 11 months; the last three were born in Inverness. No further record of the family has been found.

RICHARD LOCKWOOD STEWART 1812–87

Richard Lockwood Stewart was the son of Thomas Stewart, goldsmith in Elgin and later Inverness, and Mary Lockwood; he was their first child, born in Elgin on 9 November 1812.

The first evidence of Richard Stewart is when he advertises in the *Inverness Courier* of 4 March 1840: 'TO BE DISPOSED OF BY SUBSCRIPTION. RICHARD L. STEWART, Jeweller, Petty Street, begs leave most respectfully to acquaint the Inhabitants of Inverness and Vicinity, that he intends to dispose of the following valuable articles by Subscription Tickets, at 3s. each, to be drawn on Friday, 15th May 1840, in the Trades' Hall Inverness, N.B.– All prizes no Blanks.' There followed a long list of prizes with prices amounting to £64-13s. Another advertisement appeared in the *Inverness Courier* of 13 May 1840 (below).

Richard Lockwood Stewart, jeweller, was recorded as living with his parents in Petty Street in the 1841 Inverness census.

The *Inverness Parish Register* recorded that Richard Stewart, jeweller, Petty Street, and Margaret McLennan, Castle Street, both of Inverness, were married on 31 May 1847 by Rev Henry Hastlings, Wesleyan Minister.

The Inverness 1851 census for 18 Petty Street noted Richard Stewart, watchmaker and jeweller, aged 38, born in Elgin, living with his wife, Margaret, 46, from Kilmorack, near Beauly, which is west of Inverness. They appear not to have had any children.

On the death of his father in 1856, Richard took over the family business, being described in *Slater's Directory* 1860 as a watch and clock maker at 14 Petty Street.

The 1861 Inverness census recorded Richard, aged 48, a jeweller and watchmaker, with his wife, aged 56, at 18 Petty Street, together with three apprentices:

RICHARD L. STEWART,
JEWELLER, PETTY STREET,

BEGS leave to acquaint his Subscribers, and the Inhabitants of Inverness and the surrounding Counties, that owing to the Returns not having arrived from the different parts of the country, and as there is a small quantity of Shares still to be disposed of, he is under the necessity of postponing the Drawing of the Subscriptions to Friday 5th June.

All those who have not supplied themselves with Shares, are requested to apply as soon as possible.

May 12, 1840.

Alexander Robertson, aged 18, born in Inverness; Donald Ritchie, aged 18, born in Lochgorm, and David MacGillivray, aged 16, born in Nairn. The *Inverness Directory 1866/67* recorded Richard Stewart at 18 Petty Street, a watchmaker and jeweller. He was not listed in *Slater's Directory 1867* nor in the *Inverness Directory 1873/74*. The death of Margaret Stewart occurred on 31 May 1877 at 1 Mitchell Street, Dundee. She had been married twice; first to John Fraser, a road contractor. Her parents were given as Duncan McLennan, a linen weaver, and Margaret McQueen. The 1881 Dundee census for 1 Mitchell Street recorded Richard Stewart as a widower and jeweller, aged 68, born in Elgin. Also living at that address were three boarders, Margaret McL or Crow, aged 48, and Susan Montange, aged 24, together with George Crow, aged 4 years. Richard Stewart, journeyman jeweller, died at 3 Mitchell Street, Dundee, on 23 March 1887. The informant was his niece, Ann Samson. There are no known marks for Richard Stewart.

JOHN PRATT c1820–1901

John Farlaha[92] Leith Pratt was born in Aberdeen around 1820; his father was John Pratt, a woollen weaver, and his mother Isabella Douglas. A burial was noted, in the Aberdeen Spital Burial Ground, of a William, aged 2½ years, son of John Pratt, weaver in Aberdeen, on 12 May 1820. Nothing more is known of John Pratt junior until he arrived in Inverness. The *Inverness Parish Register* recorded that John Pratt, a jeweller, from Castle Street, married Rebecca Fletcher, from the 'same place', on 10 September 1844, in Inverness. John Pratt must have arrived in Inverness shortly before this date as there is no record of him in the 1841 census. John and Rebecca had ten known children: Isabella Ann, born 20 January 1845; John, born 18 October 1846, died 20 April 185(2); Jemima McDonell Fletcher, born 22 October 1848, died 6 August 1849; Thomas Fletcher[93], born 20 December 1850; John, born c1853[94], Rebecca Macdonell, born 3 June 1855; Andrew Alexander, born 3 October 1857, died 22 November 1857[95]; Lydia Sutherland, born 23 December 1858, died 15 March 1913; Caroline McDonell, born 21 August 1861, and, James, born 20 November 1864, died 31 October 1865.

John Pratt was recorded in the 1851 Inverness census living with his family at 34 Castle Street; he was aged 28, a master jeweller employing two men, and born in Aberdeen. His wife, Rebecca, was aged 26, born 'N.A.[96] British Subject', with two children born in Inverness; Ann Isa, aged 6, and Thomas, aged 3 months. Also at the same address as lodgers were his wife's parents: Thomas Fletcher, aged 60, late merchant, born in Red Castle, Ross, and Ann Fletcher, born in Inverness. The *Inverness Advertiser* of 6 July 1852 announced, 'INTIMATION is Hereby Made, that the PARTNERSHIP between the Subscribers, as JEWELLERS and WATCHMAKERS in Inverness, was DISSOLVED upon the second day of June current, 1852, since which time the Business has been carried on solely for behoof of Mr Pratt, who intends to conduct it in future, he trusts, to the satisfaction of his employers.' The subscribers were John MacRae and John Pratt. The *Inverness Courier* of 12 August 1852 carried another advertisement (see page 92).

Slater's Directory 1852 recorded the business in the name of John Macrae, under 'jewellers & silversmiths' and 'watch & clockmakers', at 11 High Street.

Inverness Courier
12 August 1852

11   HIGH STREET,   11
INVERNESS.

JOHN PRATT, JEWELLER and WATCHMAKER, begs
leave to intimate to the inhabitants of Inverness
and the surrounding country, that he has commenced
Business in the above line, and, from his long practical
experience in the trade, he trusts to be favoured with a
share of public patronage. JEWELLERY and HIGH-
LAND ORNAMENTS of all descriptions made to
order. All kinds of WATCHES CLEANED and
REPAIRED.
N.B.—An experienced Watchmaker kept upon the
premises. All Watches sold by J. P. will be warranted.
Jewellery and Watches sent for repair will be punctually attended to.
Inverness, 2d August 1852.

The *Inverness Advertiser* of 1 November 1853 carried an advertisement:

JOHN PRATT, JEWELLER AND WATCHMAKER, 11 HIGH STREET, 11, Takes this opportunity of returning thanks to the public in general, for the liberal share of patronage he
has received since he commenced Business, and begs to state that he still continues to
make all kinds of HIGHLAND ORNAMENTS and JEWELLERY, BROOCHES, and BONNET
CRESTS of every description. J. P. always keeps a first-rate Watchmaker for repairing all
kinds of Foreign and British Watches and Clocks. Jewellery and Watches of every kind
Repaired. All Watches sold by J. P. are warranted to be good time-keepers. An APPREN-
TICE WANTED.

Civil Registration began in Scotland in 1855 and the certificates issued in that
year give many details not recorded before or after. Rebecca Macdonell Pratt was
born on 3 June 1855. The family lived at 34 Castle Street, Inverness; the father's full
name was John Farlaha Leith Pratt, a master jeweller, aged 33, born in Aberdeen.
The mother was Rebecca Forbes MacDonell Fletcher, aged 27, born at Fort Dair,
Hudson Bay Territory. They had two boys and one girl living, one boy and one girl
were deceased.

It appears that the business carried on by John Pratt at 11 High Street ceased
somed time after 1853 as *Slater's Directory* 1860 noted Roderick McKenzie, watch
and clockmaker, at that address.

The 1861 Inverness census listed the family living in Aultnaskiach Cottage: John
Pratt, aged 38, a jeweller; Rebecca, aged 35, born in Red River, North America;
Ann I, aged 14; Thomas, aged 9; John, aged 7; Rebecca, aged 5; Lydia, aged 2;
Thomas Fletcher, aged 72, born Rosskeen, Ross-shire, and Ann Fletcher, aged 65,
who was born on the Island of Guernsey.

John Pratt is not mentioned in the *Inverness Directory* 1866/67; however, he is in
the 1873/74 *Directory*, living at 5 Albert Place, listed as a jeweller.

The 1871 Inverness census recorded the family at 5 Albert Place: John, aged 50,
jeweller; Rebecca, aged 45, born in America, British Subject; Annabella, aged 23,
teacher; Thomas, aged 19, jeweller; John, aged 16, message boy; Rebecca, aged 14;

Lydia, aged 9, and Caroline, aged 7; there was also a grandson, Alexander Stewart[97], aged 1 year, living with them.

The 1881 Inverness census found the family at 6 Albert Place; John, aged 61, a jeweller; Rebecca, aged 56, born at Red River, North America; Lydia, aged 18, an upholsteress; Rebecca, aged 21, a machinist; Caroline, aged 16, an upholsteress, and the grandson Alex[r] P Stewart, aged 10 years.

Thomas Pratt, son of John Pratt, and his family were also recorded in the 1881 census living at 43 Castle Street; Thomas Pratt, aged 27, a jeweller/silversmith, Jessie, his wife, aged 27, and Rose, aged 2 years, all born in Inverness.

John's wife, Rebecca, died on 18 February 1889, aged 71, at 6 Albert Place.

The 1891 Inverness census showed John to be an 'employed jeweller', aged 72, living with his daughter, Lydia, aged 24, an unmarried housekeeper and a grandson, Thomas Mackintosh[98], aged 9.

John Pratt, jeweller journeyman, died on 24 May 1901, aged 82, at 6 Albert Place. The informant was Thomas Pratt, his son, who lived at 3 Factory Court, Inverness. It would appear that John Pratt was a journeyman jeweller for most of his working life. He was a master jeweller in early 1851 but by January 1859 he was a journeyman once more. There are no known maker's marks for John Pratt.

A family gravestone was found in the Chapel Yard, Inverness; the inscription as follows:

ERECTED by JOHN PRATT jeweller Inverness, and his wife REBECCA FLETCHER to the memory of their children JAMIMA who died 6TH August 1849 aged 9 months. JOHN who died 20TH April 185(2) aged 5½ years ANDREW ALEX[R]. who died 7TH Nov[R] 1857 aged 7 weeks.

ROBERT NAUGHTEN JUNIOR 1830–99

Robert Naughten was born in Inverness on 23 May 1830, first-born child of Robert Naughten, jeweller, and Sarah Greenslade Nicholson. When Robert Naughten senior died in 1857, his son Robert took over the business. Robert junior was recorded in *Slater's Directory* 1860 as a 'jeweller and silversmith (& goldsmith)' at 14 Church Street, Inverness. Robert Naughten junior married Mary Ross Grant on 10 November 1858 at Inverness; Robert, aged 28, lived in Church Street, and Mary, aged 25, lived in Telford Street. Mary was born on 7 April 1832, in Elgin; her parents were John Grant, a painter[99], and Janet Ross. John Grant was a widower at the time of his daughter's marriage, residing at Meynar Cottage, Elgin.

Robert and Mary had five children: Robert Nicholson, 5 September 1859; Mary Jane, 26 January 1861; Alexander Grant, 19 February 1863; Frederick Thomas, 19 August 1864, and William Ross Grant, 11 July 1871, who died on 18 August 1871 and was buried in Tomnahurich cemetery.

The *Inverness Courier* of 12 July 1860 carried an advertisement which read, 'FOR SALE. A SOLID SILVER TEA URN, beautifully chased; will be Sold at a moderate price. Apply to R. Naughten, jeweller, Inverness.'

The 1861 Inverness census listed the family at 13 Church Street: Robert was recorded as a jeweller, aged 30, employing three men & a boy; Mary, aged 28, born in Elgin; Robert N, aged 18 months, and Mary Jane, aged 2 months, both born in

Inverness. Also at the address were Grace and Eliza MacDonald, domestic servants.

The *Inverness Courier* of 3 July 1862 advertised the business (below). The *Inverness Advertiser* of 18 March 1864 carried this small but interesting advertisement: 'R. NAUGHTEN, JEWELLER, begs to inform his Friends and Customers that, during alterations to be immediately commenced to his Shop, the STOCK will be REMOVED to his HOUSE (immediately above the Shop), where the business will be conducted as usual. The WORKING DEPARTMENT will be carried on without interruption. 14 Church Street, March 3d, 1864.' Therefore, his business was at 14 Church Street, while his house was 13 Church Street above the shop, with the workshop probably behind. These alterations must have been quite extensive as they lasted two months, the *Inverness Advertiser* of 10 May 1864 carrying the following: 'R. NAUGHTEN, JEWELLER, begs to inform his Friends and Customers that the alterations on his Premises being now completed, the SHOP has been OPENED for Business as formerly. Inverness, 9th May 1864.'

The *Inverness Courier* of 21 July 1864 carried a very similar advertisement (see p95) to that for 3 July 1862 but added 'Silver Mounted Quaighs. Ram's Head, and other Snuff-Mulls. Best English Jewellery. SILVER PLATE and Best ELECTRO-PLATED GOODS. An Experienced Engraver kept.'

(see p95)

Inverness Courier
3 July 1862

ROBERT NAUGHTEN,
JEWELLER, SILVERSMITH, & MANUFACTURER OF HIGHLAND ORNAMENTS,
14 CHURCH STREET, INVERNESS,
(Near the Caledonian Hotel),
ESTABLISHED FIFTY YEARS.

In whose possession are the Original Models of ANCIENT HIGHLAND BROOCHES.

Scotch Pebble and Cairngorm Ornaments for the Highland Brooches and Bracelets, in Gold and Silver.	Dress.
	Dirks, Sporrans.
Scotch Pebble and Cairngorm Studs, Sleeve Links, and Vest Buttons.	Powder Horns.
	Shoulder and Waist Belts and Buckles.
Scotch Pebble Ear-rings.	Pistols.
Pebble Vinaigrettes.	Shoulder Brooches.
Pebble Dirk and Claymore Brooches.	Kilt Brooches.
	Skene-dhus.
Silver Crests and Frosted Silver Clan Badges.	Shoe Buckles, Buttons.
	Silver-Mounted Quaighs, with Gaelic Mottos.
All the Patterns of Ancient Silver Heart Brooches, Queen Mary Brooches, &c.	Ram's-head Snuff Mulls.
	Silver-Mounted Snuff Mulls, Cairngorm Tops.
Ancient Highland Double Heart Wedding Rings, in Gold and Silver, and Scotch Pearl Rings.	Granite Curling Stone Paper Weights, &c.

JEWELLERY, SILVER PLATE, AND PLATED GOODS.
All kinds of Plain and Ornamental ENGRAVING executed in the best style.
3d July 1862.

94

The *Inverness Directory* 1866/67 recorded Robert Naughten, jeweller and silver-smith, working at 14 Church Street, adding his home address, 13 Church Street, in the 1873/74 edition.

An advertisement in the *Inverness Courier* of 21 July 1870 recorded that Naugh-ten was still working at '14 CHURCH STREET, INVERNESS (Near the Caledonian Hotel and same side of the Street)'.

The family were at 13 Church Street in the 1871 census: Robert Naughten, aged 40, a jeweller; Mary, aged 37; Robert, aged 11; Mary Jane, aged 10; Alexander, aged 8, and Frederick, aged 6. There were two domestic servants.

The *Inverness Courier* of 24 February 1876 carried an advertisement:

ESTABLISHED FIFTY YEARS. ROBERT NAUGHTEN, JEWELLER, SILVERSMITH, & MANUFAC-TURER OF HIGHLAND ORNAMENTS. 27 CHURCH STREET, INVERNESS, (Near the Cale-donian Hotel and same side of the Street).' The advertisement continued, 'The 'CADBOLL BROOCH', Registered September 1869, a reproduction in Sutherland Gold, of the finest specimen of early Celtic Brooch discovered in the North. The 'CROMAR-TIE' BROOCH and PENDANT, Registered December 1869. Reproductions in Gold and Native Stone of various other ancient Brooches, recently discovered in the North. Correct copies of all the Pictish Stone Crosses found in Sutherland, and of the best specimens of Argyll-shire Crosses.

The *Inverness Courier* of 13 July 1876 carried a similar advertisement but this stated that the business had been 'ESTABLISHED SIXTY YEARS.' The previous week's issue of the *Inverness Courier* still stated 'ESTABLISHED FIFTY YEARS'. This would broadly tie in with the partnership between Charles Jameson and his father which had commenced in August 1813. However, it might also indicate that 1816 was the year in which Robert Naughten's father parted from Charles Jameson.

It would appear, on first sight, that Robert Naughten moved sometime in 1875. However, the description of the premises seems to be the same; it is possible that Church Street was renumbered and his address changed from 14 to 27.

The *Inverness Advertiser* of 29 June 1880 advertised as follows: '20 PER CENT. DISCOUNT. R. NAUGHTEN, GOLDSMITH, 27 CHURCH STREET, begs to intimate to his

ROBERT NAUGHTEN,
JEWELLER, SILVERSMITH, & MANUFACTURER OF
HIGHLAND ORNAMENTS,
14 CHURCH STREET,
(Near the Caledonian Hotel,)
INVERNESS.
In whose Possession are the ORIGINAL MODELS of
Ancient Highland Brooches.
ESTABLISHED FIFTY YEARS.
CAIRNGORM and SCOTCH PEBBLE BROOCHES
and BRACELETS in Gold and Silver.
Silver Enamelled BROOCHES, &c.
Ancient Silver HEART BROOCHES.
Frosted Silver Crest, Badge, and Slogan Brooches.
HIGHLAND MOUNTINGS.
Silver Mounted Quaighs.
Ram's Head, and other Snuff-Mulls.
Best English Jewellery.
SILVER PLATE and Best ELECTRO-PLATED GOODS.
An Experienced Engraver kept.

Inverness Courier
21 July 1864

*Inverness Courier 17 December 1881 and
20 July 1882*

Customers and the Public that the above advantageous rate of
Discount will be discontinued at the end of the present month,
and therefore respectfully solicits an early inspection from those
who wish to obtain really good articles at very moderate prices.'

The 1881 Inverness census recorded the family as living at
25 Church Street: Robert, aged 50, a jeweller, employing one
man and a boy; Mary R., his wife, aged 48; Mary J, aged 19;
Alexander G, aged 18, architects assistant; Frederick T, aged 16,
scholar, and Catherine McLean, a domestic servant.

Mary Ross Naughten, wife of Robert Naughten, master
jeweller, died on 1 August 1881, at 25 Church Street, Inverness, aged 49. The informant was Robert Naughten.

The *Inverness Courier* of 17 December 1881 had a sale
advertisement (above). Another advertisement of 29 Decem-
ber 1881 stated 'CLEARING SALE OF JEWELLERY. The Whole
Stock of MR. R. NAUGHTEN, 27 CHURCH STREET, Is now
Offered, for a few Weeks, at 33½ (sic) per cent. or one third
Below Regular Selling Prices, and some things at Half Price.'
The last advertisement concerning Robert Naughten was in
the *Inverness Courier* of 20 July 1882 (above).

As *Slater's Directory* 1882 recorded P G Wilson with a shop
at 27 Church Street, it would appear that Robert Naughten
sold his business to P G Wilson in the first half of that year.
Robert retired to Milton, near Drumnadrochit, close to
Urquhart Castle on the banks of Loch Ness.

The 1891 census for Urquhart and Glenmoriston listed
Robert Naughten at Temple, as a boarder, widower, aged 60;
he was recorded as a retired jeweller, born in Inverness. The
head of the household was a widow named Catherine
Cameron, aged 67, who was living on private means.

Robert Naughten died at Milton on 12 February 1899,
aged 69. The marks illustrated are attributed to Robert Naughten junior; they are: 'R N, INS, thistle' or 'R N, INS'. Nevertheless
he may have continued to use his father's punches after 1857.

JAMES FERGUSON 1834–1910

(Ferguson Brothers, Ferguson & Son)

James was born on 9 September 1834 at Gairloch[100], Ross-shire; his parents were John Ferguson, a master mason[101], and Isabella Brotchie[102].

The 1851 census for 4 Celt Street, Inverness, recorded Isabella B Ferguson as a 41 year old widow and midwife, who was born in Chelmsford, England. Four children were listed: Elizabeth, aged 20, born in Dingwall; Alexander, aged 18, an apprentice jeweller, born in Dingwall; James B, aged 16, an apprentice watchmaker, born in Gairloch, and William, a 14 year old scholar, born in Dingwall.

It would appear that James was apprenticed to an Inverness watchmaker from 1848 to around 1855 and then, to gain experience, spent some time with a leading London watchmaker.

James Ferguson commenced business in Inverness at 15 Bridge Street in May 1857. The opening advertisement appeared in the *Inverness Courier* of 28 May 1857 (below).

The following year his address was 15 & 17 Bridge Street, Inverness; the *Inverness Courier* of 13 May 1858 carried his advertisement as a watch and chronometer maker and manufacturing jeweller at that address, and he was also listed working there in *Slater's Directory* 1860, as both a jeweller and silversmith and watch and clockmaker.

The 1861 census for 15-17 Castle Street, Inverness, listed Isabella Ferguson, a widowed midwife, aged 51, with two sons living with her: James, aged 26, a watchmaker and jeweller employing 5 men and 4 boys, and William, aged 24, a jeweller.

An advertisement placed in the *Inverness Courier* of 24 July 1862 recorded James Ferguson working at the above address and detailed his stock, which included 'sterling SILVER SPOONS. 7s. 6d. per ounce.'

CHRONOMETER AND WATCHMAKER.

JAMES FERGUSON begs respectfully to inform the Public of INVERNESS and the surrounding country, that he has commenced Business as above, in the Shop, 15 BRIDGE STREET, where he has a good selection of GOLD and SILVER WATCHES, English and Geneva; Repeating Watches in Hunting Cases, with all the latest improvements; French and English TIMEPIECES; EIGHT-DAY CLOCKS, &c.

Also, a new and highly fashionable assortment of Gold Guards and Albert CHAINS, SEALS, KEYS, &c.

J. F. having, during his recent engagement in one of the first Establishments in London, added considerably to his knowledge of his trade, and having a Choice Stock of Watch Material, suited for all kinds of Repairs, he can guarantee the skilful performance of the same. He hopes by strictly attending to Business, and in giving satisfaction to those who may honour him with their favours, to obtain that share of patronage which he will study to deserve.

Inverness, 27th May 1857.

Inverness Courier
28 May 1857

The Inverness Advertiser of 14 July 1863 announced:

WATCHMAKING & JEWELLERY ESTABLISHMENT DINGWALL. The very encouraging
Support received from the Nobility, Gentry, and Inhabitants of Ross-shire generally,
has induced the SUBSCRIBER to OPEN a BRANCH of his ESTABLISHMENT in DINGWALL;
and he trusts this arrangement will meet with a continued and extended Patronage,
and hopes the Opening of a First-Class Jewellery and Watchmaking Establishment in
the centre of an important district will meet the public approbation and support.
Efficient workmen always in attendance. JAMES FERGUSON, 15 & 17 BRIDGE STREET,
INVERNESS.

In August 1866 James and his brother William entered into a partnership, trading
as Ferguson Brothers, and were listed in the *Inverness Directory* 1866/67 working at
41 Union Street, James living at 74 Church Street with William living at 8 Drummond Street.

The Ferguson Brothers advertised in the *Inverness Courier* of 23 August 1866
that they were working at the corner of Union Street, opposite the Caledonian
Hotel; they were listed at the same address in the 1867 *Slater's Directory*.

James married Mary Anne Combe[103] on 17 October 1866 in Edinburgh; her
father was Matthew Combe, a tailor, and her mother Anne Conochie. Their first
child was John, born 11 September 1867 at 16 Seton Place, Grange, Edinburgh;
next was Matthew on 1 March 1869, at 10 Rankeillor Street, Edinburgh; Ann, born
on 18 January 1871 at Broadstone Park, Inverness; Isabella, 10 November 1872, at
Denny Street; James, 4 May 1874, at 4 Laurel Terrace (died of bronchitis 19 March
1875); James Combe, 13 January 1876, at 5 Friars Place (died 4 April 1880); Elizabeth, 11 January 1878; Mary Jane, 21 April 1880; Agnes, 23 July 1882, at 43 Huntly
Street, and William, 20 July 1884, at 2 Huntly Place.

It appears that James Ferguson had taken his younger brother into partnership
with the intention of expanding the business by opening a new branch of Ferguson Brothers in the south of Scotland. Following his marriage in October of 1866
he opened new premises in Glasgow, and the *Scotsman* of 21 August 1867 advertised
Ferguson Brothers at 3, Renfield Street, Glasgow. This must have been short-lived
for the *Edinburgh & Leith Post Office Directory* 1868-69 listed Ferguson Brothers at
18 South St Andrew Street, Edinburgh, and an advertisement in the same *Directory*
stated that Ferguson Brothers, jewellers, watchmakers and goldsmiths to His Royal
Highness the Prince of Wales, were the sole agents in Inverness and the North for
Elkington & Co, plate manufacturers to Her Majesty the Queen. James Ferguson's
home was given as 10 Rankeillor Street, Edinburgh. Ferguson Brothers were listed
for the year 1868-69 only, and it appears that soon after the birth of his second
child, in March 1869, James Ferguson returned to Inverness with his family.

The *Inverness Courier* of 6 January 1870 carried an advertisement for Ferguson
Brothers, Inverness, stating that they had, 'an excellent assortment of SUTHERLAND
GOLD JEWELLERY, of their own Design and Manufacture.'

The *Inverness Courier* of 19 May 1870 advertised:

BY SPECIAL APPOINTMENT TO HIS ROYAL HIGHNESS THE PRINCE OF WALES. FERGUSON
BROTHERS, in submitting the following as their PRICE LIST of ELECTRO-PLATED
SPOONS, &c., beg to draw particular attention to the fact that all the articles are made
of the best material, plated by the most approved process with all the recent improvements, and for extreme purity and durability cannot be surpassed, while from their

silvery whiteness, the most minute scrutiny cannot distinguish them from sterling silver.

The price of table spoons and forks, fiddle pattern, A1 was 48s per dozen, while usual quality was 36s per dozen.

The address was corner of Union Street (opposite the Caledonian Hotel).

An interesting advertisement in the *Inverness Courier* of 10 November 1870 read: 'The CHARLES DICKENS PICKWICK PUNCH (OR TODDY) LADLES, REGISTERED. MANUFACTURED IN SILVER AND ELECTRO PLATE TO be had from FERGUSON BROTHERS.' It transpires that these ladles had stems surmounted with modelled figures of the most prominent characters from Charles Dickens' *Pickwick Papers*.

James Ferguson was listed in the 1871 census living at Grange Villa, Broadstone Park, aged 36, a watchmaker and jeweller, born in Gairloch, with Mary Ann, his wife, aged 26, born in Edinburgh, John, aged 3, and Matthew, aged 2, both born in Edinburgh, and Ann, aged 2 months, born in Inverness. Also living with the family was Elizabeth Saunders Combe, James' unmarried 17 year old sister-in-law from Edinburgh.

In the *Inverness Directory* 1873-74 the business was still at 41 Union Street; James had moved home to 4 Laurel Terrace, Denny Street, and William was living at Primrose Villa, Charles Street. An advertisement for the FERGUSON BROTHERS in the *Inverness Courier* of 24 February 1876, gives the business address as CORNER OF UNION STREET (Opposite the Caledonian Hotel), 'DESIGNERS AND MANUFACTUR-ERS OF NATIONAL SCOTTISH JEWELLERY AND HIGHLAND DRESS ORNAMENTS, WATCH AND CHRONOMETER MAKERS, AND GOLDSMITHS.' Another advertisement in the *Inverness Courier* of 28 September 1876 mentioned a 'Time Ball in connection with Greenwich Observatory, by which the rates of Chronometers are accurately determined. A Kew-Observatory-accurately-tested-Standard Barometer, for comparing Aneroid and Mercurial Barometers.'

The *Inverness Courier* of 13 May 1880 advertised the Ferguson Brothers' business with the address of 'CORNER OF UNION STREET' and 'REDUCTION AND REALISING SALE OF JEWELLERY, WATCHES, CLOCKS, AND PLATE, AT A DISCOUNT OF 20 PER CENT .FROM USUAL PRICES.' The same newspaper of 1 July 1880 announced:

THE FIRM of FERGUSON BROTHERS, carrying on Business as Goldsmiths, Watchmakers, and Manufacturers of Highland Ornaments, at No. 41 Union Street, Inverness, in the County of Inverness, Scotland, of which the Subscribers, JAMES FERGUSON and WILLIAM FERGUSON were the Sole Partners, has this day been DISSOLVED by mutual consent. The Subscriber, William Ferguson, is authorised to collect the Outstanding Debts due to, and will discharge all Obligations of, the late Firm. Inverness, 4th May 1880.

James opened new premises trading as James Ferguson & Son[104]. The *Inverness Courier* of 4 and 9 September 1880 carried an advertisement on the front page: 'Will Open in a Few Days. JAMES FERGUSON & SON, WATCH AND CHRONOMETER MAKERS, JEWELLERS, Designers and Manufacturers.' The address was 'MACDOUGALL & CO's BUILDINGS (Royal Tartan Warehouse). Entrances – From centre of Union Street, from centre of High Street, Inverness.' On 9 September 1880, just below James Ferguson's advertisement, appeared another, headed 'HIGH-CLASS WATCHES. FERGUSON BROTHERS.' Presumably this was William Ferguson still trading under the old business name.

The *Inverness Courier* of 4 August 1881 carried an advertisement for James Ferguson & Son 'REMOVING TO LARGER PREMISES. WHOLE STOCK TO BE SOLD OFF. Discount - 20 per cent. from the usual Marked Selling Prices. JAMES FERGUSON & SON, JEWELLERS AND WATCHMAKERS, LOMBARD STREET, INVERNESS.' It continued 'Having arranged to Remove into Larger Premises for the purpose of extending their Business, and to enable them to utilise the Fittings of their present Shop, their WHOLE STOCK Must be Sold Off, or Reduced to a convenient amount.' The *Inverness Advertiser* of 16 August 1881 recorded the business of James Ferguson and Son, watchmakers and jewellers, at MacDougall & Co's Buildings, Lombard Street (below).

The 1881 census listed James, aged 46, living at 46 Charles Street, a watchmaker employing one man. His wife was recorded as Mary Ann, aged 36, born Edinburgh; their children were John, aged 13, born in Edinburgh; Matthew, 12, born in Edinburgh; Ann, 10; Isabella, 8; Elizabeth, 3, and Mary Jane, 11 months; all born in Inverness.

Slater's Directory 1882 listed the firm James Ferguson & Son under 'Jewellers & Manufacturers of Highland Ornaments' and 'Watch and Clockmakers' at 18 Church Street, Inverness.

Inverness Advertiser 16 August 1881

SPECTACLES AND WATCH GLASSES.

A Saving of 30 Per Cent. to Customers.

JAMES FERGUSON & SON,

WATCHMAKERS & JEWELLERS,

MACDOUGALL & CO.'S BUILDINGS,

LOMBARD STREET, INVERNESS,

Desire to state that they have been successful in producing direct from the Best Makers in the Trade (thus saving Agency and Factors Commission), a very carefully SELECTED STOCK of SPECTACLES, Concave and Convex, and Hooksides, Invisible Concave, Double-spring and Grooved; Shell, Steel, and Ebonite Folders, Drilled and Milled Eye Glasses; Preserves in Neutral, Blue, and Green Glasses.

A fair comparison of quality and prices will show the advantages offered.

WATCH GLASSES.

The fitting of WATCH GLASSES require great care. It is well known that the bezils of Watches are frequently irretrievably damaged by inexperienced workmen.

The following are the prices charged for Watch Glasses properly fitted:—

Common High Glasses..................2d each.
Patent, Patent-flat and Lunette Glasses
    for open faced Watches............3d each.
Superior Annealed Glasses for Hunters
    and Gold work reduced to..........6d each.

JAMES FERGUSON & SON,

LOMBARD STREET.

The *Inverness Courier* of 3 January 1884 recorded the business at 18 Church Street. It concluded, 'JAMES FERGUSON & SON (Late Ferguson Brothers) WATCH-MAKERS & JEWELLERS, Business Established 1857.' A further advertisement in the *Inverness Courier* of 10 August 1886 recorded their address as 24 Union Street.

The *Inverness Courier* of 20 March 1888 carried an advertisement:'THE CHEAP-EST HOUSE for everything in JEWELLERY, WATCHES, CLOCKS, and SPECTACLES, 24 Union Street. James Ferguson and Son.'

The same newspaper of 5 July (repeated on 12 July 1889) carried an adver-tisement for James Ferguson & Son stating that they had 'REMOVED from Union Street to 22 CASTLE STREET, excellent Premises, especially for the Watch and Jewellery repairing and manufacturing trades.' It concluded '22 CASTLE STREET, Directly opposite Raining's Stairs.' However, the following month in the *Inver-ness Courier* of 23 August 1889, Ferguson Brothers were advertising at 22 Castle Street. It would appear that the business had been renamed again. Another adver-tisement on 2 May 1890 recorded the business address as 22 Castle Street, but a further advertisement in the *Inverness Courier* of 4 July 1890 stated, 'FERGUSON BROTHERS, WATCHMAKERS, JEWELLERS, AND OPTICIANS' and recorded them at 9 and 11 INGLIS STREET. They were advertising that they were 'the Cheapest in Town'.

The Inverness 1891 census listed James Ferguson as living at 1 Murray Place, aged 56, a watchmaker, born Kintail; his wife Mary A, aged 46, born in Edinburgh; John, aged 23, living on private means; Matthew, 22, a watchmaker; Ann, 20, a dress-maker; Isabella, 18, a general servant; Elizabeth, 13; Mary J, 10; Agnes, 8, and William, 6 years.

The *Inverness Courier* of 5 July 1892 recorded the business at the usual address but also stated: 'Have fitted up their Premises with excellent Workshops, and have added every requisite adapted to the requirements in the various Departments of their Business.'

The *Northern Chronicle* of 1 January 1896 advertised: 'FERGUSON BROTHERS, WATCHMAKERS, JEWELLERS, AND OPTICIANS, 9 AND 11 INGLIS STREET, INVERNESS', The advertisement continued by highlighting the various watch making facilities and optical goods for sale.

The *Highland News* of 8 October 1898 carried an advertisement for Ferguson Brothers with an address at '55 CHURCH STREET (Next Door to Messrs Logan & Company).'

The *Inverness Courier* of 3 January 1899 noted that they: 'HAVE REMOVED TO 4 DRUMMOND STREET (A very Central position, and well suited for their Business).' The *Highland News* of 21 October 1899 carried an important advertisement for 'FERGUSON BROTHERS, OPTICIANS, WATCHMAKERS, AND JEWELLERS (By Special Appointment to H. R. H..The Prince of Wales) 4 DRUMMOND STREET (Two Doors up from Music Hall) INVERNESS. ESTABLISHED 1857.' This makes it clear that the firm Ferguson Brothers was the continuance of James Ferguson's business estab-lished in 1857.

Slater's Directories 1900 and 1903 recorded the business under 'Watch & Clock Makers' at 4 Drummond Street.

The *Inverness Courier* of 8 April 1904 carried a small advertisement: 'REMOVAL NOTICE. FERGUSON BROTHERS will REMOVE at Whitsunday to No. 8 EAST GATE.'

An advertisement in The *Highland News* of 7 January 1905 records the intended closure of the business. The same newspaper of 11 February 1905 recorded the address as 8 Eastgate. The last business address for Ferguson Brothers was recorded in the *Inverness Burgh Directory* 1905-06. They were listed under watchmakers and jewellers at 19 Bridge Street. It appears that James Ferguson retired from business in 1906 or early 1907 as the firm Ferguson Brothers was not recorded in the 1906-07 *Directory*. James Ferguson, watchmaker, was listed at his home address of 39 Church Street, but 'no longer of Ferguson Brothers, jewellers'. The business was not recorded in *Slater's Directory* 1907.

James Ferguson died at 39 Church Street, Inverness, on 25 May 1910, aged 75. His obituary was in *The Highland Leader and Northern Weekly* of 26 May 1910, 'Many will hear with regret of the death of Mr. James Ferguson, jeweller, which took place at 39 Church Street yesterday. The deceased gentleman, who was at one time a member of the well-known firm of Ferguson Bros., was well known and highly respected in Inverness. For some time he carried on business on his own account, but latterly he retired from active work. He was in his 76th year.'

Mary Ann Ferguson died on 17 March 1930 at 5 Ness Walk, Inverness, aged 85, widow of James Ferguson, watchmaker; her daughter Bessie Ferguson was the informant. The family gravestone in Tomnahurich Cemetery reads as follows: 'JAMES FERGUSON WATCHMAKER DIED 25TH MAY 1910, HIS WIFE MARY ANN COMBE DIED 17th MARCH 1930, JOHN DIED 25. dec. 1932, MATTHEW DIED 3rd NOV. 1904 INTERRED IN CAIRO, JAMES DIED IN INFANCY 1875, ISABELLA DIED 27th NOV 1945,

*Highland News
7 January 1905*

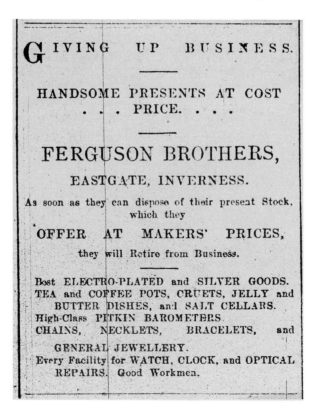

GIVING   UP   BUSINESS.

HANDSOME   PRESENTS   AT   COST
. . . PRICE. . . .

FERGUSON BROTHERS,

EASTGATE, INVERNESS.

As soon as they can dispose of their present Stock,
which they

OFFER   AT   MAKERS' PRICES,

they will Retire from Business.

Best ELECTRO-PLATED and SILVER GOODS.
TEA and COFFEE POTS, CRUETS, JELLY and
BUTTER DISHES, and SALT CELLARS.
High-Class PITKIN BAROMETERS.
CHAINS,   NECKLETS,   BRACELETS,   and
GENERAL JEWELLERY.
Every Facility for WATCH, CLOCK, and OPTICAL
REPAIRS. Good Workmen.

Luckenbooth by James Ferguson.
Private collection

JAMES COMBE DIED 4th APRIL 1880, AGNES, DIED 17 JANUARY 1935. WILLIAM DIED 25TH MAY 1939, ON VOYAGE TO U. S. A. BURIED AT SEA.'

James Ferguson made very fine plaid brooches, one of which is in the National Museums of Scotland. Another, a Luckenbooth, is illustrated above. His mark was 'J F, INS'. Ferguson Brothers used the mark 'F. B[s]' and 'FERGUSON BROS, INVSS'.

A James Ferguson clock remains inside the Old High Church, Inverness.

WILLIAM FERGUSON 1836–1898
(Ferguson Brothers, Ferguson & MacBean)

William Ferguson was born on 6 June 1836 in Dingwall, Ross-shire, the son of John Ferguson, a master mason, and Isabella Brotchie[105] (see p97).

William Ferguson, aged 28, married Elizabeth McBean, aged 21, in Inverness on 6 December 1865. William's occupation was recorded as jeweller. Elizabeth's parents were Alexander McBean, a clothier, and Elizabeth Ross. There were no known children of the marriage.

William Ferguson entered into partnership with his established brother, James, forming the company of Ferguson Brothers in August 1866. The *Inverness Courier* of 16 August 1866 showed James Ferguson advertising alone, but in the following

Billhead for Ferguson Brothers 1881

week's *Courier* the company was advertising as Ferguson Brothers, their shop situated on the corner of Union Street (41 Union Street). The Ferguson Brothers used the mark 'F. B^s'.

The *Inverness Directories* 1866/67 and 1873/74 listed them as 'Jewellers and Watchmakers' at 41 Union Street, Inverness. William's home was recorded as 8 Drummond Street in the 1866/67 *Directory* and Primrose Villa, Charles Street, in 1873/74.

William Ferguson was listed in the 1871 census, aged 32, born Dingwall, and living at Primrose Villa, 12 Charles Street with his wife Elizabeth, aged 26, who was also born in Inverness. The census also recorded that William was a master jeweller employing 8 men and 3 boys.

On the 15 November 1878 the *General Register of Sasines for Inverness* recorded the annexation to William Ferguson by Feu Charter dated 29 October 1878 of 3 roods of land by the road leading to Tomnahurich Cemetery; here at Fernbank, Cemetery Road, (now Bruce Gardens), William's wife, Elizabeth, died on 23 January 1881.

Just prior to his wife's death William Ferguson's partnership with his elder brother was severed, and it was with his brother-in-law, James MacBean, who had recently returned to Inverness following thirteen years in Canada, that William entered into a new partnership as 'Ferguson and MacBean'.

Inverness Courier 11 December 1880

MESSRS FERGUSON & MACBEAN,
Successors to
FERGUSON BROTHERS,
WATCHMAKERS, JEWELLERS, AND
HIGHLAND ORNAMENT MAKERS,
CORNER OF UNION STREET,
INVERNESS.
Beg to announce that they have acquired the whole Stock and Book Debts of their predecessors, and will carry on the Business as formerly, and trust by strict attention and courtesy to merit a continuation of that patronage so liberally bestowed on their predecessors.

In the *Inverness Courier* of 11 December 1880 (opposite), Ferguson and MacBean advertised as successors to Ferguson Brothers. The same newspaper of 14 December 1880 carried three separate advertisements for the new partnership.

The 1881 census for Inverness recorded William at Fernbank as a 43 year old widowed jeweller, employing 3 men. Also listed were Mary MacGillivray, housekeeper, and Mary MacDonald, general servant.

The *Inverness Courier* of 20 July 1882 recorded the business as Ferguson & MacBean (successors to Ferguson Brothers), corner of Union Street, Inverness, and *Slater's Directories* 1882 and 1893 recorded the company trading as jewellers, watch and clockmakers at that address.

The *Inverness Courier* of 3 January 1884 carried an advertisement for 'THE HIGHLAND JEWELLERY ESTABLISHMENT By Special Appointment to H. R. H. the Prince of Wales.' It concluded, 'FERGUSON & MACBEAN (Successors to Ferguson Brothers), MANUFACTURERS OF HIGHLAND ORNAMENTS AND JEWELLERY, CORNER OF UNION STREET, INVERNESS.'

William Ferguson remarried on 4 November 1884 at 24 Gilmore Place, Edinburgh. He was described as a widowed master jeweller, aged 46, from Fern Bank, Inverness. His wife was Helen Christie, a spinster, aged 36, from 11 Academy Street, Inverness, the daughter of a deceased confectioner, Henry Christie, and Grace Salmond. There were no known children from this union.

In the *Inverness County Directory* 1887 Ferguson and MacBean advertised:

> 'The Highland Jewellery Establishment'
> by special appointment to
> His Royal Highness the Prince of Wales.

The 1891 census for Bruce Gardens, Inverness, listed William Ferguson as a 52 year old jeweller with his wife, Helen, aged 42, born in Kirkcaldy, Fifeshire; also listed were Mary McGillivray, a visitor, and Christina Ross, a general domestic servant.

The *Highland News* of 2 January 1892 carried another advertisement (overleaf).

William died on Saturday 3 December 1898 at the New Hotel, Gullane, County of Haddington, while on a golfing holiday with his wife and friends. His obituary in the *Northern Chronicle* of 7 December 1898 stated, 'He was best known as an enthusiastic Volunteer and marksman; as a matter of fact, his name and fame is national in this connection. He entered the Volunteer force at its inauguration in 1860, and at once manifested a strong interest in shooting'. Among the trophies William won at Wimbledon were the St Georges Vase in 1862, The Wimbledon Cup for Match Rifles in 1869, The Albert in 1871, The Daily Telegraph Cup in 1872, The Wimbledon Cup for Service Rifles in 1874, The Olympic in 1876, The Association Cup for Match Rifles in 1883 and 1886, and the All-Comers' Aggregate in 1885. He also represented Scotland in the Elcho Team for 34 years, being one of the original members. The obituary also mentioned that 'He passed through the ranks to a commission, and was appointed junior major in his regiment in August this year'.

The *Sheriff Court Books of the County of Inverness* recorded on 15 June 1899 that William Ferguson had died on 3 December 1898, testate, and that the value of his personal estate was £1,822-0s-10d. His wife, Helen, was the executrix nominate of the deed; in this instance a contract of marriage.

THE HIGHLAND JEWELLERY ESTABLISHMENT.

BY SPECIAL APPOINTMENT TO H.R.H. THE PRINCE OF WALES.
HIGHLAND AND CAIRNGORM JEWELLERY.

ALL the old Patterns and many Registered Novelties New this Season.

HIGHLAND DRESS ORNAMENTS.

Dirks, Sporrans, Shoulder Brooches, Skean Dhu , and every Requisite for this Picturesque Dress.

SOLID SILVER AND ELECTRO-SILVER PLATE.

The Latest Specialities for Wedding, Birthday, and Complimentary Presents, at Moderate Prices. Selections of Goods sent for approval.

ANTIQUE SILVER PLATE, CLOCKS, &c.

Fine Gold Jewellery. Gold and Silver Watches. Clocks in Brass, Bronze, Enamels, Marbles, and Fine Woods.

Presentation Committees met with on Liberal Terms.

Watches, Clocks, and Jewellery Carefully Repaired by Thoroughly Experienced Workmen.

Electric Time Ball in Direct Communication with Greenwich Observatory.

Highest Price given for Old Gold and Silver.

FERGUSON & MACBEAN,
CORNER OF UNION STREET,
INVERNESS.

Helen Ferguson died on 7 October 1923 at 37 Albert Street, Aberdeen, aged 75 years. The death certificate stated that she was the widow of William Ferguson, jeweller.

Ferguson Brothers used the mark 'F. B', and 'FERGUSON BROS, INVSS' whilst Ferguson and MacBean used the marks 'F & M, INVS', which sometimes included a 'CAMEL'.

The dates of the various businesses associated with this family were as follows:

James Ferguson	1857-66 (James Ferguson working alone)
Ferguson Brothers	1866-80 (James & William Ferguson)
Ferguson and MacBean	1880-1906 (William Ferguson (d 3 Dec 1898) & James MacBean (d 8 Dec 1905))
Fraser, Ferguson and MacBean	1906-45 (Alexander William Fraser)
James Ferguson and Son	1880-89 (James Ferguson & Son)
Ferguson Brothers	1889-1905 (James Ferguson & Sons)

ALEXANDER DALLAS 1838–1906

Alexander Dallas was born in Inverness on 7 January 1838; his parents were Peter Dallas, a painter, and Isabella Cameron. The Dallas family were first recorded living on the East side of Church Street in the 1841 Inverness census: Peter Dallas, aged 30, a journeyman painter, born in England; Isabella, aged 25; Alexander, aged 3, and Margaret aged 11 months; all born in the county. The family was detailed in the 1851 Inverness census in Academy Street: Isabell Cameron[106], aged 34; Alexr, aged 13, a scholar; John, aged 8; Margaret, aged 10; Jane, aged 6, and Peter, aged 6 months; all born in Inverness.

Alexander Dallas placed an advertisement in the *Inverness Courier* of 11 July 1861 (below). Robert Smith had been advertising in the *Inverness Courier* over the previous months at the business address of 76 Church Street.

Alexander Dallas cannot be found in the Inverness 1861 census, which was taken on 7 April; however, some pages are missing from that census or he may have been still resident in Edinburgh.

The next advertisement for Alexander was recorded in the *Inverness Courier* of 25 December 1862. It was repeated in the *Courier* of 30 July 1863: 'ALEXANDER DALLAS, CHRONOMETER, WATCH, AND CLOCKMAKER, 77 CHURCH STREET, INVERNESS.' Further advertisements in the *Inverness Courier* of 21 July 1864, *Inverness Courier* of 23 August 1866 and *Inverness Advertiser* of 9 October 1866 only stated: 'ALEX DALLAS, WATCHMAKER, 77 CHURCH STREET, INVERNESS.'

Alexander Dallas married Margaret McDonald on 12 September 1866; he was recorded as a watchmaker aged 25, while Margaret was aged 21. Margaret was born at Hill Place, Inverness, on 10 October 1844 and her parents were recorded as Ewen[107] Macdonald, a house proprietor, and Ann McIntosh.

Alexander was listed in the *Inverness Directory* 1866/67 living at 66 Church Street and working at 77 Church Street. The 1871 census recorded him living at 2 Church Street, a 31 year old watchmaker, born in Inverness, with his wife Margaret, aged 26, also born in Inverness, and their son, Evan, aged 2 years. All his children were born in the town: Peter, 1 July 1867, at 2 Church Street (died 8 January 1868); Evan, 4 February 1869; John, 16 April 1871 (died 22 December 1916)[108]; Alexander, 25 December 1873; Donald, 17 November 1875, at 3 Church Street; Isabella, 15 August 1877, at 16 Market Brae; James, 12 December 1879; Peter Stewart, 28 January 1882, and Annie Margaret, 26 October 1888.

CHRONOMETER, WATCH, & CLOCK MAKING,
77 CHURCH STREET, INVERNESS.

ALEXANDER DALLAS (from Messrs R. BRYSON & Sons, Edinburgh) begs to intimate that he has commenced business in that Shop, 77 CHURCH STREET, as CHRONOMETER, WATCH, and CLOCK MAKER, lately occupied by Mr R. Smith.

From past experience, and by close attention to the working department of his business, he hopes to be favoured with a share of public patronage.

Inverness Courier
11 July 1861

The *Inverness Directory* 1873/74 recorded him living at 2 Church Street with his shop still at 77 Church Street. Alexander's shop remained there until around 1874 when he moved to 30 Church Street; the business remained at that address until around 1902.

The 1881 Inverness census recorded the family at 16 Market Brae; Alexander was listed as a watchmaker employing a man and a boy; his wife Margaret, aged 36, with their five sons: Evan, aged 12; John, aged 9; Alick, aged 7; Donald, aged 5, and James, aged 1, all born in Inverness. There was also a domestic servant living with them, Alexina MacKenzie, aged 19, born in Kirkhill, Inverness.

In the 1882 and 1893 *Slater's Directory* he was listed under 'watch and clock makers' and also 'jewellers & manufacturers of highland ornaments' at 30 Church Street.

The Inverness 1891 census found the family still living at 16 Market Brae: Alexander, aged 51, a watch and clockmaker; Margaret, aged 46; John, 19, a general clerk; Alexander, aged 17, a watchmaker; Donald, aged 15, also a watchmaker; James, aged 11; Peter S, aged 9, and Annie M, aged 2 years. There was also a domestic servant, Ida Barclay, aged 19. The business removed to 44 Church Street around 1902 and Alexander was in business there until his death in 1906.

Slater's Directory 1900 recorded the business under 'jewellers' and 'watch and clock makers' at 30 Church Street. By the 1903 *Directory* the business was recorded at 44 Church Street. Slater's 1907 *Directory* recorded the business at 48 Church Street, however, the 1911 edition recorded it under 'watch and clock makers' only, at 44 Church Street. In the 1915, 1921 and 1928 *Kelly's Directory* it was at 50 Church Street. The business was recorded under watchmakers and jewellers in the *Inverness Burgh Directory* 1928-29 as Alex Dallas working at 50 Church Street.

Alexander Dallas, master watchmaker, died at 4 Hill Place, Inverness, on 29 September 1906, aged 66; the informant was his son Don Dallas. The *Inverness Courier* of 2 October 1906 reported the death notice. The *Highland News* of 6 October 1906 carried an obituary:

THE LATE MR ALEXANDER DALLAS. WELL-KNOWN CITIZEN PASSES AWAY. Another well-known citizen has passed away in the person of Mr Alexander Dallas, watchmaker. He was one of Inverness's earliest photographers, and his work in this connection revealed the artistic side of Mr Dallas, who, it may be said, paved the way for budding knights of the camera. Mr Dallas carried on a successful business as a watchmaker and jeweller in Church Street, and it was a source of great pleasure to step into his shop and have a chat with him on old Inverness-a subject on which he could speak with a vividness that never failed to interest the listener. Mr Dallas had a rich fund of anecdote, and his reminiscences of the old town in which he was born delighted the many residenters with whom he used to converse. Some time ago he was laid aside by a serious illness, from which he never recovered. He died at his residence, Hill Terrace, on Saturday. Mr Dallas is survived by his wife and grown-up family, to whom many tokens of sympathy have been extended in their sad bereavement. The funeral, which took place on Tuesday, was largely and representatively attended.

The business was carried on by his son Alexander Dallas junior. Margaret, widow of Alexander, died on 15 January 1911, aged 66; the informant was her son, John. The family gravestone was located in Tomnahurich cemetery and the inscription reads:

IN MEMORY OF ALEXANDER DALLAS WATCHMAKER, INVERNESS WHO DIED 29. SEP. 1906, AGED 66 YEARS, AND HIS WIFE MARGARET MACDONALD WHO DIED 15 JANY 1911,

AGED 66 YEARS. ALSO THEIR CHILDREN PETER, WHO DIED 8. JAN. 1868, AGED 6 MONTHS ISABELLA, WHO DIED 17. NOV. 1879 AGED 2 YEARS. ERECTED BY THEIR SIX SONS AND DAUGHTER. IN MEMORY OF JOHN DALLAS, WRITER, SECOND SON OF ALEXANDER DALLAS, WHO DIED 22 DEC. 1916 AGED 45 YEARS.'

Some silver work was produced by Alexander Dallas, but he was primarily a watch and clockmaker, and it is postulated that he worked from his workshop on the corner of Queensgate and Church Street; his silver is very rare and consists mainly of items with small silver presentation plates. The marks used were 'A • D, INV^{SS}' or 'A • D, INV^{SS}' and sometimes with a 'CAMEL'.

An Alexander Dallas clock is still visible today in the roof of the indoor market between Union Street and Queensgate, Inverness.

PETER GEORGE WILSON 1843-1925

Peter George Wilson was born in New Keith, Banff-shire on 2 April 1843, the son of Peter Wilson, a watchmaker, and Helen Duff. He was apprenticed to his father in about 1856. His two younger brothers were also apprenticed to their father but they went to America in the late 1860s or early 1870s. Alexander Wilson[109] remained in New York while Charles Duff Wilson, returned to Elgin[110]; both became very successful watchmakers and jewellers.

The Keith 1851 census detailed Peter G Wilson, aged 7 years, living in Bridge Street with his parents: Peter Wilson, aged 34, a watch and clockmaker; Helen, aged 36; with his two brothers and two sisters. The 1861 Keith census recorded him as an 18 year old watchmaker living in Moss Street. He was listed as a lodger with Margaret McDonald, and with him was his younger brother, Charles, aged 11 years, a scholar. Meanwhile, Peter's father and mother were recorded in the Village of Dufftown: Peter Wilson, aged 44, a clock and watchmaker; his wife, Helen, aged 48, and their four other children: Magdalene, aged 16; Alexander Duff, aged 14, an apprentice watchmaker; Helen aged 9, and Margaret aged 3 years.

It seems that Peter George Wilson set up business in Inverness in about 1865; however, no opening advertisement has been found for 100 Church Street, which was probably his first shop in Inverness. Nevertheless, an advertisement was noted in the *Banffshire Journal* of 3 January 1865: 'P. WILSON & SON RESPECTFULLY announce that they have just received a large Stock of NEW GOODS, purchased personally in London by Mr WILSON, Jun., on the most advantageous terms.' The address for the business was recorded as 'MID STREET, KEITH (next door to the Gordon Arms Hotel), AND DUFFTOWN.' It is not clear which son this refers to; Peter George was aged 22, and Alexander would have been aged 18 years.

P. G. WILSON, WATCHMAKER, JEWELLER, &c., will REMOVE in a FEW DAYS to that NEW SHOP,

No. 8 UNION STREET,

and previous to that time, in 100 CHURCH STREET, Offers, at REDUCED PRICES, his Stock of—

Gold and Silver Watches, Gold Guard and Albert Chains, Brooches, Bracelets, Armlets, Ear-Rings, Finger Rings, Lockets, Scarf Pins, and a variety of other articles in Gold, Silver, and Jet.

An assortment of Clocks, Barometers, Telescopes, Opera and Field Glasses, and Spectacles of all kinds.

Peter George Wilson's business was first noted in the *Inverness Advertiser* of 23 May 1865 (above), and the *Inverness Courier* of 25 May 1865. In the *Inverness Advertiser* of 27 June 1865 he announced, 'will REMOVE on the 1st of JULY to that NEW SHOP, NO. 8 UNION STREET and previous to that time, in 100 CHURCH STREET.' Later, in the *Inverness Advertiser* of 1 August 1865, he advertised: 'P. G. WILSON, WATCHMAKER, JEWELLER, &c., has OPENED that New Shop, No. 8 UNION STREET (Fourth Door from the Railway Station), and has just to hand an Assortment of the most FASHIONABLE LONDON-MADE JEWELLERY'. In the *Inverness Advertiser* of 9 October 1866 it stated, 'We understand that Mr P. G. Wilson, jeweller, 8 Union Street, who was recently fortunate in obtaining the patronage of Baron Rothschild and party on their passing through Inverness, has had the honour of supplying several articles of jewellery to their Royal Highnesses the Prince and Princess of Wales at Dunrobin.'

He was recorded in the *Inverness Directory* 1866/67 working at 8 Union Street, as a jeweller, silversmith and watchmaker; his home was at 15 Union Street where he was listed as a watchmaker.

The *Inverness Advertiser* of 13 September 1867 reported:

HIGHLAND JEWELLERY PATRONISED BY THE QUEEN:–We understand that last week Mr P. G. Wilson, jeweller, Union Street, had the honour to receive Her Majesty's order to visit Balmoral with specimens of his Highland jewellery, when Mr Wilson was favoured with large orders from the Queen, Prince and Princess Christian, Princess Louise, Prince Leopold, Princess Beatrice, and other visitors presently at Balmoral. At the desire of Her Majesty and of Madame Van-de-Weyer, Mr Wilson also paid a visit to Abergeldie, where his Excellency Mr Van-de-Weyer, the Belgian Ambassador, is at present residing, and received there orders for various articles from Madame Van-de-Weyer and family. These transactions, it need scarcely be said, are highly creditable to our Inverness manufactures and to the enterprise of Mr Wilson.

The *Inverness Advertiser* of 12 December 1868 reported, 'APPOINTMENT.–We have seen the following communication which Mr P. G. Wilson [sic], jeweller, has had the honour to receive:– 'Kensington Palace, December 7th. Colonel Clifton is desired by the Princess Mary Adelaide to inform Mr Wilson that, in compliance with his request, her Royal Highness and the Prince of Teck have much pleasure in appointing him as their jeweller and goldsmith'.

Peter again advertised in the *Inverness Courier* of 6 January 1870 with his business address as 8 Union Street (opposite). By this date he was advertising nearly

NEW-YEAR PRESENTS.

P. G. WILSON,
THE COURT GOLDSMITH AND JEWELLER AT INVERNESS.

Has much pleasure in soliciting attention to his present Stock of JEWELLERY and PLATE, which embraces a large number of articles of merit, and may be said to be the best selection of JEWELLERY he has yet offered for Sale.

Mr WILSON has made special arrangements for New-Year Presents, and there will be found in his collection articles suited for those of moderate income as well as for the first in the kingdom.

LADIES GOLD RINGS in great variety, from 10s. to £2 10s., and with fine Gems from £2 to £5 each. DIAMOND RINGS, Seven, Ten, Fifteen, Twenty, and Thirty Guineas each. Ladies and Gentlemen's GOLD LOCKETS, in good Gold, from 10s. to 25s. ; in fine Gold, from £1 to £10. Gentlemen's Gold SCARF PINS, from 7s. 6d. to £5.

A choice Selection of Bracelets, Brooches, Ear-rings, Necklets, Studs, Sleeve Links, Pen and Pencil-Cases, Smelling Bottles, &c., &c., in the newest and most fashionable styles.

GOLD GUARD & ALBERT CHAINS,
In a variety of Patterns, at Prices from £2 to £10 each.

P. G. WILSON is well known as the Purchaser of the SUTHERLANDSHIRE GOLD, and has in Stock a number of Articles made of it, by his own workmen, in his Establishment at Inverness. Any article of Jewellery made to order of the SUTHERLAND GOLD, and sent safe by Post to any part of the world.

A beautiful Stock of
SILVER ELECTRO-PLATE,
Including all the Articles required for Table use, and many Ornamental Articles suitable for Presentation.

An Elegant Assortment of
WATCHES & CLOCKS
of the best quality.

P. G. WILSON would call attention to the fact that, while his Goods are of the best quality, his charges are not higher than those of inferior Establishments—his object being to secure a large amount of Patronage, and at the same time the approval of his Customers.

Orders by Post receive prompt and careful attention from P. G. WILSON, JEWELLER, SILVERSMITH, and MANUFACTURER of HIGHLAND ORNAMENTS to HER MAJESTY THE QUEEN, &c., &c., &c., 8 UNION STREET, INVERNESS.

Inverness Courier 6 January 1870

every week, usually in the top right hand corner of the front page; each advertisement stated 'by Special Appointment to Her Majesty the Queen'.

The 1871 census listed Peter Wilson at 9 Union Street, aged 28, a jeweller employing 6 men; he was living with his sister, Helen D, aged 19, a shop keeper, and Margaret Thomson, a domestic servant.

The *Inverness Courier* of 4 January 1872 carried another advertisement for P G Wilson, 8 Union Street, which stated he was 'THE COURT GOLDSMITH AND JEWELLER AT INVERNESS.'

The *Inverness Advertiser* of 18 March 1873 reported that Peter Wilson intended to move from 8 Union Street to 44 High Street 'in two weeks from this date', and the same newspaper of 29 April 1873 advertised: 'P. G. WILSON HAS REMOVED TO HIS FINE PREMISES 44 HIGH STREET.' The *Inverness Directory* 1873/74 stated that his business was at 44 High Street, with his home given as 43 High Street.

The *Inverness Advertiser* of 5 January 1875 recorded Wilson advertising at 44 High Street:

> VISITORS Are freely admitted to INSPECT the SHOP and MANUFACTORY, although they may not wish to purchase anything. The interior is about one hundred and twenty feet long, the front part of which is fitted up in the style of an Exhibition Room or Museum, thereby allowing the Visitor to walk round and see conveniently everything contained in the Shelves and Cases. The press has described "the whole as forming one of the finest places of business in the Jewellery and Watchmaking trade in the kingdom".

The business featured again in the *Inverness Courier* of 28 September 1876 (below).

Peter married Helen Whyte on 27 March 1879, in Aberlour[111]; Helen was born in 1844 and her parents were Archibald Whyte, a house proprietor, and Mary Findlay.

The *Inverness Advertiser* of 18 February 1881 carried an advertisement for his

*Inverness Courier
28 September 1876*

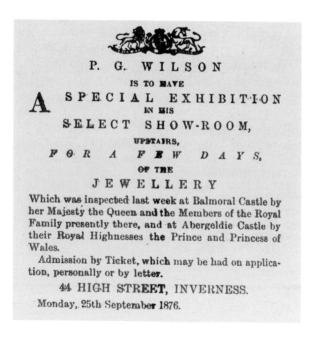

business but no address was printed. 'Has a large and beautiful Stock of JEWELLERY, in the most fashionable and correct Styles; and which have been patronised as Works of Art by many distinguished persons of taste.'

The 1881 Inverness census listed Peter Wilson at 22 High Street, Inverness, aged 38, a jeweller employing five men and three boys. It was this census which first recorded his wife, Helen; she was aged 37, from Cortachy in Forfarshire. They had a son called Peter G Wilson, aged 1, who was born in Inverness, and a servant called Alexandrina Fraser, aged 37.

In the 1882 *Slater's Directory* Wilson was listed under two addresses, one at 44 High Street, the other 27 Church Street. An advertisement in the *Inverness Courier* of 20 July 1882 was as follows: 'WILSON (LATE NAUGHTEN), JEWELLER AND SILVER-SMITH, 27 CHURCH STREET, INVERNESS. JEWELLERY and SILVER PLATE, &c., at very Moderate Prices for Ready Money.' Robert Naughten had been advertising in the *Inverness Courier* from 15 December 1881 that he was conducting a 'GREAT CHEAP SALE OF JEWELLERY. The Whole Stock of Mr R. NAUGHTEN, 27 CHURCH STREET.'

Helen and Peter Wilson's children were: Peter George Wilson junior, born 2 January 1880; William Charles, born 3 February 1884, and Elizabeth Mary, born 11 March 1886, died 8 March 1887, aged 12 months. On each occasion the father was recorded as a master jeweller living at 44 High Street.

The *Inverness Courier* of 25 June 1885 carried an advertisement: 'Apprentice WANTED, for the JEWELLERY BUSINESS. Apply to P. G. Wilson, High Street.'

The *Highland News* of 25 May 1889 stated that he had taken 'a Lease of the CORNER SHOP, NO. 1 HIGH STREET' (below). The *Highland News* of 1 June 1889 stated that he had 'REMOVED to his NEW SHOP (The Corner Shop), NO. 1 HIGH STREET (Opposite the Town Hall).' He advertised again in the *Inverness Courier* of 1 July 1890 at 1 High Street, adding '(Corner opposite the Town Hall),' and this was repeated in the *Inverness Courier* of 1 July 1892.

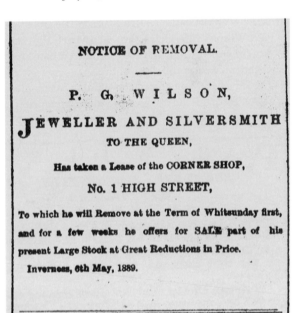

Highland News 25 May 1889

Buckle by P G Wilson.
Private collection. Ewen Weatherspoon

Luckenbooth by P G Wilson.
Private collection. Ewen Weatherspoon

The 1891 Inverness Census listed him living at 106 Castle Street, aged 48, a jeweller and watchmaker, born in Keith, with Helen, his wife, aged 47, recorded as born in Clova, Forfarshire, and their two boys, 'Pattie' George, aged 11, and Charles William, aged 7, both born in Inverness. Also at that address was Margaret Forbes, a 38 year old housemaid, born in Kilmorack.

In the 1893 *Slater's Directory* his business address was still recorded at 1 High Street; this was the shop which had formerly been occupied by Alexander McLeod, William Mason and William Fraser.

The *Inverness Courier* of 2 January 1900 carried the following: 'P. G. WILSON, JEWELLER & SILVERSMITH TO HER MAJESTY THE QUEEN, &c., &c. 1 HIGH STREET.'

Peter Wilson's wife, Helen, died on 9 March 1901, aged 57, at 5 High Street.

Slater's Directories 1900 and 1903 recorded Wilson's business still at 1 High Street, listed under jewellers and silversmiths.

The last advertisement for Peter Wilson was recorded in the *Inverness Courier* of 15 March 1904; this did not give an address, presumably still 1 High Street, and the

Inverness Courier 15 March 1904

P. G. W I L S O N,
JEWELLER, SILVERSMITH, AND
WATCHMAKER,
I N V E R N E S S.
SPECIAL SHOW and BARGAINS in SILVER
ELECTRO-PLATE in his SHOWROOMS upstairs.
SPOONS and FORKS, &c., of Superior Quality in
all the Best Patterns, and every Article required for
Table use.
Watches, Clocks, and Jewellery cleaned and repaired
in the best manner, and at Moderate Charges.

advertisement did not indicate that he was about to move his business. However, the *Inverness Courier* of 15 April 1904 carried an advertisement for 'CAMPBELL'S GREAT REMOVAL SALE (FROM TOWN HALL BUILDINGS), OF HIS ENTIRE, LARGE, AND VALUABLE STOCK … The whole Stock must be cleared out previous to Removal to those Central Premises NO. 1 HIGH STREET (OPPOSITE TOWN HALL).' *Slater's Directory* 1907 and 1911 recorded the business, under jewellers, at 50 Church Street; however, *Slater's Directory* 1915 recorded his address as 58 Church Street.

The *Inverness Courier* of 14 December 1915 detailed the sale of Wilson's business:

SALE OF Jeweller's, Antique Dealer's Stock-in-Trade & Fittings On THURSDAY, 16th Dec., at 2 p. m., AND THREE FOLLOWING DAYS. To be SOLD, by Public Auction, the Entire STOCK-IN-TRADE of P. G. WILSON, The Court Jeweller, within the Premises, 58 CHURCH ST., INVERNESS. … P. G. WILSON is the Oldest Established Jeweller in Inverness, being commanded Jeweller to her Late Majesty Queen Victoria, H. R. H. the Duke of Edinburgh, H. R. H. Princess Alice, to Their Royal Highnesses Prince and Princess Christian, and many other members of the Royal Family. The auctioneer has every confidence in recommending the quality of the Stock, although the Goods and Premises have been neglected on account of the Proprietor's ill-health.

Peter George Wilson died on 18 or 19 January 1925, aged 81, at 34 Church Street, Inverness, a widowed, retired watchmaker and jeweller. His brother, Charles Duff Wilson, who lived at 9 West Road, Elgin, was the informant.

C D Wilson, who was also a jeweller, worked at 124 High Street, Elgin; his home was in King Street in 1889 but by 1925 he had moved to The Cottage, West Road, Elgin. He was Lord Provost of Elgin from 1908-13.

Peter Wilson's obituaries appear in the *Inverness Courier* of 23 and 27 January 1925. He was buried in Tomnahurich cemetery; the grave was located but there is no gravestone to mark the spot. A clock in the ticket office of the Strathspey Steam Railway, at Boat of Garten, is inscribed with his name (P G Wilson, Inverness). Another is on the wasll of nairn Railway Station.

His marks were either 'P. G. W., INS' or 'P. G. WILSON, INVERNESS'.

JAMES MACBEAN c1847–1905
(Ferguson & MacBean)

James MacBean was born in Inverness around 1847, son of Alexander MacBean, a tailor and clothier, and Elizabeth Ross. In the 1851 census for 38 High Street, Inverness, Alexr. McBean was listed as a 39 year old tailor and clothier, born in Croy, Inverness-shire, with his wife, Elizabeth Ross, aged 37, also born in Croy; their son James was recorded, aged 4, born in Inverness, together with six further sons and one daughter. A niece, Jessie McBean, aged 9, and 2 house servants, Lesly McPherson and Elisabeth McKenzie, completed the household.

The 1861 census for 23 Inglis Street, Inverness, recorded Alexander MacBean as a 49 year old tailor and clothier, born in Croy, Inverness-shire, with his wife Elizabeth, aged 46, born in Resaurie, Inverness-shire; also listed were 2 daughters and 7 sons including James, a 14 year old scholar, born in Inverness, plus a domestic servant, Margaret Urquhart, aged 19.

James MacBean was apprenticed to James Ferguson around 1861 and was still an apprentice when his sister, Elizabeth, married James Ferguson's brother William in December 1865. The following year William Ferguson joined his brother James to form the company of Ferguson Brothers. James MacBean left Ferguson Brothers around 1867 as a young journeyman to continue his career in Canada. During the thirteen years spent there it appears he married, but he returned to the Highland capital in 1880.

James entered into partnership with his brother-in-law, William Ferguson, in December 1880, to form the new company of Ferguson and MacBean. In the *Inverness Courier* of 14 December 1880 they advertised as successors to Ferguson Brothers, corner of Union Street, Inverness. (William Ferguson's previous partner, his elder brother James, had shortly before started a new company of watchmakers and jewellers called Ferguson and Son.)

Menu Holder by Ferguson & MacBean.
Private collection. Ewen Weatherspoon

The 1881 census for 8 Abban Road, Inverness, listed James MacBean as a boarder at the home of his brother, William, and family. James was noted as a 32 year old widower, watchmaker, born in Inverness.

James MacBean, jeweller, aged 37, a widower, married Elspet Marjory Smith[112], aged 25, the daughter of Farquhar Smith, a deceased Episcopal clergyman, and Elizabeth Cardno, also deceased, on 22 October 1885 at St. Andrew's Episcopal Church, Aberdeen. James was described as a 'Jeweller (Master)' at the birth of their first child, Reginald James, on 2 April 1887, at 6 Telford Terrace, Inverness. Their next child was called Winniefred Marks MacBean, who was born at the same

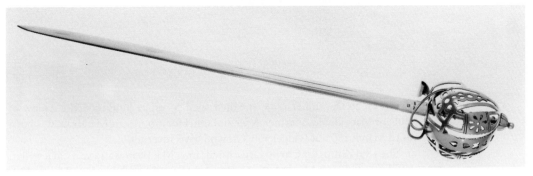

Paper Knife by Ferguson & MacBean.
Private collection. A C Cooper, London

address on 20 December 1888. She died, aged 75, on 22 June 1964, the widow of William Macgillivray, a farmer. A second son, Horatio Alistair MacBean, was born on 16 March 1892, at Ridgeleigh, Crown Drive, Inverness.

The 1891 census for Crown Drive listed James MacBean as a 42 year old jeweller, with his wife Elspet M, aged 31; son Reginald J, aged 4, and daughter Winifred M, aged 2 years; also listed was a general servant, Margaret Buchanan.

James MacBean continued the business following the death of William Ferguson in 1898. The *Inverness Courier* of 13 January 1899 carried an advertisement 'THE HIGHLAND JEWELLERY ESTABLISHMENT, FAMOUS FOR ARTISTIC HIGHLAND JEWELLERY. FERGUSON & MACBEAN, CORNER OF UNION STREET, INVERNESS.'

Slater's Directories 1900 and 1903 recorded this partnership as Jewellers, Silversmiths, Watch and Clockmakers at 41 Union Street, Inverness.

James MacBean died at Ridgeleigh, Crown Drive, on 8 December 1905, aged 57, and his death certificate described him as a Master Jeweller and Goldsmith. He was buried on 12 December 1905 in Tomnahurich Cemetery and the *Inverness Courier* of that date carried an obituary: '...being at the head of the firm of Messrs. Ferguson & Macbean, jewellers and watchmakers, Union Street, he was a well-known townsman'. In its conclusion it noted: 'We understand that the eldest son succeeds Mr. Macbean in the business.'

The *Sheriff Court Books of the County of Inverness* recorded on 3 April 1906 that James MacBean had died on 8 December 1905 and was the sole partner of the firm of Ferguson and MacBean. His wife was executrix nominate of the will. A gravestone in Tomnahurich cemetery has the inscription: 'SACRED TO THE LOVING MEMORY OF JAMES MACBEAN RIDGELEIGH, CROWN DRIVE, INVERNESS, DIED 8TH DECEMBER 1905 AND HIS WIFE ELSPET MARJORY DIED 3RD AUGUST 1918.'

The *Inverness Courier* of 27 July 1906 carried an advertisement headed:

GREAT JEWELLERY, &c., SALE. THE HIGHLAND JEWELLERY ESTABLISHMENT, UNION STREET CORNER, INVERNESS. FERGUSON & MACBEAN'S Whole Stock to be Cleared at practically Cost Price. The Stock comprises JEWELLERY of all descriptions. PLATE, CLOCKS, WATCHES, ANTIQUES, CURIOS, &c., as well as a Fine Collection of HIGHLAND JEWELLERY and ORNAMENTS. TERMS–CASH.

The marks used by Ferguson & MacBean were 'F & M, INVS', or 'F & M, I.N.V.S.' which sometimes included a 'CAMEL'. Ferguson and MacBean registered punches at the Birmingham Assay Office on 11 October 1886, 30 September 1895 and 12 May 1903.

ARTHUR MEDLOCK 1852–1930
(Medlock & Craik)

Arthur Medlock was born in the parish of Cockpen, Midlothian, in a hamlet called Polton Street, on 17 June 1852. His father was John Medlock, a butler, and his mother Grace Minow[113] who married 23 November 1845 in Dalmeny, West Lothian. Arthur was the third of five known children.

The family, without the father, were located in the 1851 census for Cockpen living in Polton Street[114]; Grace Medlock, aged 34, born in S Queensferry; John, aged 3, born in Lasswade[115], and James, 8 months, born in Cockpen. The 1861 census described Grace Medlock as a wife, but her husband, John, was not recorded at that address on the night of the census. Grace was aged 44, given as born in Dunfermline, with her children: John, aged 13; James, aged 10; Arthur, 8; Grace E, 6, and William, 4.

Before Arthur was married, he was recorded in the Inverness 1871 census as an bachelor, watchmaker, from Cockpen, aged 18; he was a lodger at 12 Richard's Alley with Hellen McLennan, a 50 year old married housekeeper.

The *Inverness Directory* 1873/74 listed Arthur Medlock living at 2 Nicols Alley, at Mrs Maclennan's lodging-house, Church Street, Inverness. He married Anne Ferguson on 22 April 1874. He was a 21 year old journeyman watchmaker, living at the above address; Anne was aged 23 living at 6 Inglis Street with her parents, Daniel Ferguson, a master watchmaker, and Margaret MacBean. Their first child was called Margaret Grace, born 12 May 1875, at 27 Telford Road. Next was Daniel John[116], born, 21 August 1877, but he died on 31 March 1879; his gravestone is located in Tomnahurich cemetery, Inverness. The inscription reads as follows: 'Sacred to the memory of Daniel John son of Arthur and Anne Medlock died 31st March 1879 Aged 20 months.' The remaining children were: Arthur Charles, born 8 January 1880, at 30 Innes Street; Rose Anne, born 11 November 1881, at 80 Church Street; Frederick William, born 7 October 1883, at 14 Innes Street; Helena Charlotte, born 26 June 1886, at 14 Innes Street, and Elizabeth Gertrude, born 3 December 1890, at Victoria Circus.

It is postulated that Arthur Medlock was apprenticed to Daniel Ferguson, in Inverness, and later worked as a journeyman to him until starting his own business, in about 1876, probably at 35 Castle Street; however, no opening advertisement has been found in any of the regional newspapers.

The 1881 census recorded Arthur Medlock as a watchmaker, aged 28, born in Cockpen, Midlothian, employing 3 boys. He was living at 30 Innes Street with his

Clan Badge by Arthur Medlock.
Private collection

Inverness Courier 31 May 1883

NOTICE OF REMOVAL.
———
ARTHUR MEDLOCK,
WATCHMAKER, JEWELLER, &c.,
Begs to Intimate that he has REMOVED to more
Central Premises,
No. 6 BRIDGE STREET.
A. M. takes this opportunity of thanking his numerous Customers and the Public for the liberal support he has had in the past, and he would draw special attention to his very carefully Selected and Fashionable Stock of
JEWELLERY, WATCHES, ELECTRO-PLATED GOODS, CLOCKS, &c.,
Only from the Best Houses in the Trade.
Best Class WATCH REPAIRING, and Jewellery Manufactured and Repaired on the Premises.
INSPECTION RESPECTFULLY INVITED.
Inverness, 28th May 1883.

wife Anne, 29, born in Nairn, and their children, Margaret Grace, aged 5, and Arthur Charles, aged 1 year. Also in the household was a general servant called Margaret Gray, aged 24, from England.

Slater's Directory 1882 recorded him under Jewellers & Manufacturers of Highland Ornaments, and, Watch and Clock Makers, working at 35 Castle Street; this appeared to be the first occasion that his business address was listed. The *Inverness Courier* of 31 May 1883 carried the first noted advertisement for Medlock which stated: 'NOTICE OF REMOVAL. ARTHUR MEDLOCK, WATCHMAKER, JEWELLER, &c., Begs to Intimate that he has REMOVED to more Central Premises, No. 6 BRIDGE STREET.'

The Edinburgh Assay Office recorded on 13 April 1890 that 'Mr Medlock sent punch which was impressed on the plate.'

The Inverness 1891 census listed the Medlock family living at Cathian Cottage, Victoria Circus; Arthur, aged 38, a watchmaker and jeweller; Ann, aged 41; Arthur C, 11; Rose Ann, 9; Fred W, 7; Helen C, 4, and Elizabeth G, aged 4 months. Also living with the family was Flora Sutherland, 22, a general servant.

Slater's Directory 1893 recorded Medlock as a watchmaker at 6 Bridge Street and his residence as Charlcot, Crown Drive, Inverness.

Arthur Medlock was the informant when his mother-in-law, Margaret Ferguson née MacBean, died in June 1902; his address was Ashlyn, Crown Drive. This was his address from about 1898 until at least 1918.

Slater's Directories 1900, 1903 and 1907 recorded the business under Jewellers, and, Watch & Clock Makers, at 6 Bridge Street and the 1911 *Directory* listed him as a jeweller, at the same address.

The next noted newspaper advertisement was in the *Inverness Courier* of 31 July 1906 headed: 'IMPORTANT ANNOUNCEMENT' (p121). The final advertisement noted for the business of Arthur Medlock was in the *Highland News* of 27 September 1913; it reported the following:

IMTIMATION. Mr ARTHUR MEDLOCK begs to intimate that he has TRANSFERRED his BUSINESS to Mr JAMES R. CRAIK, who will continue to conduct it as hitherto, under

Arthur Medlock c1910. Highland Photographic Archives, Inverness

Inverness Courier 31 July 1906

the Firm Name and designation of MEDLOCK & CRAIK GOLD-SMITHS, JEWELLERS, WATCHMAKERS, ENGRAVERS, AND OPTI-CIANS, 6 BRIDGE STREET, INVERNESS. Mr MEDLOCK takes this opportunity of tendering his sincere thanks to his many Customers and the Public generally for the liberal patronage bestowed on him for the past 38 years[117]. Mr JAMES R. CRAIK desires to intimate that he has acquired the said Business, and that he will carry it on as stated for his own behoof. It will be his object, by the same strict attention to business, to merit the Patronage enjoyed by Mr Medlock, and he trusts the present Clientele will continue to give him the same confidence which they extended to his predecessor. Inverness, 22nd September, 1913.

A photograph of Arthur Medlock taken before 1920, probably around 1910 (above). The marks Arthur Medlock used on his silver were 'MEDLOCK, INV^{ss}'.

Details of the marriages of Arthur Medlock's children are as follows: Margaret Grace married G A Ross, a farmer from Rhynie on 17 March 1898; Helena Charlotte married Gerrard Finnie, Bank Agent from Fortrose, in 1917, when Arthur was recorded as a retired master jeweller; Elizabeth Gertrude married Edwin Stevenson, linen merchant from Lisburn,

Ireland, on 10 April 1918. Arthur Charles, linen manufacturer, married Martha Charlotte Stevenson in Belfast on 11 February 1920.

Arthur's wife, Anne, died on 11 February 1923, aged 72, at Braeside, Henderson Street, Bridge of Allan; the informant was Gerrard Firnie, son-in-law, his address was the Bank of Scotland, Kirriemuir. Anne's husband was recorded as Arthur Medlock, jeweller (retired). In the records of the Personal Estate of Mrs Ann Medlock, Arthur Charles Medlock, Linen Manufacturer, from Ardavory, Craigavad, County Down, was recorded.

This was the clue to finding where Arthur Medlock settled after his wife's death. It would appear that he travelled to Ireland where two of his children made their homes; he died on 4 August 1930, recorded as a retired jeweller, aged 78, from Redholme, Craigavad, County Down.

WILLIAM REID CHRISTIE 1863–c1916

William Christie was born on 10 September 1863 at McVicar's Lane, Perth Road, Dundee. His parents were Alexander Christie, a journeyman baker, and Isabella McIntosh, who married in Dundee on 26 November 1862.

The Arbroath 1881 census listed William Christie with his parents, two brothers and three sisters at 18 Jamieson Street. He was recorded as a jeweller's apprentice, aged 17 years, born in Dundee.

William was recorded in the Inverness 1891 census living at 5 Charles Street as a lodger, unmarried; he stated that he was a jeweller's assistant, aged 27, born in Dundee.

The *Highland News* of 4 June 1892 carried an advertisement for 'W. R. CHRISTIE, MAUNUFACTURING GOLDSMITH, WATCHMAKER, AND OPTICIAN, 1 QUEEN'S

QUEEN'S GATE
JEWELLERY ESTABLISHMENT.

W. R. CHRISTIE
(LATE WITH FERGUSON & MACBEAN)

Would respectfully invite attention to his Stock of WATCHES,
CLOCKS, JEWELLERY, and ELECTRO-PLATE.

CHRISTIE'S Popular Keyless Hunting Lever, £4 2s 6d—a
genuine and reliable timekeeper. Prize Medal Keyless Lever,
£4. Ladies' Watches from 15s ; choice designs. The Victoria
Knockabout Watch, in strong cases, with crystal glass and
self-winding, 14s 6d—suitable for the Holidays, Cricket,
Cycling, &c.
The now favourite PEPPER CASTORS in Oak, with Silver
Mounts, from 1s each ; a variety of very pretty designs to
choose from.
TEA-POTS, best Electro-Plate, 15s and upwards.
The Largest Selection of New and Original Designs in
CAIRNGORM and PEBBLE JEWELLERY in the North.

Parcels of all Goods sent on approval.
Watches, Clocks, and Jewellery receive genuine treatment
from Practical Workmen.
CHARGES MODERATE.

GATE BUILDINGS, Has now OPENED the above PREMISES with a Stock replete with
the Latest Novelties in JEWELLERY, SILVER, and ELECTRO-PLATE. &c.' On 25 June
1892 another advertisement (above) appeared. A further advertisement of 5
November 1892 recorded him as a watchmaker and optician at Queens's Gate
Buildings.

On 11 November 1896 at 74 Church Street, Inverness, William, aged 33,
married Mary Ann Mackintosh, aged 28. Their residence was recorded as 74
Church Street. Mary Ann's parents were Donald Mackintosh, house painter, and
Mary Ann Ferguson.

The *Highland News* of 16 September 1899 carried the following advertisement:
'WATCH YOUR EYES. FROM 1s TO 50s. CHRISTIE'S Spectacles and Folders are recom-
mended for weak and failing eyesight.' It concluded, 'W. R. CHRISTIE, OPTICIAN TO
THE FACULTY, 1 QUEENSGATE, INVERNESS.'

William Christie was recorded in *Slater's Directories* 1900, 1903 and 1907 under
watch and clockmakers, working at 1 Queensgate. The 1911 *Directory* recorded his
business at 32 Queensgate but he was missing from the 1915 *Directory*, Commercial
Section, being only listed under 'Private Residents' at Arbirlot, Montague Row,
Inverness.

William was recorded in the *Inverness Burgh Directory* 1905-06 as a jeweller at 32
Queen's Gate, Inverness, his house being Arbilot (sic), Montague Row, Inverness.
These addresses remained the same for all *Inverness Burgh Directories* up till 1909-10.

The *Highland News* of 1 April 1911 reported as follows: 'W. R. CHRISTIE,
JEWELLER, QUEENSGATE, Begs to thank his numerous Patrons and Friends for the
splendid support they have given him during the last Two Weeks of his GENUINE
CLEARANCE SALE and hereby intimates that he has re-arranged the remainder of his
Stock at STILL FURTHER REDUCTIONS.' There followed a long list of items from his

stock with relevant prices. The same newspaper of 13 May 1911 carried the following advertisement: 'CHRISTIE'S REMOVAL SALE Tell your Father and Mother that W. R. CHRISTIE has decided, at the request of a number of his Customers, to extend his SWEEPING REDUCTION IN PRICES TO HIS SPECTACLE DEPARTMENT.' It then listed various items and prices and finished with, 'NOTE ADDRESS AFTER MAY TERM – 1 DRUMMOND STREET.'

The *Highland News* of 17 June 1911 carried an advertisement which simply said, 'CHRISTIE, JEWELLER REMOVED TO 1 DRUMMOND STREET.' The *Highland News* of 16 March 1912 carried a witty advertisement for wedding rings:

> Christie, The Ring Leader. FOR YEARS AND YEARS. Your wife-to-be will wear the sacred emblem of matrimony which you have placed upon her finger ... Standard Quality and Sterling Value, at an establishment where the "magic circles" are sold by weight, is what you want. With every ring we present the bride with a small memento of the occasion. W. R. CHRISTIE, MANUFACTURING JEWELLER. 1 DRUMMOND STREET, INVERNESS.

A further advertisement of 7 December 1912 showed examples and prices of the jewellery that he sold; he was still advertising as a manufacturing jeweller at 1 Drummond Street.

The *Highland News* of 27 September 1913 carried the following headed: 'ANNUAL SALE. W. R. CHRISTIE, JEWELLER, DRUMMOND STREET, INVERNESS, Begs to

Jewellery box top for W R Christie.

Highland News 6 May 1916

GIVING UP BUSINESS
ON ACCOUNT OF THE WAR

Mr W. R. Christie

WATCHMAKER AND JEWELLER,
1 DRUMMOND STREET,

HAS Decided to Retire from the RETAIL BUSINESS, and now Offers his ENTIRE STOCK at 50 Per Cent. under Usual Prices. As the Stock, which is in Excellent Condition, must be Cleared by TUESDAY, the 22nd current, the Public are respectfully invited to secure such Articles as they may require at this GENUINE SALE.

NO REASONABLE OFFER REFUSED.
SEE WINDOWS FOR BARGAINS.

1 DRUMMOND STREET,
INVERNESS.

intimate his FOURTH ANNUAL SALE, Which will commence on THURSDAY, October 2ⁿᵈ. The WHOLE STOCK will be marked in Plain Figures at tempting prices.' His address was recorded as Lombard Street when he advertised in the same newspaper on 6 June 1914 and 5 December 1914; however, it was 1 Drummond Street on 18 December 1915.

The *Highland News* of 8 April 1916 ran the following advertisement headed 'REMOVAL NOTICE', which continued 'W. R. CHRISTIE Begs to intimate that he will Remove to NO. 3 LOMBARD STREET, A Few Doors up, at the May Term. Before doing so, he proposes having a CLEARING SALE of his Whole Stock.' His address was Drummond Street.

The last advertisement for W. R. Christie was recorded in the *Highland News* of 6 May (opposite) and each issue until 27 May 1916, when he stated that he was giving up business on account of the war; his address was 1 Drummond Street. It appears that John Fraser, draper & outfitter, (late 3 Lombard Street) , became the new shopkeeper at 1 Drummond Street.

The *Inverness Burgh Directory* 1916-17 listed him as a jeweller with only the house address; the implication was that he had retired. There is no record of his death in Scotland.

An example of one of W R Christie's clocks is on the outside of the booking office at Boat of Garten Railway Station. The only mark noted for him is as follows: 'W.R.C, INS'.

Inverness Museum and Art Gallery

ALEXANDER WILLIAM FRASER 1863-1945
(Fraser, Ferguson & MacBean)

Alexander William Fraser was born on 27 June 1863 at 18 Church Street, Inverness, the son of Alexander William Fraser, a photographer, and Helen McKenzie. The *Inverness Courier* of 13 October 1864 carried an advertisement:

> PHOTOGRAPHIC STUDIO, 18 CHURCH STREET, INVERNESS. A.W. FRASER, PHOTOGRAPHER, in thanking the Public for past favours, begs most respectfully to intimate that, in consequence of the great increase of his business, he has, in order to meet the Public demands, considerably enlarged his Premises, and added all the newest and most approved Apparatus to his Establishment.

A W Fraser junior was a trained watchmaker, but we do not know to whom he was apprenticed; however, we do know that aged 24, now a master watchmaker, he married Charlotte Thomson, aged 19, the daughter of William Thomson, a master draper, and Jessie Robertson, on 13 December 1887 at Grantown-on-Spey. Tragically Charlotte died in pregnancy

Jewellery box top for Fraser, Ferguson & Macbean

on 13 July 1888, aged 20; the address given was Corner of Square, Grantown, her parents' home. Her gravestone was located in the Inverallan Graveyard, Grantown, Lair 378; the inscription on the gravestone reads: 'In Memory of Charlotte Thomson, wife of Alex Wm Fraser, Grantown, Born 17th May 1868, Died 13th July 1888.' The lair was bought by Mr A W Fraser, Fern Cottage, for his first wife.

The 1891 census for Fern Cottage, New South Street, Grantown-on-Spey listed Alexander Fraser, aged 27, as a watchmaker and a widower; living with him was his 18 year old sister, Nellie, who was housekeeper, and Jessie Grant, a domestic servant, aged 16 years.

Alexander remarried at the age of 35, on 12 October 1898, at the Grand Hotel, Aberdeen. His bride was Isabella Sim, a 37 year old spinster, from Westwood, Grantown, the daughter of Alexander Sim, a feuar, and Jane Grant. Alexander and Isabella had at least three daughters: the eldest was Alison Emily who was born 23 September 1899, then Jean Helen Jessie, on 5 March 1901, and Leslie on 14 June 1903, all born at Fern Cottage, Grantown. It would appear that whilst he was in Grantown he studied to be an optician, combining this with his profession as a watchmaker and jeweller.

The *Grantown Supplement Extra* of 11 August 1906 carried an advertisement headed: 'FRASER'S HIGHLAND JEWELLERY ESTABLISHMENT.' It concluded 'A.W. FRASER, Goldsmith, Jeweller and Highland Ornament Maker, GRANTOWN-ON-SPEY.'

The *Grantown Supplement* throughout 1906 carried the same advertisement headed 'DEFECTS OF VISION' (below). Unfortunately there was no address given, however, we do know his business premises were in the High Street.

The Grantown Supplement 13 October 1906

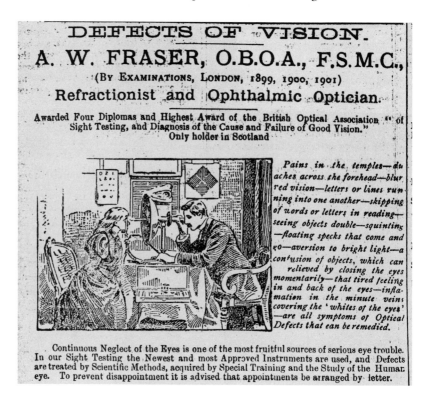

126

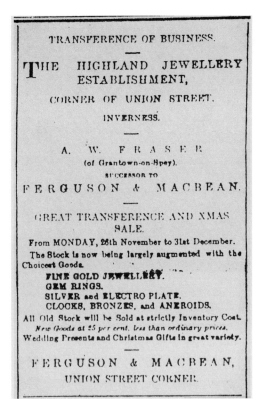

The *Grantown Supplement* of 13 October 1906 reported that among the names recorded for the County of Elgin, A W Fraser, Jeweller, had been added to the Roll of Justices of the Peace on the recommendation of his Grace the Duke of Richmond and Gordon, K G, Lord Lieutenant of the County.

Meanwhile on the 13 November 1906, the *Inverness Courier* carried an advertisement for a transference of business (above). It would appear from this that the new firm was to be named A W Fraser, but at the change of advertisements in the *Inverness Courier* on Tuesday 4 December 1906, the new business was, for the first time, called Fraser, Ferguson and MacBean's Highland Jewellery Establishment (above).

The *Grantown Supplement* of 24 November 1906 carried an advertisement for the sale of Alexander Fraser's home:

House Property for Sale. GRANTOWN-ON-SPEY. For sale by private bargain the desirable villa known as Ardconnel standing in its grounds with southern exposure, containing 3 public rooms, 7 bedrooms, servant's bedroom, bathroom, lavatories, servant's hall, kitchen, scullery, pantries, wash-house, &c. Hot water circulation throughout. Tennis Green and large garden. For further particulars apply to Mr. A.W. Fraser, 41 Union Street, Inverness, or the Subscribees.

Shortly after this his household furniture was advertised for sale. On the same page another advertisement stated: 'HOUSE TO LET at No 41 HIGH STREET, above shop. Apply A.W. FRASER, Ardconnel.'

left: *Inverness Courier 13 November 1906*

right: *Inverness Courier 4 December 1906*

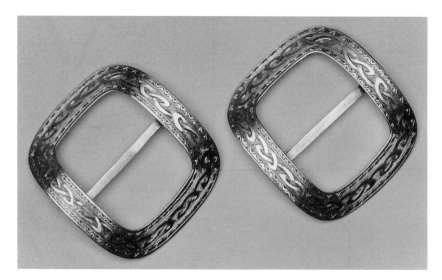

The *Grantown Supplement* of 26 January 1907 reported that Mr John A Fraser, who had been 15 years in business in Dufftown as a watchmaker and jeweller, had acquired[118] the Grantown business of his brother, Mr A W Fraser. John Fraser had become ill in March 1907 and went to Edinburgh for special treatment, unfortunately, he died there on 2 September 1907, aged 42 years. Meantime the business of A W Fraser had continued as advertisements were still noted in the local newspaper of 11 and 18 May and 15 June 1907.

The *Strathspey News & Grantown Supplement* of 6 July 1907 carried another advertisement headed 'FRASER'S HIGHLAND JEWELLERY ESTABLISHMENT, GRANTOWN ON SPEY AND AT FRASER, FERGUSON & MACBEAN'S, Union Street Corner, INVERNESS.' It concluded, 'A. W. FRASER, Designer and Manufacturer of Highland Jewellery.'

The *Grantown Supplement* of 27 July 1907 reported that Mr A W Fraser, Jeweller of Grantown, Inverness and Dufftown, had sold the Dufftown business to Mr MacDonald, Alloa, formerly of Inverness. Mr MacDonald had served his apprenticeship with an Inverness firm.

Throughout 1907 the *Grantown Supplement* carried advertisements for A W Fraser and one of 21 December 1907 stated: 'WEDDING, CHRISTMAS, and NEW YEAR GIFTS IN LARGE VARIETY AT A.W. FRASER, JEWELLER.' This would imply that Alexander Fraser continued the Grantown business together with the larger Inverness branch, although by *Slater's Directory* 1915, the Grantown branch was missing.

The *Highland News* of 4 January 1913 carried an advertisement for the Inverness business headed: 'Eyesight Testing for Spectacles and Eyeglasses. FRASER, FERGUSON & MACBEAN Refractionists and Ophthalmic Opticians. A.W. FRASER, F.B.O.A., F.S.M.C., Principal.' It concluded with the usual address, 'UNION STREET, INVERNESS'.

On 12 May 1926 Alexander Fraser's eldest daughter, Alison Emily, aged 26, married Horatio Alistair MacBean, aged 34, son of deceased James MacBean[119], master jeweller. His occupation was recorded as bank accountant and his residence given as Calcutta.

Slater's 1907, 1911, 1915, 1921 and *Kelly's* 1928 *Directories* listed the business at 41 Union Street, initially under Jewellers, Silversmiths, and Watchmakers & Clockmakers; however, from 1911 onwards they were detailed as jewellers. The *Inverness Burgh Directory* 1928-29, *MacDonald's Scottish Directories* 1935-36 and 1936-37, *Murray's Aberdeen, Inverness and North of Scotland Trades' Directory* 1936-37 all recorded the business still at the same address but it was not found in *MacDonald's Scottish Directory* 1941-42. Fraser, Ferguson & MacBean was situated where the Lloyds T S B bank is at present located, on the corner of Church Street and Union Street. Latterly the address was given as 24 Church Street (Union Street Corner), ophthalmic opticians and photographic dealers.

Alexander's wife, Isabella, died at 11 Drummond Crescent, Inverness, on 2 September 1944, aged 84. The death was registered by her daughter, Alison MacBean. Alexander William Fraser, jeweller and optician, died at 11 Drummond Crescent on 1 January 1945, aged 81. His death was registered by his son-in-law, Horatio MacBean.

Alexander's obituary in the *Northern Chronicle* on 3 January 1945 stated:

> We regret to record the death on New Year's Day at his residence, Birchwood, Inverness, of Mr. Alexander William Fraser, J.P., of the firm of Messrs. Fraser, Ferguson and MacBean, jewellers, Inverness. He was an octogenarian, and his illness was of brief duration. Before coming to Inverness about forty years ago he was in business in Grantown-on-Spey.

The *Strathspey Herald & Grantown Advertiser* of 5 January 1945 also carried a death notice as follows: 'Fraser. – at Birchwood, Inverness, on 1st January, 1945, Alexander William Fraser, J.P., of Fraser, Ferguson and MacBean, jewellers.'

A gravestone in Tomnahurich cemetery reads: In loving memory of Alexander W. Fraser, J.P., Birchwood, Inverness died 1st January 1945. And of his wife Isabella Sim, died 2nd September 1944.

The marks used by Fraser, Ferguson & MacBean were 'F.F & M, INVSS', and sometimes included a 'CAMEL'. They also registered a punch at the Birmingham Assay Office on 7 May 1929.

William Morrison, who had served his apprenticeship as a watchmaker with this firm in the 1930s said that the watchmaking department was run by Walter Buchanan, a strict Irishman, and the jewellery manufacturing was managed by John Horne. The workshop was over the shop, towards the back, with the opticians also upstairs. He related that in the 1930s, the 'Time Ball' was still over the front door of the shop and was religiously released at 11 o'clock, on the precise time of the P O signal from Greenwich. It was a common sight to see gentlemen with their pocket watches standing outside at midday to check the time.

The firm was managed by David Scott, after the death of Alexander Fraser, until about 1947, when the business ceased to trade and the shop was taken over by Howden's, the florists and nurserymen.

Jewellery box top for Donald MacRae

DONALD MACRAE c1866-c1929

Donald MacRae was first noted in *Slater's Directory* 1900 as a watchmaker working at 28 Eastgate. He was recorded at the same address in *Slater's* 1903, 1907, 1911, 1915, 1921 and *Kelly's* 1928 *Directories*, always as a watchmaker.

The *Inverness Courier* of 18 January 1910 carried an advertisement for MACRAE, Jeweller, Eastgate, Inverness. '1887 – ESTABLISHED TWENTY-THREE YEARS – 1910.'

The *Highland News* of 6 January 1912 carried an advertisement (below). The shop address was recorded as Eastgate in the *Highland News* of January 1914 and 2 January 1915.

Donald MacRae was listed in the *Inverness Burgh Directory* 1928-29 under watchmakers and jewellers, working at 28 East Gate.

The following mark is attributed to Donald MacRae: 'DMCR over INV^{ss}' with a pellet over the M, a pellet under the c, a pellet under the V and a dash under the ss. The mark is reproduced from the Edinburgh Assay Office plates.

Courtesy of the Edinburgh Assay Office

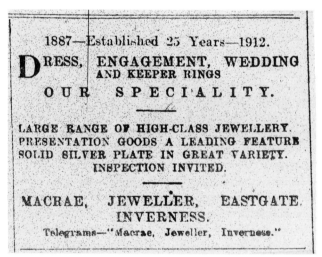

Highland News 6 January 1912

JAMES ROBERTS CRAIK 1874-1948
(Medlock & Craik)

James Roberts Craik was born on 9 March 1874 at 32 Arthur Street, Edinburgh, son of James Craik, a typefounder, and Mary Munro. James Craik, aged 26, of 5 Victoria Square, Inverness, married Margaret Fulton Kidd, aged 27, of 21 Upper Gray Street, Edinburgh, on 28 March 1900 in Edinburgh. Margaret was the daughter of John McDougall Kidd, a baker, and Mary Gillies. James and Margaret had two known daughters: Norah Roberts, who was born on 7 January 1901 at 21 Upper Gray Street, Edinburgh (their domicile was recorded as 2 Redfern Terrace, Inverness); and Patricia Roberts, born on 30 October 1908 at 27 Ness Bank, Inverness. James Roberts Craik was recorded as an engraver and designer, for the former, and engraver for the latter. James Craik was also the brother-in-law of William B Taylor.

The *Highland News* of 27 September 1913 (right) reported a transfer of business from Medlock to Craik.

The *Highland News* of 3 January 1914 carried the following advertisement:

> PERFECT WORKMANSHIP Is the Best Possible Advertisement and the Secret of our Success. THAT IS WHY We give the closest attention to even the most insignificant Repair or Order. WE KNOW A Casual Customer will thereby become a Regular Patron. That is what We Want. If you are not Satisfied, therefore, COME TO US, WE CAN, and Will, Satisfy You both in Workmanship and Prices. Medlock & Craik, Practical Watchmakers, Jewellers, Engravers & Opticians, 6 Bridge Street, Inverness.

The *Highland News* of 23 January 1915 carried an advertisement (below).

Slater's 1915, 1921 and *Kelly's* 1928 *Directories* listed the business under jewellers, as Medlock and Craik, at 6 Bridge Street, with Jas R Craik as the proprietor. The *Inverness Burgh Directory* 1928-29 and *MacDonald's Scottish Directory* 1935-36 still recorded the business at 6 Bridge Street, whilst *MacDonald's Scottish Directory* 1936-37 detailed it at 33 Bridge Street. The same *Directory* for the year 1941-42 also listed the business

IMTIMATION.

Mr ARTHUR MEDLOCK begs to intimate that he has TRANSFERRED his BUSINESS to Mr JAMES R. CRAIK who will continue to conduct it as hitherto, under the Firm Name and designation of

MEDLOCK & CRAIK,

GOLDSMITHS, JEWELLERS, WATCHMAKERS, ENGRAVERS, AND OPTICIANS,

6 Bridge Street, Inverness.

Mr MEDLOCK takes this opportunity of tendering his sincere thanks to his many Customers and the Public generally for the liberal patronage bestowed on him for the past 38 years.

Mr JAMES R. CRAIK desires to intimate that he has acquired the said Business, and that he will carry it on as stated for his own behoof. It will be his object, by the same strict attention to business, to merit the Patronage enjoyed by Mr Medlock, and he trusts the present Clientele will continue to give him the same confidence which they extended to his predecessor.

Inverness, 22nd September, 1913.

Highland News 27 September 1913

If You Appreciate Good Jewellery
.. We are Indispensible to You. ..
TWO SPECIAL LINES.

Our Special SIX SHILLING LEVER WATCH, either in Oxydised or Solid Nickel Cases. It is quite impossible for you to know how satisfactory a Cheap Watch can be until you have tested Medlock and Craik's.

Our New Army Solid Nickel Silver SHAVING MIRROR is just the thing for the Man at the Front. They are Unbreakable and will not rust. Price 2s each, in Pocket Protective Case.

Quality for Quality, Finish for Finish, our Prices are as low, and in most cases lower, than other Establishments.

Special Attention given to ENGRAVING, WATCH, CLOCK AND JEWELLERY REPAIRS, all of which are executed on the Premises.

MEDLOCK & CRAIK,

Watchmakers, Jewellers, Engravers & Opticians,

6 BRIDGE STREET, INVERNESS

Telephone 3 y 1.

Highland News 23 January 1915

Cairngorm House,
Bridge Street,
Inverness, c1950.
Courtesy of the
Highland Photographic
Archives, Inverness

address as 33 Bridge Street. Medlock & Craik remained at that address until the early 1950s; a photograph of the business address, Cairngorm House[120], is illustrated . The *Inverness Burgh Directories* 1956-57 and 1960-61 listed the concern as Medlock & Craik, jewellers, at 2, 3 Exchange Place.

Margaret Fulton Craik died on 27 May 1936, at the Royal Infirmary, Edinburgh, aged 63 years. Her residence was given as 34 Broadstone Park, Inverness.

James Craik, master engraver, died on 4 June 1948, recorded as a widower, aged 74, at 34 Broadstone Park, Inverness. The *Inverness Courier* of 8 June 1948 recorded the death as follows: 'CRAIK- At 34 Broadstone Park, Inverness, on 4 June 1948, James Roberts Craik, engraver, designer and jeweller, of the firm of Medlock and Craik, Cairngorm House, Inverness, beloved husband of the late Margaret Fulton Kidd. Interred in Tomnahurich Cemetery.' In the same newspaper his obituary was printed:

> By the death of Mr James Roberts Craik, at his residence in Inverness on Friday, a well-known jeweller and designer, who conducted business in the town for many years, has passed away. He had the distinction of being the only skilled engraver north of Aberdeen, and he had a large clientele in the Highlands who entrusted him with special work, which he performed with taste and skill. He was greatly interested in Freemasonry. Mr Craik was for some years the Right Worshipful Master of St Mary's Lodge, and he was also interested in vocal music. For some time Mr Craik had not enjoyed good health, but he had carried on his skilled work until recently. In the busi-

ness, known as Medlock and Craik, Bridge Street, his daughter, Miss Norah Craik, was associated with him as a partner, and she intends to carry on the business. Mr Craik, who was 74 years of age, was a native of Edinburgh, and came to Inverness about 1896. He is also survived by a daughter who holds an important post in England.

His daughter, Norah Craik, continued the business until 1961. She lived at the same house but renamed it Duddingston. A Mr Allan finally took over the business until his eventual death in 1980. *MacDonald's Scottish Directory* 1965-66 recorded the concern at Cairngorm House, 20 Queensgate.

The business 'Cairngorm House (Medlock & Craik)' ceased to exist when the hotel in Queensgate burnt down in 1992.

Norah Roberts Craik died at the Royal Infirmary, Perth, on 28 June 1993, aged 92. Her residence was given as Duddingston, Golf Course Road, Rosemount, Blairgowrie.

Their marks were 'M & C, INVSS' or 'MEDLOCK & CRAIK INVERNESS', 'MEDLOCK & CRAIK incuse.'

WILLIAM BUCHANAN TAYLOR 1876-1942

William Buchanan Taylor was born on 25 November 1876 at 7 Gordon Street, Leith, the son of James Taylor, a journeyman mason, and Mary Ann Buchanan. William was first noted in the 1891 Edinburgh census for 34 Upper Gray Street as a 14 year old scholar living with his father, James, mother, Mary Ann, and three brothers, James, Alexander and Robert.

Having served his apprenticeship in Edinburgh William Taylor commenced business around July 1899 in the Tolbooth, on the corner of Church Street and Bridge Street, Inverness. The earliest noted working date for William B Taylor was in the *Inverness Burgh Directory* 1901-02; he was recorded as a Jeweller at 10 Bridge Street, Inverness. *Slater's Directory* 1903 listed him as a working jeweller at the same address.

He married Mary Aitchison Munro Craik at 17 Gladstone Terrace, Edinburgh, on 3 September 1903. He was described as a jeweller, aged 26, from 63 Church Street, Inverness. Mary was aged 30, from 17 Gladstone Terrace, Edinburgh; her parents were James Craik, a type founder, and Mary Aitchison Munro. Mary Craik was born on 25 November 1872, at 32 Arthur Street, Edinburgh, and was sister to James Roberts Craik (of Medlock & Craik).

It would appear that when William Taylor commenced business in the Tolbooth, (10 Bridge Street) he was helped by

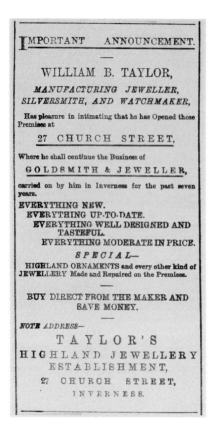

Inverness Courier 31 July 1906

Jewellery box top

his wife who ran the shop while he concentrated on repairs. In those days he was one of about twenty jewellers in the town where the trade was directed at tourists, especially Americans. William Taylor was described by a family member as a very personable man who was always smartly dressed; he had a waxed moustache and was normally dressed in jacket and trousers, grey spats and highly polished shoes.

There was only one surviving child from this union, Magdalene Buchanan born on 9 June 1904 at 28 Queen's Gate, Inverness, where her father was described as a working jeweller. The only other known child was born and died on the same day, 8 August 1910, at Silverfjord, 5 Ness Bank, Inverness; William Taylor was described as a master jeweller.

The *Inverness Courier* of 31 July 1906 carried an advertisement headed IMPORTANT ANNOUNCEMENT (left). The business at 27 Church Street was on three floors; the workshop was on the top floor and split into two workshops, one for clockmaking and the other jewellery. The shop at 27 Church Street was situated where the Caledonian Hotel now stands.

The *Inverness Courier* of 19 April 1910 carried an advertisement for William B Taylor 27 Church Street: 'GREAT JEWELLERY STOCK REDUCING SALE NOW IN PROGRESS, SPECIAL BARGAINS. SPECIAL DISCOUNT of 4s in every Pound. SEE OUR WINDOWS FOR PRICES.' Another in the same newspaper of 13 May 1910 stated: 'Taylor's Annual Sale. GREAT BARGAINS IN Watches, Clocks, Jewellery, Silver Ware and Electro-Plate.'

The *Highland News* of 7 January 1911 ran an advertisement:

The Purchasing of Jewellery Is not necessarily such an expensive job as some people imagine it to be. It depends where you go for these things. The wise buyer invariably comes to us knowing that Our Stock represents the Highest Quality and the Greatest Value. In every type of Jewellery and Silver-ware. A glance over our stock is the most fascinating way of passing a spare half-hour. WILLIAM B. TAYLOR, 27 CHURCH STREET, INVERNESS.

The same newspaper of 23 March 1912 carried an advertisement headed: 'GREAT JEWELLERY SALE. AN EXCELLENT OPPORTUNITY TO PURCHASE WEDDING PRESENTS AT MUCH BELOW USUAL PRICES. Every article will be subject to a Cash Discount of 3s in every £1. All Goods Booked will be charged Usual Prices. W. B. TAYLOR, 27 Church Street, INVERNESS.'

The *Highland News* of 4 January 1913 carried a large advertisement: 'ENGAGEMENT RINGS 10s 6d to £50. SELECTIONS SENT ON APPROVAL. W. B. TAYLOR, 27 Church Street, INVERNESS.' The *Highland News* of 27 December 1913 carried an advertisement (right).

The same newspaper of 23 January 1915 advertised: 'Rings etc. 10/6 to £50 RINGS & JEWELLERY form a section of our display which will interest every present seeker.'

An even bigger advertisement, which could not be missed, appeared in the *Highland News* of 1 January 1916: 'W.B.TAYLOR, THE SHOP FOR NOVELTIES, 27 Church Street.'

His shop was at 27 Church Street, from 1906; a photograph of W B Taylor and two of his employees, was taken there in 1931 (below) and the calendar on the wall clearly recalls the date. A further two photographs show the front of the shop (p136) and a close up of the window illustrating the Prince of Wales Freedom Casket, presented in June 1931, which pinpoints the date quite accurately.

Slater's Directory 1907 listed the business under Jewellers, Silversmiths, and Watch & Clockmakers, at 27 Church Street and 10 Bridge Street, whilst *Slater's Directory* 1911 recorded the concern at 27 Church Street with the workshop at 10 Bridge Street, listed as: jewellers, watch & clock makers, goldsmith & silversmith. *Slater's* 1915 and 1921, *Kelly's* 1928 and the *Inverness Burgh Directory* 1928-29 recorded the business at 27 Church Street only. *MacDonald's Scottish Directory* 1935-36 and 1941-42 noted the business at 25 and 27 Church Street, although *Murray's Aberdeen, Inverness and North of Scotland Trades' Directory* 1936-37 still listed only 27 Church Street.

All kinds of Presents that will open the door of the New Year pleasantly for your Friends

—dainty little Jewellery ideas for ladies, useful suggestions for the men, distinctive items in Silver and Electro-plate that would give satisfaction to any of your friends. We offer a selection that is a pleasure to choose from, and our prices range upwards from 1s.—representing excellent value always.

The Right Present at the Right Price is Easy to Find Here

W. B. TAYLOR,
27 CHURCH STREET, INVERNESS.

Highland News 27 December 1913

The casket presented to HRH the Prince of Wales on 26 June 1931, in W B Taylor's Workshop, June 1931. From left to right: Willie Matheson, Dan MacKinlay, Willie Taylor. Highland Photographic Archives, Inverness

*W B Taylor's Shop
Window 1931 and
c1945.* Private collection

His marks were 'W.T., INVSS', 'W. B.T, SILVER, INV[ss]' and 'W. B. TAYLOR, SILVERSMITH, INVERNESS'.

William Taylor died on 9 February 1942, aged 65, at 7 Ballifeary Road, Inverness, described as a watchmaker and jeweller. The informant was his brother, Robert B Taylor of 25 Attadale Road, Inverness. The *Inverness Courier* of 20 February 1942 carried the following: 'BUSINESS ANNOUNCEMENT Owing to the death of Mr Taylor, the business premises of W. B. TAYLOR JEWELLER 27 CHURCH STREET, INVERNESS Will be CLOSED until about MARCH 2nd, when Business will be carried on as usual.' The same newspaper of 3 March stated that the 'BUSINESS WILL REOPEN ON TUESDAY 5th MARCH, PLEASE NOTE – PREMISES WILL BE CLOSED EACH WEDNESDAY UNTIL FURTHER NOTICE when Business will be carried on as usual.' Finally, another business advertisement in the same newspaper of 17 March stated: 'THE PREMISES OF W. B. TAYLOR WATCHMAKER AND JEWELLER 25 and 27 CHURCH STREET, INVERNESS. Will Remain Closed All Day WEDNESDAY and FRIDAY Until Further Notice.'

His gravestone in Tomnahurich cemetery reads as follows:

IN MEMORY OF MY BELOVED HUSBAND WILLIAM BUCHANAN TAYLOR, JEWELLER, SILVERSMITH & WATCHMAKER DIED AT ELMGROVE HOUSE, BALLIFEARY ROAD, INVERNESS, 9TH FEBRU-ARY 1942. ALSO MY BELOVED SISTER SUSANNA LOGAN CRAIK, WHO DIED 16TH DECEMBER 1963. AND HIS BELOVED WIFE MARY A. M. CRAIK WHO DIED 21ST JUNE 1969, AGED 96 YEARS.

The business was carried on after his death by his wife, Mary, and her sister Susanna Craik together with Robert Taylor[121] until about 1954, when Ian Kinnear, his grandson, took over the indirect management until the eventual sale of the business in 1965. *MacDonald's Scottish Directory* 1965-66 recorded the business at 25-27 Church Street, under jewellers and watch repairers.

Glengarry cap badge by W B Taylor

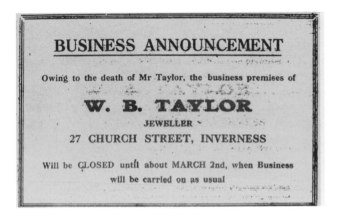

Inverness Courier 20 February 1942

CHARLES DOHERTY 1859–c1912

Charles Doherty was born in Edinburgh on 7 March 1859, the son of James Doherty, hawker, and Mary McLauchlan.

The Edinburgh 1881 census recorded Charles as a working jeweller, aged 22, living at 4 Milne Square with his brother, John, an unemployed carver and gilder, aged 30, and two sisters, Margaret Jane, a photographer, aged 26, and Isabella, a sewing machinist, aged 19; all born in Edinburgh. Also living with them was a cousin, James McLaughlan, aged 8, born in Glasgow.

On 22 October 1884 at St Patrick's Church, Cowgate, Edinburgh, Charles Doherty, working jeweller, aged 25, who lived at 13 Home Street, Edinburgh, married Elizabeth Gilchrist, aged 23, whose home was at 18 Bristo Street, Edinburgh. His father was recorded as James Doherty, tailor, deceased. Her parents were Mark Gilchrist, cabman, and Elizabeth Cummings. Witnesses were Patrick Charles Kelly and Isabella Doherty. There was one known child from the union of Charles and Elizabeth, James Mark Doherty, born on 29 January 1885 at 40 North Richmond Street, Edinburgh; his father was recorded a jeweller.

The Edinburgh 1891 census recorded the family living in two rooms at 19 Jamaica Street: Charles Docherty, a jeweller, aged 32; Elizabeth, a book folder, aged 31, and James, aged 6; all born in Edinburgh.

Charles Doherty was first noted in Inverness in the *Inverness Burgh Directory* 1904-05; he was listed as Charles Docharty (sic), watchmaker, at 4 Carlton Terrace, Millburn Road, in the alphabetical section, and as Charles Docherty, jeweller, at the same address, in the street section. The 1906-07 *Directory* recorded him at the above address as a watchmaker, but also at 16 Union Street as a jeweller. The 1907-08 *Inverness Directory* listed him as a jeweller at 22 Union Street only but the 1910-11 *Directory* noted two addresses for him, 22 and 24 Union Street. The *Inverness Burgh Directory* 1912-13 listed him for the last time, as a jeweller, at 24 Union Street only. He was also entered in *Slater's Directories* for this period.

It appears that the family left Inverness and probably Scotland sometime after 1912 as record of their deaths cannot be found.

His punches were noted on a pair of shoe buckles in the Inverness Museum and Art Gallery and marked as follows: 'C.D, camel, INV^{ss}' (above).

CHAPTER FOUR

INVERNESS CRAFTSMEN NOTED FROM OTHER SOURCES

JOHN McLEOD c1801–72

JAMES JACK c1803–c1839

ALEXANDER FALCONER c1810–37

WILLIAM FRASER c1869–c1883

APPRENTICES AND CRAFTSMEN NOTED IN THE 1841 CENSUS

APPRENTICES AND CRAFTSMEN NOTED IN THE 1851 CENSUS

APPRENTICES AND CRAFTSMEN NOTED IN THE 1861 CENSUS

APPRENTICES AND CRAFTSMEN NOTED IN THE 1871 CENSUS

APPRENTICES AND CRAFTSMEN NOTED IN THE 1881 CENSUS

APPRENTICES AND CRAFTSMEN NOTED IN THE 1891 CENSUS

OTHER CRAFTSMEN NOTED IN THE INVERNESS NEWSPAPERS

WILIAM GRANT

DONALD SABISTON 1840–1872

HAROLD CHISHOLM

DUNCAN MACRAE

JOHN ALEXANDER MACPHERSON 1867–1926

ALEXANDER FRASER

JOHN MACKENZIE

MACKENZIE BROTHERS

MACKENZIE & Co

JOHN FERGUSON 1858–c1900

Other less well-documented goldsmiths, silversmiths and jewellers worked in Inverness during the period 1800–1900. The majority of these craftsmen and their families are described in the notes that follow.

139

JOHN MCLEOD c1801–1872

John McLeod was born in Inverness around the turn of the nineteenth century; the first note of him was when he was recorded in the *Inverness Hammermen Minute Book*. He was apprenticed to Robert Naughten and his indenture was registered on 5 August 1823.

The 1841 census detailed John McLeod as a 30 year old jeweller living in King Street with his father, also John McLeod, a 75 year old army pensioner.

The *Inverness Parish Register* recorded the marriage of John MacLeod, jeweller, of King Street, Inverness, to Lillias MacArthur of Church Street, Inverness, on 23 December 1842. John McLeod, jeweller in King Street, and Lillias MacArthur had a son called John, on 19 March 1843, and another, Thomas, on 22 March 1848. John McLeod and family were listed in the Inverness 1851 census living at 29 Church Street: John, a jeweller, aged 50; Lilly, aged 39; John, 8; James, 6, and Margaret, 2; all born in Inverness. John was probably a journeyman jeweller, but it is also possible that he worked independently for one or more of the larger jewellers in Inverness. He was listed in the 1866/67 *Inverness Directory* as living at 10 Raining Stairs (Castle Street). In the 1871 census John McLeod was noted at 82 Castle Street, a widower, a 73 year old working goldsmith, with his unemployed son, Robert, aged 18, and his unemployed niece, Elizabeth Reed, aged 50.

John McLeod died on 15 July 1872 at the Northern Infirmary. On his death certificate his father was given as John McLeod, nurseryman; his mother was unknown. His death was reported by a neighbour who lived at 9 Church Street.

There are no known marks for John McLeod.

JAMES JACK c1803–c1839

The *Inverness Hammermen Minute Book* recorded James Jack as an apprentice to Robert Naughten and his indenture was registered on 5 August 1823.

His marriage is in the *Inverness Parish Register* for 9 November 1829: 'James Jack Jeweller Inverness and Mary Macniel of Dingwall By the Revd. Mr Beathune of Dingwall.' They had a son, Lewis, baptised on 28 November 1829, the father given as a 'Jeweler Shore.' Then followed James, born 11 November 1831, father noted as a goldsmith in Shore Street where a daughter, Isabella, was born on 8 January 1834, the father's occupation on that occasion was given as a silversmith; Sarah Nicholson Jack was born on 6 August 1836. It is interesting to note that Robert Naughten's wife was named Sarah Nicholson.

The 1841 Inverness census listed the family living in Glebe Street, Margaret (Mary) aged 30; Lewis aged 10; James 6; Sarah 3, and Jesse Ann 1 year, but James Jack[122] was not recorded.

The 1851 census recorded the family still living in Inverness but now at 40 Friar's Street; Mary Jack was a widow and householder, aged 45, born in Edinburgh; Lewis Jack, the eldest son, was listed as a 21 year old jeweller, his brother, James, 19, a plumber, and two sisters, Sarah, 14, and Jessie Ann, aged 12.

Mary Jack died on 22 April 1893, aged 94, at 83 Church Street, recorded as the widow of James Jack, master jeweller. Her parents were not recorded on the death certificate. The informant was Kenneth Fraser, her son-in-law, who had married Jessie Ann Jack in Inverness on 12 September 1862.

There are no known marks for James Jack.

ALEXANDER FALKNER (FALCONER) c1810–1837

The *Inverness Hammermen Minute Book* recorded Alexander Falkner as an apprentice to Alexander MacLeod (he was possibly Alexander MacLeod's brother-in-law); the indenture was registered on 4 May 1830.

The *Inverness Parish Register* detailed the marriage of Alexander Falconer, a jeweller, in High Street, to Christian/Christine Munro, 'of the same place', on 30 November 1835.

The *Parish Register* recorded the birth of Alexander on 9 October 1837, to Christine, relict of the late Alexander Falconer jeweller'.

The are no known marks for Alexander Falconer.

WILLIAM FRASER c1869–c1883

An advertisement appeared in the *Inverness Advertiser* of 23 November 1869:

GOLDSMITH, WATCHMAKER, & JEWELLER. WILLIAM FRASER, 1 HIGH STREET, INVERNESS, has a large well selected Stock, COMPRISING – JEWELLERY OF SUTHERLAND GOLD. CAIRNGORM AND PEBBLE BROOCHES AND BRACELETS. LONDON-MADE JEWELLERY OF CHASE DESIGN. SILVER-ELECTROPLATED GOODS OF BEST QUALITY.

This would appear to be the address formerly used by William Mason, jeweller.

He was advertising in the *Inverness Courier* of 6 January 1870: 'GOLDSMITH, WATCHMAKER, & JEWELLER.' Among his wares he was recorded as selling Sutherland gold jewellery and London-made jewellery as well as electro-plated goods. Electro-plating and gilding was undertaken on the premises.

An advertisement in the *Inverness Courier* of 10 November 1870 recorded Fraser at 1 High Street: 'WATCH AND CHRONOMETER MAKER, GOLDSMITH, JEWELLER & MANUFACTURER OF HIGHLAND ORNAMENTS;' in this advertisement he details the names of Celtic Pendants, Crosses and Brooches 'most of them copied from Ancient Bronzes found when making the SUTHERLAND RAILWAY'.

In the 1871 census a William Fraser was living as a lodger at 35 High Street; he was aged 31, unmarried, and recorded as a goldsmith, jeweller and watch maker, born in Kilmorack.

Another small advertisement appeared in the Inverness Journal of 19 June 1873 for 1 High Street.

In the 1873/74 *Inverness Directory*, William Fraser was listed as a jeweller working at 1 High Street and living at 35 High Street.

William Fraser was declared bankrupt in January 1875. A further advertisement was in the *Inverness Courier* of 24 August 1876: 'THE GREAT CLEARING SALE OF JEWELLERY, WATCHES, AND CLOCKS, ELECTROPLATED GOODS &C., 1 HIGH STREET (Corner of Church Street)'. It continued 'The Bankrupt Stock of WILLIAM FRASER was bought at more than one-third below value, and a lot of first class Goods have been secured at such low prices as enables the whole to be offered at prices unprecedented in the Capital of the Highlands.'

There was, however, there was a second William Fraser, a jeweller, who lived at 8 North Church Lane according to the 1873/74 *Directory*. He did not own a business, and probably worked for one of the other jewellers or watchmakers in Inverness.

The *Inverness Courier* of 17 July 1883 carried an advertisement: 'Notice of Removal. -W^m. FRASER, Watchmaker and Jeweller begs to intimate that he has REMOVED from 33 Bridge Street to 5 LOMBARD STREET, INVERNESS.'

APPRENTICES AND CRAFTSMEN NOTED IN THE 1841 CENSUS

Name	Address	Age	Occupation
Bain, John	3 Tap Lane	20	Jeweller's apprentice
Mackenzie, John	East Side of Church St	30	Jeweller

APPRENTICES AND CRAFTSMEN NOTED IN THE 1851 CENSUS

Ferrier, James	10 Grants Close	19	Jeweller
Fraser, Hugh	61 Castle Street	14	Jeweller's apprentice
Forbes, Alexander	Midmills	19	Jeweller
McPherson, Alexander	Millburn	14	Apprentice jeweller

APPRENTICES AND CRAFTSMEN NOTED IN THE 1861 CENSUS

McKenzie, Malcolm	57 Petty Street	35	Jeweller
McPherson, Hugh	10 Rose Street	15	Apprentice jeweller

APPRENTICES AND CRAFTSMEN NOTED IN THE 1871 CENSUS

Chisholm, Joseph	Lombard Street	26	Lapidary
Clark, William	9 Church Street	54	Working goldsmith
Couper, William	38 Friars Street	27	Jeweller
Faller, Adolf	63 Petty Street	28	Watchmaker, Goldsmith & Jeweller
Faller, Otto	63 Petty Street	31	Watchmaker, Goldsmith & Jeweller
Forbes, Alexander	Kingsmills Road	38	Jeweller
Forbes, Alexander	44 Huntly Street	17	Jeweller
Fraser, William H.	Crown Street	26	Jeweller
Grant, John Edward	Stephens Brae	20	Jeweller
Hauser, Philip	63 Petty Street	34	Watchmaker, Goldsmith & Jeweller
Hauser, Premus	63 Petty Street	31	Watchmaker, Goldsmith & Jeweller
Henry, William	5 Tap Lane	33	Journeyman jeweller

Hossack, Donald	Village of Clacknharry	21	Goldsmith
McBean, Paul	39 Friars Street	21	Lapidary
McCulloch, James	17 Castle Street	45	Jeweller
McDonald, Alexander	13 Glebe Street	34	Jeweller
Macdonald, Donald	4 Celt Street	21	Goldsmith
Macdonald, William	4 Celt Street	18	Goldsmith
McGregor, Alexander	2 Church Street	15	Goldsmith
McKenzie, John	Cuthberts Close	18	Jeweller
McKenzie John	11 Beatons Lane	59	Jeweller (out of employ)
McPherson, Alexander	Argyle Street	32	Jeweller
McPherson, John	7 Gilbert Street	20	Jeweller
McPherson, William	Lombard Street	26	Jeweller
McRae, Alexander	2 Friars Street	21	Jeweller
Miller, Thomas	12 Anderson Street	14	Jeweller
Munro, James	30 Chapel Street	23	Jeweller
Murray, John	39 High Street	14	Jeweller
Norrie, William	21 Haugh Road	19	Jeweller
O'Gow, John	18 Douglas Row	38	Jeweller
Sim, Alexander	Kingsmills Road	56	Engraver
Sim, Alexander	Kingsmills Road	24	Engraver
Stewart, John	16 Bridge Street	22	Jeweller & optician
Storah (sic), Dougall	2 Anderson Street	16	Apprentice Jeweller
Thompson, Robert	5 New Bldgs, Queen Street	36	Jeweller

APPRENTICES AND CRAFTSMEN NOTED IN THE 1881 CENSUS

Forbes, Alexander	34 Kingsmills Road	49	Jeweller
McKenzie, John	Inverness Poor House	68	Working jeweller
MacPherson, Hugh	17 Rose Street	33	Jeweller
McPherson, William	29 Charles Street	35	Jeweller (visitor)
Norris, unknown	17 Glebe Street	unknown	Jeweller (away on census night)
Slorah (sic), Donald	32 Chapel Street	25	Jeweller

APPRENTICES AND CRAFTSMEN NOTED IN THE 1891 CENSUS

Macpherson, Alexander	Castle Court	52	Jeweller
Macpherson, William	11 Bridge Street	45	Jeweller

Other Jewellers noted in the Inverness Newspapers

William Grant

The *Inverness Journal and Northern Advertiser* of 28 December 1832, reported under the deaths column: 'At Inverness, on the 18th current, after a lingering illness, which he bore with patience and resignation, Mr. Wm. Grant, Jeweller, aged 23.'

Donald Sabiston 1840–72

The *Inverness Parish Register* detailed the birth of Donald Sabiston, son of Benjamin Sabiston, a ship's captain, and Margaret MacKenzie, on 13 December 1840 at Glebe.

The *Inverness Courier*, of 7 July 1870 (right) carried an advertisement.

The 1871 Inverness census, for 37 Friars Street, recorded Donald Sabiston, aged 26, an unmarried jeweller, living with his mother Margaret, a widow, aged 50; both were born in Inverness.

Donald Sabiston, jeweller, age given as 31 years, died on 22 April 1872 at 37 Friars Street. He died of pulmonary consumption from which he had been suffering for two years. The informant was Alex Dallas, a neighbour and watchmaker whose shop address was 77 Church Street (see page 107).

Harold Chisholm

The *Inverness Courier* of 25 December 1862 carried an advertisement as follows: 'HAROLD CHISHOLM, WORKING JEWELLER, 58 ACADEMY STREET, INVERNESS. – Work done for the Trade and Public in general. All orders punctually attended to, and the very Lowest Prices charged.' The *Inverness Courier* of 3 August 1876 carried another advertisement (right).

Duncan MacRae

The Inverness 1881 census recorded Duncan MacRae, aged 23, unmarried, a watch maker and jeweller, born in Inverness; he was living at 36 Friar's Street with John McRae, a blacksmith, and Catherine McRae.

The *Inverness Advertiser*, of 18 February 1881, carried an advertisement for Duncan MacRae, Chronometer & Watch Maker, Jeweller and Optician. The address recorded in the newspaper was Town Hall Buildings, Inverness: 'Begs to return his sincere thanks to his numerous Customers and the Public generally for the liberal support accorded to him in the past, and while soliciting a continuance of their kind patronage, would mention that, owing to the large amount of support and encouragement he has received since commencing business, he has greatly increased his Stock in all departments.'

The *Inverness Courier* of 4 January 1883 carried the following: 'REDUCTION PRIOR TO STOCKTAKING. D. MACRAE, WATCHMAKER, JEWELLER, AND OPTICIAN, TOWN HALL BUILDINGS INVERNESS.'

The *Inverness Courier* of 9 July 1885 ran an advertisement (right).

Inverness Courier
7 July 1870

GOLDSMITH, JEWELLER, & WATCHMAKER,
17 BRIDGE STREET, INVERNESS.

DONALD SABISTON, for several years principal JEWELLER to the late Mr MASON, and subsequently to Mr FRASER, 1 High Street, here, begs to inform the Ladies' and Gentlemen of Inverness and surrounding country, and the public generally, that he has opened business on his own account in the above shop, and trusts to be favoured with a share of their support.

D.·S., from his past experience, flatters himself that he is in a position to execute, with promptness and neatness, all orders intrusted to him.

Gold and Silver WATCHES ; French and Alabaster CLOCKS, with and without Shades ; Gold and Silver BROOCHES ; BRACELETS, EARRINGS, SCARF PINS, Ladies' Gem, Wedding, and Guard RINGS, and a well selected Stock of other Jewellery, in new and tasteful designs.

Best ELECTRO-PLATED GOODS, of every variety, and at very moderate prices. WHITBY JET, carefully selected.

Any article not in Stock, made to order on short notice. Special designs furnished. Crest and Monogram Brooches to order. All repairs executed neatly.

17 Bridge Street. Inverness.

Inverness Courier
3 August 1876

SHEFFIELD CUTLER.

MR CHISHOLM has pleasure in informing his Friends and the Public generally, that he has secured the services of a First-class CUTLER from SHEFFIELD ; and as all the general Work of a Cutler will now be done on the Premises, in the Best Style of Workmanship, he hopes to supply a long felt want.

Pocket, Pen, and Table Knives, Scissors, and Surgical Instruments Ground and Repaired, Razors Ground and Set, general Cutlery Work done.

General Furnishing Ironmongery Warehouse,
8 Church Street, Inverness.

Inverness Courier
9 July 1885

MACRAE'S
HIGHLAND JEWELLERY
ESTABLISHMENT,
15 CHURCH STREET, INVERNESS,

Manufacturer of HIGHLAND DRESS ORNA-MENTS and CELTIC JEWELLERY, comprising new and orignial designs in Cairngorm, Amethyst, Pearl, and other Scotch Stones, set in Gold and Silver.

A large and carefully selected Stock of BRITISH and FOREIGN CLOCKS and WATCHES, ELECTRO PLATE, &c., from the leading Manufacturers in the Trade.

All Goods marked in plain figures.

Repairs of all kinds done on the Premises.

Charges Moderate.

15 CHURCH STREET
(Opposite Northern Meeting Rooms),
INVERNESS.

145

The *Inverness Courier* of 6 July 1886 carried the following advertisement: 'REAL-ISING SALE OF JEWELLERY, WATCHES, CLOCKS, ELECTRO-PLATE and OPTICAL GOODS at one-half the usual Selling Prices, at D. MACRAE'S, 15 Church St.

Duncan MacRae, watchmaker, died on 22 July 1892, aged 35, at the Northern Infirmary, Inverness, his usual address was 5 Lower Kessock Street, Inverness. He was married to Margaret Ann Munro, who was the informant, and his parents were noted as John McRae, blacksmith, and Catherine Fraser.

JOHN ALEXANDER MACPHERSON 1867–1926

John Alexander Macpherson was born on 3 January 1867 at Barnhill Buildings, Inverness. His father was Alexander McPherson, a jeweller, and his mother was Jessie Barron, who married on 23 July 1866 in Glasgow.

The *Highland News* of 18 January 1890 recorded:

OPENING ANNOUNCEMENT. JOHN A. MACPHERSON, WATCHMAKER AND JEWELLER. Begs to announce to the Inhabitants of Inverness and District that he has opened that

JOHN A. MACPHERSON
16 AND 18 BRIDGE STREET,
INVERNESS
(*CHEAPEST AND BEST SHOP IN THE TRADE*),
Has a Large and Well-Selected Stock of
WATCHES, CLOCKS, JEWELLERY,
ELECTRO-PLATE, MUSICAL BOXES (Latest Airs),
TELESCOPES, MICROSCOPES.
OPERA, FIELD, and MARINE GLASSES.
Non-Acromatic Lenses, from 3s 9d ; very powerful Acromatic Lenses, from 8s.
Real Ivory, Solid Silver LORGNETT, White Pearl and other Fancy OPERAS, suitable for Presents.
WATCHES—The Exhibition Keyless, 10s ; pure White Metal Watches, from 16s ; Silver Watches, from 20s ; Silver Levers, from £2 10s ; English Levers, from £4 ; Gold Watches, from £3 10s. Second-hand Gold and Silver Watches always in Stock.
CLOCKS—The Burmah Lever Nickel Timepiece, from 3s 6d ; Alarm, from 5s 6d ; also, American and French Marble Clocks, suitable for Presentations.
SPECTACLES, EYE-GLASSES, PRESERVES — Splendid Selection to select from. Sights tested by the new Test Types never fails. Steel-framed Spectacles, from 6d. Interchangeable Cork-Nosed Eye-Glasses, from 1s 6d. Pebble Spectacles and Eye-Glasses, from 4s 6d. Tortoiseshell Lorgnett Eye-Glasses for Ladies also in Stock, at various prices.
Inspection Invited.
WATCHES, CLOCKS, and JEWELLERY sent from the Country will receive Strict Attention, and returned Post or Carriage Paid ; also, every Job guaranteed and upheld free of charge for One Year.

EXPERIENCED WORKMEN SENT TO ANY PART OF THE COUNTRY.

J. A. MACPHERSON has added a Fresh Supply to his Stock of FISHING TACKLE, RODS, REELS, LINES, BASKETS, BAGS, SATEEN TROUSERS, STOCKINGS, HOOK-BOOKS, CLIPS, NETS, TROUT and SALMON FLIES of every Description (any Pattern made to Order at Shortest Notice), &c.
TROUT and SALMON RODS Made and Repaired.
Send for Price List, Free on application.

JOHN A. MACPHERSON,
WATCHMAKER, JEWELLER, OPTICIAN,
AND DEALER IN FISHING TACKLE,
The Central Jewellery Establishment,
17 BRIDGE STREET.

A very choice selection to choose from. All the latest designs. Inspection respectfully invited. Watches, Clocks, Jewellery, &c., repaired by experienced workmen on the premises. Charges moderate.

Highland News 16 September 1899

Highland News 2 January 1892

SHOP, 18 BRIDGE STREET, with a large and well selected Stock of First-class CLOCKS, WATCHES, JEWELLERY, PLATE &c., CRESTS, GROUSE CLAWS, and all kinds of HIGHLAND ORNAMENTS made to Order on Shortest Notice.

The *Highland News* of 12 April 1890 carried an advertisement for 'JOHN A. MACPHERSON, WATCHMAKER AND JEWELLER, 18 BRIDGE STREET, INVERNESS, Begs to call the attention of the Inhabitants of Inverness and District to his varied Stock of WATCHES, CLOCKS, JEWELLERY, and PLATE.' A further advertisement in the *Highland News*, of 2 January 1892 (far left), reported that: 'JOHN A. MACPHERSON 16 and 18 BRIDGE STREET, INVERNESS (CHEAPEST AND BEST SHOP IN THE TRADE).'

The same newspaper of 12 November 1892 advertised:

JOHN A. MACPHERSON, THE JEWELLERY ESTABLISHMENT, 3 CASTLE STREET (Late of Bridge Street), OPPOSITE TOWN HALL, INVERNESS, Begs to inform his numerous Customers in Town and Country that, since he REMOVED to the above LARGE and CENTRAL PREMISES, he has added to his former Stock a choice selection of GOLD and SILVER BROOCHES, EARINGS, BRACELETS, BANGLES, NECKLETS, GEM RINGS, BREAST PINS, STUDS, CHAINS.

Slater's Directory 1893 detailed John A Macpherson as a watchmaker and jeweller at 3 Castle Street.

In the *Highland News* of 29 April 1899 he advertised:

GREAT CLEARING SALE, WATCHES, JEWELLERY, SILVER & ELECTRO PLATED GOODS, FISHING TACKLE &c., AT MACPHERSON'S JEWELLERY ESTABLISHMENT, CASTLE STREET. No reasonable offer refused, a very choice selection to choose from. The Sale will be only for a few weeks, as we are removing from present shop to a more suitable one. No. 17 BRIDGE STREET. TERMS–CASH.

Another advertisement (left) in the same newspaper of 16 September 1899 recorded the business now established at 17 Bridge Street.

Slater's Directory 1900 recorded his business under jewellers and watchmakers at 17 Bridge Street, but he was listed as John A. Macpherson & Co. at the same address in the 1903 *Directory*.

The *Inverness Courier*, of 5 April 1904, carried a front page advertisement which read:

JEWELLERS STOCK FOR SALE. For SALE the Whole STOCK and FITTINGS belonging to the Sequestrated Estate of J. A. MACPHERSON & COY., Jewellers, 17 Bridge Street, Inverness. Offers to be lodged with the Trustee, J. D. Wallace, solicitor, 29 High Street, Inverness, who will exhibit the Inventory, or the undersigned, on or before Tuesday, 5th April. W. CHARLES MACBEAN, Solicitor, York House, Church Street, Inverness.

Slater's Directory 1915 recorded him as a watchmaker under the appellation of Jn. A. Macpherson at 61 Castle Street; the 1921 *Directory* confirmed this, but added, '& Antique Dealer 56 Castle Street'.

John Alexander MacPherson died on 14 March 1926 at 16 Gordonville, Haugh, Inverness, aged 59. His death certificate recorded him as an art dealer and his parents were given as Alexander MacPherson, a jeweller, and Jessie Barron. He had been married twice; his first wife was given as Marion Morrison and his second as Catherine MacKenzie.

A George Macpherson was noted at 61 Castle Street in *Kelly's Directory* 1928 under watchmakers.

ALEXANDER FRASER

The *Highland News* of 4 June 1892 advertised:

> NOTICE OF REMOVAL. ALEXANDER FRASER, WATCHMAKER AND JEWELLER, TAIN. I beg to intimate that I intend REMOVING early in June to the Shop, No. 37 PETTY STREET, INVERNESS, where I intend carrying on all the Branches of my Business, as formerly in Tain. While making the above announcement, I take this opportunity of thanking my numerous Customers and Friends for the liberal support accorded to me during the past Twelve Years, and I would respectfully solicit a continuance of the same at the above address. Tain, 10th May, 1892.

JOHN MACKENZIE

The *Inverness Courier* of 1 July 1884 carried an advertisement for John MacKenzie (below right). *Slater's Directory* 1900 recorded this watchmaker at 15 Inglis Street, Inverness.

MACKENZIE BROTHERS

The *Inverness Advertiser* of 15 March 1881 carried an advertisement (below left) for Mackenzie Bros, Manufacturing Jewellers and Watchmakers, 17 Lombard Street, Inverness. The *Highland News* of 19 July 1890, advertised: 'MACKENZIE BROTHERS, JEWELLERS, WATCHMAKERS, AND HIGHLAND ORNAMENT MANUFACTURERS, OF 17 LOMBARD STREET, HAVE REMOVED TO 22 UNION STREET.'

MACKENZIE & CO

Slater's Directories 1903 and 1907 record this business under jewellers and watch makers at 11 Lombard Street, Inverness; it was missing from the 1911 *Directory*.

MACKENZIE BROS.,
MANUFACTURING JEWELLERS
AND WATCHMAKERS,
17 LOMBARD STREET,
INVERNESS.

The only Establishment for BROOCH PINS at TWO-PENCE EACH, manufactured from the best quality of German Silver Wire.

We would also draw the special attention of the Public to the fact that since we have been the means of originating a great reduction in the price of WATCH GLASSES, as hitherto charged in Inverness, we would take this opportunity of returning our sincere thanks to our numerous customers and the Public for their liberal support and patronage which has thus enabled us to crown our efforts, with success. We have much pleasure in being able to make a STILL FURTHER REDUCTION by offering our WATCH GLASSES, which are of the Best Quality, at the Nominal Charge of TWOPENCE EACH.

No common quality of Glasses kept in Stock; all guaranteed of the Best Quality and Manufacture.

None but Workmen of First-Class Experience Employed both in the Jewellery and Watchmaking Departments.

☞ OBSERVE THE ADDRESS—

THE LOMBARD STREET
MANUFACTURING JEWELLERY AND
WATCHMAKING ESTABLISHMENT.

JOHN MACKENZIE,
WATCHMAKER,
5 CASTLE STREET
(*Opposite the Town Hall*),
INVERNESS.

Any description of Work, in the above Business, carefully and promptly executed at London Trade Prices

Inverness Courier 1 July 1884

Inverness Advertiser 15 March 1881

JOHN FERGUSON 1858-c1900

John Ferguson was born on 15 July 1858, the son of Daniel Ferguson, watchmaker and jeweller, and Margaret McBean (see Daniel Ferguson p181).

The *Inverness Courier* of 7 December 1888 advertised his business:

WATCH, CLOCK, AND JEWELLERY REPAIRS. The SUBSCRIBERS beg to inform the Public that they have fitted up the Shop, NO. 4 PETTY STREET (Three Doors from Post-office), INVERNESS. ... JOHN & A. FERGUSON, WATCH AND CLOCK MAKERS & JEWELLERS, 4 PETTY STREET, JEWELLERY WORKSHOP, NO. 6.

The *Highland News* of 12 January 1889 carried an advertisement (below). The same newspaper of 5 July 1890 advertised:

41 CASTLE STREET, INVERNESS. JOHN FERGUSON, WATCHMAKER, JEWELLER, AND OPTI-CIAN. Respectfully begs to tender his thanks to the Gentry and Inhabitants of Inverness and neighbourhood for the patronage bestowed upon him during the two years he has been in business in Castle Street, and to inform them that his Stock has been enlarged, improved, and entirely refitted, to meet the requirements of his Extended Business, and he trusts to be able, by showing a larger and more varied Stock, and having ample accommodation for the execution of Special Orders and Repairs, &c., to receive the patronage of old friends, and an increased connection from the general public who may not yet have given him a trial.

Two further advertisements for John Ferguson were noted in the *Highland News* in 1892. The first, of 2 January, recorded him as a watchmaker and jeweller, at 41 Castle Street, and the second, a similar announcement, was dated 5 November.

Highland News
12 January 1889

WATCHES,

CLOCKS,

JEWELLERY, &c.

J O H N   F E R G U S O N,

WATCHMAKER, JEWELLER, AND OPTICIAN,

40 CASTLE STREET, INVERNESS,

Has pleasure in intimating to the inhabitants of Inverness and surrounding District that he has COMMENCED BUSINESS at the above address, where can be seen a well-selected Stock of

WATCHES, CLOCKS, AND JEWELLERY.

J. F.'s experience in the Watch-Repairing Department is second to none for punctuality and skilful workmanship, giving his own personal attention.

Having served his apprenticeship with his father, Mr Daniel Ferguson, Watchmaker and Jeweller, 33 Union Street, Inverness, afterwards in London, parties now entrusting him with their Orders will receive most careful attention.

40 CASTLE STREET, INVERNESS.

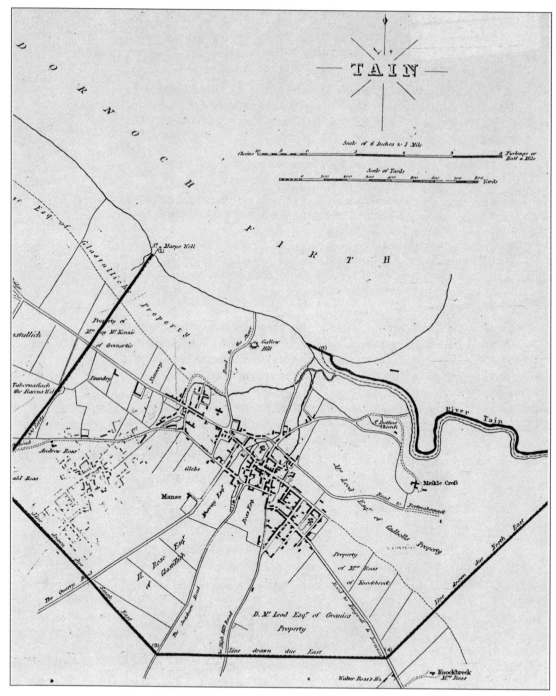

Map of Tain from Lt Dawson's Survey 1832

CHAPTER FIVE

TAIN CRAFTSMEN

★HUGH ROSS c1703–c1778[123] &

★HUGH ROSS junior c1740–c1787

★ALEXANDER STEWART c1765–c1845

★JOHN SELLAR c1801–86 (see Wick)

★WILLIAM INNES c1804–c1870

★RICHARD MAXWELL WILKIE 1806–80

  ALEXANDER STEWART 1837[124]

★WILLIAM McKENZIE c1818–79

  JAMES HOUSTON c1810–c1850

  JOHN MACKENZIE & COMPANY 1854

★Example of mark illustrated

Tain Town View
c1825

Tain is a royal burgh lying on the southern shore of the Dornoch Firth, some thirty-four miles north of Inverness. It is the county town of Ross-shire and the town silver mark is the town name in roman or italic capital letters. The Stent Roll of the burgh revealed that a goldsmith was working in Tain in 1659; he was, however, un-named.

The *Survey* conducted by Lt Dawson in 1832 reported:

> TAIN is situated on a bank at a little distance from the Southern Shore of the Firth of Dornoch. It has improved of late years, and may be considered in a thriving condition. Many new Houses have been built, and a good deal of ground has been feued. It possesses a good Academy, which has attracted a number of families to the Town for the education of their children; but it has little or no Manufacture, and the sand bars on the coast deprive it of any advantage it might have derived from its maritime situation. A new entrance into the Town from the South is contemplated.

The 1821 census calculated the population of the Burgh and Parish of Tain to be 2,861 and it had only risen to 3,078 by the 1831 census.

HUGH ROSS c1703-c1778 & HUGH ROSS junior, c1740-c1787

The earliest Tain silversmith for whom a maker's mark is known is Hugh Ross. It is said that in 1717 Robert Innes, a goldsmith in Inverness, took an apprentice by the name of Hugh Ross for five years; however, a search of the existing Inverness archives has failed, as yet, to confirm this apprenticeship. If we accept the date 1717, Hugh Ross would have been born about 1703, assuming his apprenticeship had commenced at the age of thirteen or fourteen years.

We do know that from the second quarter of the eighteenth century Hugh Ross was established as a silversmith and jeweller in Tain, and he appeared to use a series of date letters together with his other marks.

In May 1740 there is a record of Hugh Ross repairing a sword head and a pair of shoe buckles belonging to the Laird of Pitcalnie; the Laird and his family were patrons of Hugh Ross for many years. A Hugh Ross was Baillie from 1754 to 1760 but we cannot be sure that this was the goldsmith: the occupation was not stated and, of course, the name Ross was, and still is, extremely common in the area.

The goldsmith Hugh Ross was a man of property for in 1751 his name appeared in the Burgh records as owner of a 'Tenement with stables and byres' (which he built and repaired) 'Lying in the High Street north of the steeple in Little Taine'. There is a letter dated 'Tayn 7th March 1754' from Hugh Ross to the Laird of Pitcalnie in which he suggests he should take a damaged watch to be repaired in Edinburgh; he continued, 'I'm to get Some Sealls done in Scots peebles & varreity of Such, & oy^r Stones for Signets, Rings Lockets &c, So If you wint any particular impression for a Signet or any Such, Shall get you Served.' A further letter dated 19 December 1754 begins:

> Madam I Received your's of this date, I'm fond the fathion of the Spoon's please's you, I Send by the bearer one nowise to the disadvantage mark'd as you direct. I was hinder'd 'ere woud Send a Ring, you'll please Send by ist occassion the measure of the finger it's for, & afterward's may have it by ist Occasion.

The name Hugh Ross appeared on the Suit Roll of Tain in 1766.

At this point the authors suggest the introduction of a second Hugh Ross, almost certainly the son of the above. It is likely that Hugh Ross junior was born in Tain around 1740.

The *Tain Parish Registers* have been damaged, some completely missing, and it is not surprising therefore that no entry has been found for his marriage to Mary Munro. It is not known if they had any children prior to 1773, but we are certain of the four recorded as follows in the *Tain Parish Register*: 'Tain the twelfth day of August Jajvij & Seventy three. That day Hugh Ross Junr Silversmith had a Child Babtized lawfully Begot with Mary Munro lawful Daughter of Baillie Donald Munro Called John.'; 'Tain the Sixteenth Day of May Jajvij & Seventy five, That Day Hugh Ross Junr Silversmith in Town had a Child Babtized begot in the Honble Bond of Marriage with Mary Munro Lawful Daughter of Baillie Donald Munro Called Donald'; 'Tain the tenth day of March Jajvij & Seventy Seven years. Which day Hugh Ross Junr Goldsmith had a Child Babtized begot in the Honble Bond of Marriage with Mary Munro lawful Daughter of Baillie Donald Munro late of this place called Andrew. Witnesses Baillie John Reid & Mr Alexander Campbell Schoolmaster in Town.'; 'At Tain the twenty Ninth Day of September Jajvij & Seventy Nine years. The Same Day Hugh Ross Silversmith had a Child Babtized Lawfully Begot with Mary Munro Lawful Daughter of the Deceast Baillie Donald Munro Called Janet. Witnesses Baillie John Barclay & John Ross Merchant.'

It is to be noted that on 9 September 1779 Hugh Ross no longer carried the appendage 'Junr' implying that his father had died between 10 March 1777 and the above date. The *Tain Guildry Book*, dated 10 January 1780, recorded that Hugh Ross, silversmith, was put forward to be one of two key-keepers for the following year. At the same meeting 'Hugh Ross Silversmith offered himself as a member of the Society and to Contribute Quarterly to the fund But not as a member to sit in the seat in the Church The Members present accept of the said Mr. Hugh Ross as a member when he gave in as a Donation to the fund ten Shillings & Sixpence St^r'.

It is clear that there were two Hugh Rosses, probably father and son, working in Tain as gold and silversmiths; the elder from c1725 to c1775 and the younger from c1765 to c1787.

Hugh Ross junior was recorded as the 'Late Hugh Ross' in the 1787 Suit Roll and also the Burgh records. It seems likely that he died in or just before 1787 as in that year a roup of his chattels was held in Tain.

Among the articles recorded were:

1	Silver-mounted snuffbox	7s-6d
3	Pairs silver buckles	£1-8s-6d
9	Silver tablespoons (21½oz)	£5-11s-0d
47	Silver hearts (Luckenbooth Brooches[125])	£3-5s-6d
1	Gold heart	11s-6d
11	Silver rings	15s-6d
9	Teaspoons and 2 Sugar spoons	£1-2s-10d
5	Gold rings	£1-8s-3d
2	Candlesticks and 1 Caster	1s-8d
2	Coffee pots	
3	Nutmeg graters	
1	Punch ladle	

Snuff Mull by
Hugh Ross.
Christie's, Glasgow

The Suit Roll of 1801 does not detail any gold or silversmiths in Tain and we have found no evidence of a silversmith taking over from Hugh Ross junior.

There is an obvious difficulty in establishing a definite set of marks for each Hugh Ross, as it appears the punches were carried through from senior to junior; however, the style of the piece distinguishes the earlier items.

Their marks were 'HR' conjoined, either in a square or oval punch, often in conjunction with a mark depicting the upper part of the 'figure of St Duthac or Duthus' which is flanked by the capital letters 's D' (above). A 'date letter' may also be added. The sometimes quoted 's B with St Duthac' mark is a mistaken interpretation of the 's D' already noted. Jackson's Silver & Gold Marks also records an 'H·R' mark with the St Duthac punch.

ALEXANDER STEWART c1765-c1845

From information obtained from later census records it appears that Alexander Stewart was born about 1765, but no record of his birth or baptism has been found; we have been unable to ascertain where and to whom he was apprenticed.

Alexander Stewart was a successful gold and silversmith, first noted in the *Inverness Hammermen Minute Book* on 10 May 1796, when a petition was made by him to be admitted into the Incorporation. His admission as a Freeman Burgess was confirmed in the *Inverness Town Council Minutes*, dated 15 May 1797: 'Alexander Stewart Silver Smith was upon his petition received and admitted Freeman Burgess of the Hammermen Incorporation of the said Burgh upon payment of Ten pounds Scots to James Suter Treasurer to be a charge against him in his Treasury accounts'.

The *Inverness Parish Register* recorded that Alexander Stewart, silversmith, married Barbara Gibson[126], on 8 April 1797, in Inverness. They had five known children, whilst in Inverness; they were: Jean, baptised 2 March 1798; James, 5 March 1800; Alexander, 16 November 1801; Archibald, 16 June 1803, and John Byres, born 2 December 1810. The *Parish Register* recorded, on 14 March 1804, the death of a child: 'Dep a child of ... Stewart Goldsmith.'

On 31 May 1798 the *Inverness Hammermen Minute Book* recorded that Alexander Stewart had been elected to be one of the two Key-keepers, and on 27 May 1802 he was noted as the Boxmaster of the Incorporation.

The *Inverness Kirk Session Minute Book*, 1730-1824, detailed on 2 March 1802, the following:

> It was reported that the late Mr John Baillie had bequeathed in his Will to the Session, Money in their favours; the Tenor of which follows. I leave and bequeath to the Kirk Session of Inverness the Sum of Fifty Pounds ster. for the Express purpose of being applied by them to the purchase of six Silver Communion Element Cups. 'Item I leave & Bequeath to the Proprietors of the Chapel of Ease of Inverness. Thirty five Pounds str. to be applied by them to purchase four Silver Communion Element Cups And I desire and request hat the said Element Cups shall be kept by the said Kirk Session & Proprietors of the said Chapel of Ease and to be used by them on Sacramental Occasions in their respective places of worship and I hereby desire that there shall be engraved on each of the said Cups to the Kirk Session of Inverness the following, Inscription. Gift John Bailie House Carpenter in Inverness to the Kirk Session of Inverness[127].

These Cups are still in use today (opposite). The silversmith who made these wonderful silver cups was Alexander Stewart; they are marked underneath 'A·S, INS'.

The *Inverness Town Council Minutes* dated 16 September 1805 and 14 September 1807 record that Alexander Stewart had been nominated, but was not elected, Deacon of the Hammermen's Incorporation for those years. The *Town Council Minutes*, dated 25 September 1809, detailed:

> The Clerk produced a list made up by him of the Members of the different Incorporations who have been admitted to the freedom of the Town since the year one thousand seven hundred and seventy three and which list was given to the Deacon Conveener to be communicated to the different Incorporations that such of their Members as are not burgesses may furthwith apply to the Town Council in the usual manner ...

Under the Hammermen was Alexander Stewart, Silversmith, with the date 15 May 1797.

The *Inverness Hammermen Minute Book* noted Stewart as taking five apprentices during the period 1800 to 1812. The most notable was Thomas Stewart, alias McGuirman (p55) who initially went to London, probably as a journeyman, then to Elgin, and finally to Inverness in 1828. The other apprentices were: James Forbes, Hugh Macintosh, Alexander McRae and Andrew Clark.

An advertisement appeared in the *Inverness Journal* of 20 November 1812 (page 158). The Tain Suit Roll of 1801 does not mention a silversmith in the Town; it appears there were none of that trade working in Tain after Hugh Ross, junior, until Alexander Stewart, in 1812.

Inverness Communion Cups by Alexander Stewart. Private collection. J I R Martin

ALEX. STEWART, Silver-Smith, begs leave to return his moft grateful thanks to thofe who have honoured him with their employment whiie he refided in Invernefs, and to intimate to the Ladies and Gentlemen of Rofs-fhire and the Public in gener al, that he has removed to Tain, where he is to carry on, in all its branches, the bufinefs of Gold-Smith, Silver-Smith, and Jeweller.

From the fatisfaction A. S. has reafon to think his work has given to his employers in Rofs and Su therland while carrying on bufinefs at Invernefs, he anxioufly hopes to merit a continuance of their favours, and this they may reft affured he will en deavour to merit by the moderation of his charges, and the moft unremitting attention to their com mands.

N:B. Old Gold and Silver will be purchafed at the higheft prices, and old Plate exchanged, renewed, or repaired, on the moft reafonable terms.

In 1815 Alexander Stewart raised a bond for £100 on a property in the 'new town' of Tain, at the east end of the burgh. In 1818 it was 'evicted from him by regular process before the Magistrates of Tain for nonpayment of the feu-duty' to Donald MacLeod of Geanies.

The Tain Royal Academy records reveal the attendance of several of Alexander Stewart's children. In January and August 1814, Jane, Alexander, James and Thomas were noted; throughout the period 1814 to January 1819 one or more of these children attended on an irregular basis. In January 1820 John Stewart was recorded and whilst not shown in the August entry, he appeared once more in January 1821, but from this date no further entries were found.

The *Tain Parish Register* did not record any children born to Alexander and Barbara; however, at least one son, Hugh, was known to have been born there around 1814. Hugh married Margaret Stewart on 11 October 1841 in Tain; he was recorded as a tinsmith and was listed in the Tain census for 1851, 1861 and 1871, living with his family in Market Street, and noted as born in that Burgh. Hugh Stewart, master tinsmith, died on 22 October 1879 at King Street, Tain. The death certificate stated that he was aged 'about 65 years' and his parents were recorded as Alexander Stewart, working jeweller, and Barbara Gibson.

Pigot's Directory 1825 recorded Alexander Stewart as a 'working silversmith' in Tain; no further address was given. He was reputedly retailing silver throughout the north of Scotland with a possible outlet in Dingwall, although this is unproven. It is almost certain that he was the Alexander Stewart noted in the above directory as a jeweller, silversmith and umbrella maker, in East Street, Inverness.

The *Small Debt Book* for the County of Ross recorded, on 23 July 1825, that 'Alex' Stewart Goldsmith Tain' was being pursued for a debt by George Ross of Tain. Other complaints against him followed on 13 September 1825, 22 November and 5 December 1826, 8 January, 20 July, 3 September and 28 December 1827, 1 July and 11 October 1828, 7 January 1829, 24 September 1830 and 23 April 1832.

CARD.

ALEXANDER STEWART, Working Jeweller, begs leave to inform the inhabitants of Tain and the surrounding country, that he has commenced Business in the above line, at his shop, nearly opposite the Grove, and he will give punctual attention to all orders left at his Shop.

Communications and orders received by M Roderick Douglas, Bookseller.

Old Gold and Silver bought or taken in exchange.

Tain, 17th July, 1837.

An advertisement appeared in the *Inverness Journal* of 19 July and was repeated on 26 July 1837 (above). As this advertisement stated that Alexander Stewart 'commenced Business' this might indicate that this was the son of the silversmith, but as yet we have been unable to discover this son's trade or profession. There certainly would have been a need for a working jeweller once Richard Maxwell Wilkie had left Tain.

Alexander Stewart, aged 75, was last noted in the 1841 Tain census living in Lamington Street, with his wife, Barbara, aged 65 years; neither were born in the County of Ross. Lamington Street was a short extension of the High Street. There was no entry for them in the 1851 census so it must be assumed that they died during that period; no record of their burials has been found in Tain or Inverness.

Alexander was not a prosperous man whilst in Tain, but one cannot doubt the quality of much of his work. Most of his output was table silver; table and dessert spoons, forks, teaspoons, salt spoons, sugar tongs, small toddy ladles and large soup ladles. Other small items such as snuff boxes, quaichs and plaid brooches are known to have been made by him, the majority bearing the Inverness mark.

Inverness Brooch by Alexander Stewart.
Private collection

Inverness Snuff Box by Alexander Stewart (H 1.9 cm, L 6.9 cm, W 3.9 cm).
Private collection.
Ewen Weatherspoon

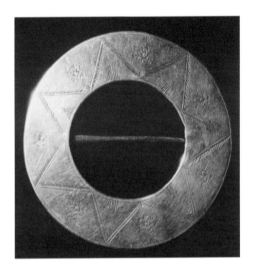

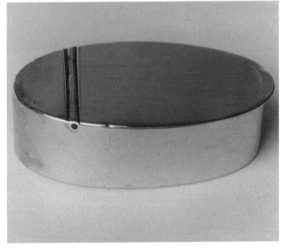

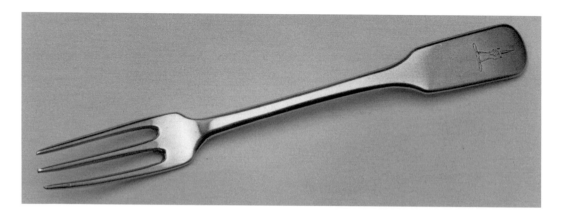

*Tain Three Pronged
Fork by Alexander
Stewart.*
Private collection.
Ewen Weatherspoon

He used a rectangular punch, 'TAIN' or 'INS', in Roman capital letters, and his initials 'A·S'; however, his mark is sometimes noted without a town mark, and if so, is generally attributed to Inverness. The Tain mark is considered much rarer than that of Inverness. His maker's mark 'A·S' is easily recognised because the pellet is closer to the 'A' at a position level with its cross-bar. There is also a narrower 'A S' punch with no pellet. Additionally, Jacksons' Silver & Gold Marks, third edition, illustrates an oval punch with 'A·S'.

Inverness and Tain silver sometimes bears a 'wheat ear' (or 'shuttle mark'); indeed Stewart, on occasions, added this feature stamped horizontally, to his usual mark, with 'TAIN' or 'INS'. Punches of this type have been referred to as 'Tinkers' marks, another of which, the so-called 'Cup & Saucer', was used on much of Stewart's work; this is, in fact, the capital letter 'C'[128], which is badly worn or was poorly struck.

WILLIAM INNES c1804–c1870

William Innes, recorded as Walter Innes in *Jackson's Silver & Gold Marks*, third edition, worked in Tain from about 1828 to 1834. The authors have had great difficulty in establishing where William was born and who his parents were. One possible candidate would seem to be the William Innes recorded, on 14 June 1804, in the *Logie Easter Parish Register*: 'William Munro (Innes) son to Alexr Innes School M. & session clerk & of Catherine Ross was born.' William Innes, 'son of Alex. Innes school master Logie', was also noted in the Tain Royal Academy roll of pupils from August 1819 to January 1821. If apprenticed in Tain, the obvious Master would have been Alexander Stewart, who had moved from Inverness to Tain in 1812. Suffice to say the records do not appear to exist to confirm the above. We do know, however, that sometime before 1832 William was working, on his own account, in Tain, but by the scarcity of his silver, this must have been for a relatively short period of time. By the middle of 1832 he was in partnership with Richard Maxwell Wilkie; the Small Debt Record Book for the County of Ross detailed, on 23 July 1832, the names of 'William Innes & Richard Wilkie Goldsmiths Tain' in a complaint brought by Alexander Ross, Blacksmith, in Tain, for a debt of eighteen shillings.

The *Tain Council Book* (8 February 1832 to 15 May 1839), minuted a meeting of the Magistrates and Council of the Burgh of Tain, dated 9 April 1834, which included the following: 'It was then stated that several persons particularly ... and Innes and Wilkie were carrying on trade within Burgh without purchasing their freedom. The Meeting direct application to be made to them to enter as Freemen.' Another meeting, of 11 June 1834, reported that, 'Mr. Taylor to make a List of unfreemen carrying on business in Town and to Send the officer to them for the entry fees according to the Scale of rates formerly agreed to.' The last noted meeting concerning the unfreemen recorded, on 25 June 1834, that, 'Mr. Taylor then stated that he gave a List of the names of persons carrying on business within the Burgh without having purchased the Freedom thereof to Alexander Ross Burgh officer to call upon them to pay the sums ordered by a former Meeting but he has got no report from him of what he has done. When it was moved by Bailie John MacKenzie that

Fish Slice by William Innes.
Private collection.
Dumfries Museum

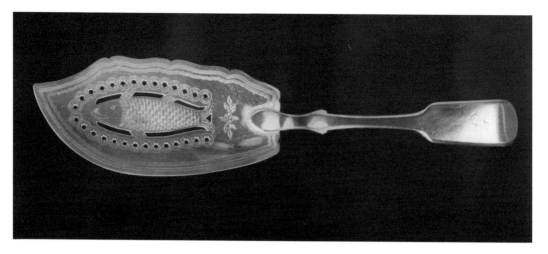

Inverness Courier
18 June 1834

DISSOLUTION OF PARTNERSHIP.

THE COPARTNERY carried on by William Innes and Richard M. Wilkie under the Firm of Innes and Wilkie, Gold and Silversmiths, in Tain, was this day dissolved by mutual consent.

Richard M. Wilkie is authorised to pay the Debts owing by, and to collect those due to the late Firm.

WILLIAM INNES.
RICHARD M. WILKIE.

JOHN URQUHART, Witness.
JOHN MACPHERSON, Witness.
Tain, 16th June, 1834.

R. M. WILKIE begs respectfully to intimate to the Inhabitants of Tain and surrounding country, that he still continues to carry on the business in all its branches, on his own account, and he is determined no exertion on his part shall be wanting, to merit a share of public patronage. R. M. W. has always on hand a neat assortment of Jewellery, Watches, Silver Spoons, fine Cutlery and Britannia Metal goods, of the newest patterns, and as he has made arrangements with a few of the most respectable houses in the South, for a regular supply of goods in the above departments, those who may favour him with their support, may depend upon them being fashionable, and on reasonable terms.

the matter be allowed for the present to lie over for further consideration which was unanimously agreed to.' Unfortunately there was no further information as to whether any of the un-freemen paid their dues.

The partnership between Innes and Wilkie terminated in 1834; the *Inverness Courier* of 18 June of that year carried an advertisement (above). The advertisement was dated 16 June 1834, the day of dissolution.

It is known that Innes marked silver with his initials 'w I' combined in a single punch with 'TAIN'; Tain being in italic capital letters. Another set of marks used by William Innes was 'W. I. *TAIN*, THISTLE, SUNBURST'. His version of the traditional

'thistle' mark might indicate that the silver conformed to standard. It is known that Richard Wilkie worked with Innes for about two years from c1832 to 1834; the partnership used the mark 'I & W'.

Despite extensive research we have been unable to trace William Innes further in Scotland. One possible explanation for this could be that William emigrated to Canada; a William Innes married Ann Larkin at St John's Presbyterian Church in Quebec City, Canada, on 27 February 1843.

The *Canada Directory, Brought Down to 1851* (published by John Lovell, Montreal), recorded William Innes, under jewellers and watchmakers, working in St John Street, without.

He was located in the 1851 Quebec census[129], in St John's Ward; the details as follows: William Innes, goldsmith, Protestant, aged 49, born in Scotland, was living with his Irish born wife, Ann, aged 34, a Catholic, and their children; Mary, 8; George, 7, and Ann, aged 1 year. All the children were Catholics and born in Quebec. It would also appear that a male child, aged 3½ years, died in 1851. Their home was built of brick, two stories high, over a jeweller's shop. William's signature is reproduced below; it was identical to that found on the 1851 Quebec census.

William Innes [signature]

The *Canada Directory 1857-58, Corrected to November, 1857*, recorded 'William Inness', goldsmith, working at 25½ St. John Street, without.'

The *Records of St Patrick's Catholic Church of Quebec* detail the baptism on 13 March 1859 of John Edward Patrick Innes, which stated that he had been 'born the day before, the son of William Innes, jeweler and Ann Larkin of Quebec.' These records also revealed that 'John Innes, aged 6, was buried on 22 September 1867, child of William Innes, jeweler, and Ann Larkin, who died 19 September 1867.'

Lovell's Canadian Dominion Directory 1871 listed a Mrs William Innes, dressmaker, living at 69½ St. John Street, without. It would appear that William Innes had died sometime before 1871; however no record of his death has been found in Quebec.

RICHARD MAXWELL WILKIE 1806-1880

Richard Maxwell Wilkie was born in Glasgow on 11 June 1806, son of John Wilkie, a merchant[130], and Elizabeth Sampson. John Wilkie had married Betty Sampson on 2 January 1789 in the parish of Eastwood, County of Renfrew. They had at least twelve children, four daughters and eight sons, Richard being their ninth recorded child.

Richard Wilkie was probably apprenticed to a jeweller and silversmith in Glasgow before going to Tain sometime after 1830; we do know that he was initially in partnership with William Innes by July 1832, but the partnership ended in June 1834 and he carried on working on his own account until about 1837.

The *Small Debt Record Book* for the County of Ross describes 'Richard M. Wilkie Jeweller Tain' being pursued, on 16 December 1833, for a debt of one pound fifteen shillings; on 29 April 1834 his name appeared again, but on this occasion he was the pursuer of a debt of ten shillings and sixpence.

The partnership with Innes was dissolved by mutual consent on 16 June 1834. The *Inverness Courier* of 18 June 1834 carried an advertisement as follows:

DISSOLUTION OF PARTNERSHIP. THE COPARTNERY carried on by William Innes and Richard M. Wilkie under the Firm of Innes and Wilkie, Gold and Silversmiths, in Tain, was this day dissolved by mutual consent. Richard M. Wilkie is authorised to pay the Debts owing by, and to collect those due to the late Firm.' It concluded, 'R. M. WILKIE begs respectfully to intimate to the Inhabitants of Tain and surrounding country, that he still continues to carry on the business in all its branches, on his own account, and he is determined no exertion on his part shall be wanting, to merit a share of public patronage. R. M. W. has always on hand a neat assortment of Jewellery, Watches, Silver Spoons, fine Cutlery and Britannia Metal goods, of the newest patterns, and as he has made arrangements with a few of the most respectable houses in the South, for a regular supply of goods in the above departments, those who may favour him with their support, may depend upon them being fashionable, and on reasonable terms.

Pigot's Directory 1837 listed 'Rd. Maxwell Wilkie' as a silversmith working in the 'Terrace'. Legend has it that Wilkie emigrated to Canada in about 1840 and returned to Tain in about 1862; although he was not found in the Tain or Edderton 1841, 1851 or 1861 census, we have discovered, from further research, information which seems to discredit the story. Although it does appear that Wilkie did go to Canada at some point, we suspect that it may have been William Innes that settled there, and that there was a confusion of names in the telling.

Fish Slice by Richard Maxwell Wilkie.
Private collection.
A C Cooper Ltd, London

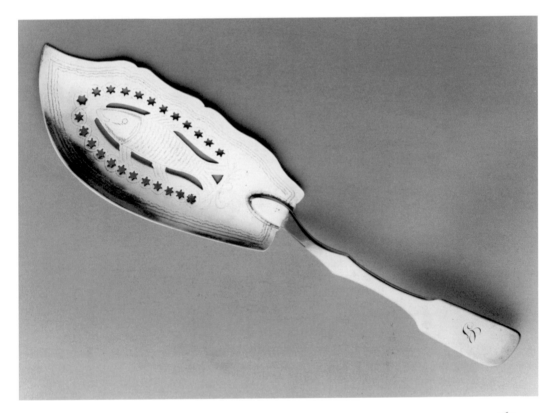

From Tain, Richard Wilkie went to Glasgow where he was recorded in the *Glasgow Post Office Directory* 1838-39 as a jeweller working at 24 Buchanan Street, with a house in Oxford Street. The next year the *Directory* recorded his business at 116 Buchanan Street and his house at 14 Renfrew Street.

Richard Wilkie was in Glasgow during April 1840, as the Blotter Register of Marriages for Glasgow, County of Lanark, recorded:

> Glasgow, 6 April 1840. We the Subscribers, Householders in Glasgow, do hereby certify, That Richard Maxwell Wilkie, Jeweller, in Glasgow & Margaret Crafford Phillips, res there are reputed unmarried persons - that they are not related or connected within any of the forbidden degrees, and that have resided, as above stated, for at least six weeks immediately preceding this date.

However, the names have been crossed through in the register and the word 'withdrawn' added.

The *Glasgow Post Office Directories* for the years 1841 to 1846 show no trace of Wilkie. During this period he may have been in London, as the next advertisement in the *Inverness Courier* of 20 and 27 May 1846 (below) suggests.

The *Glasgow Post Office Directories* 1847-48, 1848-49 and 1849-50 recorded Wilkie as a goldsmith and jeweller working at 14 Warwick Street, Glasgow. There was no further trace of him after this date in these *Directories* nor was he recorded in *Slater's Directory* 1852.

Richard Wilkie did eventually marry; the *Glasgow Parish Register* recorded, under the date of 17 December 1854, the following: 'Richard Maxwell Wilkie, Goldsmith in Glasgow, & Margaret Martin Murray residing there, Married 29th December by Dr. Duncan Macfarlan one of the Ministers of Glasgow.'

Slater's Directory 1860 listed R M Wilkie at 9 Mitchell Street, Glasgow, under Watch and Clock Makers and Jewellers and Silversmiths. Marked against his name was an asterisk recording him as a working jeweller.

Several documents were obtained from the Northern Health Services Archives, Aberdeen; the first, a medical certificate, dated 27 November 1870, stated that Richard Wilkie was in Tain prison, where he was listed as a silversmith and jeweller, and described by Dr James Vass as 'a person of unsound mind'. He was observed as having a 'Threatening and Violent Manner, Proposes marriage to several ladies at

*Inverness Courier
20 May 1846*

R. M. WILKIE,
GOLDSMITH AND JEWELLER,
GLASGOW,

BEGS respectfully to intimate to his friends and the public in general of ROSS and SUTHERLAND SHIRES, that he intends visiting these Counties about the end of May, with a choice and select assortment of GOLD and SILVER WATCHES, JEWELLERY, SILVER PLATE, &c.
R. M. W. is at present in London, and intends visiting the principal Towns in England, to select the Newest Patterns in the different branches of his business.
London, 16th May 1846.

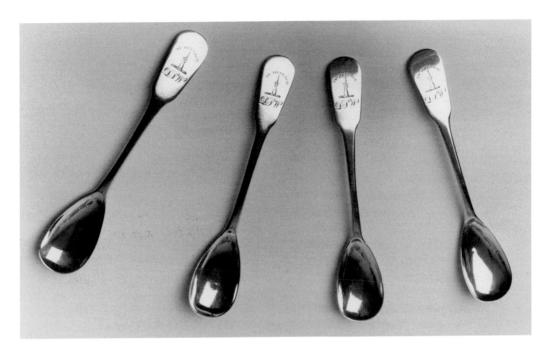

the same time (his wife, I am informed, being alive). Proposes setting out for Glasgow to buy an Elegant Carriage Equipage (while he is in poverty being supported by the gratuity of his brother) and occupying a shooting lodge at a rent of several hundred pounds a year.' Dr Vass then recorded facts, 'communicated to me by others': 'Report to Procurator Fiscal by the Inspector of Police by whom he has been arrested for threatening violence at various houses in town.'

On 28 November 1870 a further certificate was signed by Dr Alexander Walker who having examined Wilkie, reported that he was 'Very much excited talks incessantly - sometimes fails to get out the words he wishes - believes himself to be very wealthy tho' actually poor & talks of riding in carriages & other absurdities.' Dr Walker then recorded facts, 'communicated to me by others': 'Has completely changed his habits within a short time having become noisy & extravagant - has threatened violence on several occasions & is profuse in his offers of marriage sleeps little & eats most voraciously.'

On 3 December 1870 Wilkie's brother John, of 24 Blythswood Square, Glasgow, had an order granted to detain Richard as a private patient in the Royal Lunatic Asylum of Aberdeen.

In the statement dated 30 November 1870 remarks written by a third party unknown were amended by John Wilkie. Richard's age had been left blank but John added 'about 60'. Richard's status was quoted as 'Married', but this was crossed through by John and the words, 'I have no knowledge of this' added. Other details recorded that Richard was recently unemployed but was previously a jeweller, a protestant, whose previous place of abode was Canada for some years, and that he had been insane for some weeks. Richard was admitted on 5 December 1870 as a private patient at £30 per annum; he was suffering from 'mental disorder – mania'. He was described as aged 60, a jeweller with grey eyes, thin and quite grey hair, pale complexion, middle size stature with a stooping figure.

This patient was brought from Tain prison, into which he had been put at the insistence of the Procurator Fiscal having been violent and obstreperous and dangerous to the keeper. On admission here he was a good deal excited talking and jabbering (his speech at times being very thick and indistinct) incessantly about being engaged to marry sane Miss Rose - fancies he is possessed of a vast fortune-says he is to bring an action of damage, to the tune of two thousand six hundred pound, against the Sheriff and Fiscal for false imprisonment &c. &c.

It continued:

Med. Certificates testify as follows – Threatening and violent manner - proposes marriage to several ladies at the same time (his wife being alive) proposes setting out for Glasgow to bring an Elegant Carriage Equipage - he himself being in poverty and supported by the gratuity of his Brother. He sleeps little and eats most voraciously. This is said to be the first attack of a few weeks duration. – No cause assigned.

It concluded:

Considerably excited - has a broken down appearance - sight defection on right eye - wants all his teeth - both hands scarred and still sore by recent burn from his apron catching fire - bad boils on right arm.

The discharge register showed that he was discharged, recovered, on 9 May 1871, after a stay of five months and four days. He was released on the advice of Dr Jamieson, the asylum physician and superintendent. One further point of interest; although no cause of Wilkie's insanity was given in the admission register, a statistical table on cases discharged, recovered, in 1871, listed intemperance as the cause of the mental illness of the male patient, with mania, who was in for five months and four days.

The Aberdeen 1871 census listed him as a patient in the Royal Lunatic Asylum as an unmarried watchmaker and jeweller, aged 65, born in Glasgow. It is believed that Richard Wilkie returned to Tain on his release from the Asylum in May 1871. The *Register of Paupers Admitted into the Easter Ross Union Poorhouse* recorded that an order was made to admit Richard Wilkie into the Tain poorhouse on 20 November 1878. He was admitted on 22 November, and recorded (Nº 703) as infirm, aged 72 years, a jeweller from the Parish of Tain. His name appeared in three registers; the last occasion recorded his death, of natural decay, on 27 April 1880.

The St Duthus Cemetery, Tain, *Burial Register* recorded that Richard Maxwell Wilkie was interred on 29 April 1880; his residence had been Easter Ross Union Poorhouse. He was listed as a 75 year old jeweller, buried in Section G No 76. This was not a pauper's grave; however, if a stone was erected it has not stood the rigours of time.

The authors found in the Tain 1841 census a Juliet Wilkie, aged 5, living with Eppy Ross, aged 40, recorded as independent, and Betsy Ross, aged 15; all three 'born in county', with a home on the County Road. There was no record of the birth of Juliet or of a marriage between Richard Maxwell Wilkie and Eppy Ross in the *Tain Parish Register*.

On 9 February 1866, Juliet Wilkie, by now a lady's maid in Edinburgh, had an illegitimate son whom she named Richard Maxwell Wilkie[131]. Juliet died at 11 Marionville Road, Edinburgh, on 14 February 1910, aged 74. Her son, Richard, the informant on her death certificate, stated that she was unmarried and was herself illegitimate; he failed to give the names of either of her parents. Juliet was born about 1836, a period when Richard Maxwell Wilkie, the silversmith, was in Tain. No baptismal record has been found for Juliet, but it is probable that she was the daughter of Richard and possibly Eppy Ross. One last point of note was that, listed in the *Register of Paupers Admitted into the Easter Ross Union Poorhouse* was an Eppy Ross, No 702, a washerwoman admitted on 7 October 1878; she was aged 78, and reported as very frail. Her name appeared in three registers; the final entry recorded her death on 5 August 1880, of natural decay. Her death certificate stated she was aged 81 years, the widow of Alexander Ross, pensioner, and her parents were listed as David Ross, a crofter, and Christina Ross.

Richard Wilkie's marks whilst in Tain consisted of 'R W, TAIN, thistle'; the 'TAIN' punch differs slightly from that used by Alexander Stewart; the 'Thistle' mark is the same as that used by William Innes. The Wilkie 'TAIN' punch is currently on display in the Tain Museum. In 1834 Wilkie received an order for table silver from a local family and this bears the marks 'R W, TAIN, a thistle, and, a rising sun'.

WILLIAM MCKENZIE c1818–79

William McKenzie was born in Tain around 1818, the son of David McKenzie, a farm manager, and Ann McDonald. Nothing more is known about William McKenzie until he is found in the 1841 Tain census, living in Academy Street, aged 20, and recorded as a watchmaker; also at that address was Catharine Ross, aged 75, described as independent, and John Munro, aged 15 years. All were born in Ross-shire.

He married his wife, Caroline Mayrose Price, on 17 April 1852 in Down, Kent; William was recorded as a silversmith from Tain, Ross, North Britain[132], the son of David McKenzie, a farmer, whilst Caroline was the daughter of Charles Price, merchant. After their marriage they moved to Tain where their first child was born in December 1852. How they met we will probably never know.

The 1851 census for Down had recorded 'Mayrose Ca. Price'[133] living at Down Lodge[134]; she was head of the household and listed as an unmarried gentlewoman, aged 32, born in London. The remainder of the household was made up of three visitors and two servants. The 1851 Tain census revealed that William McKenzie was living in Thorn Hill, unmarried, aged 32, a watch cleaner and jeweller, born in Tain. The remainder of the household were: Margaret Ross, a visitor, aged 23; William Ross[135], aged 18, an apprentice watchmaker, and Isabella Ross, aged 55, a house servant, all born in Tain.

Slater's Directory 1852 recorded the business of William McKenzie at the 'Terrace', under Watch and Clockmakers.

The Tain Free Church of Scotland Register of Baptisms detailed the births of his children as follows: 'William Andrew lawful Son to Mr W[m]. McKenzie, Watchmaker &. Tain And his lawful Spouse Caroline May Rose Price born upon 27th Decr. 1852'; 'Louisa Caroline lawful Daughter to Mr. William McKenzie Watchmaker & Jeweller Tain And his lawful Spouse Caroline Mayrose born 24 Decr. 1854'; 'Mary Ann[136] lawful Daughter of Mr. William McKenzie Watchmaker Tain And his lawful Spouse Caroline Mayrose born 4th September 1856'; 'Edward William lawful Son to Mr William McKenzie Watchmaker & Jeweller Tain & his lawful Spouse Caroline Mayrose born 5th of July 1858'; 'Charles David[137] lawful Son to Mr. William McKenzie Watchmaker Tain And his lawful Spouse Caroline Mayrose Born upon the 14th day of February 1861'.

Slater's Directory 1860 noted the business of William McKenzie at the 'Terrace', under Watch and Clockmakers. Also in this edition of *Slater's*, under 'Miscellaneous', was a John McKenzie, a 'hair dresser & perfumer, and dealer in watches, jewellery and toys', in King Street.

The Tain 1861 census recorded William McKenzie and his family living in High Street; William, aged 43, a watchmaker, born in Tain; Caroline, his wife, aged 40, born in London; Louisa C, 7; Mary Ann, 5; Edward W, 3, and Charles D, 1 month. There were also two domestic servants in the household.

Charles David McKenzie died on 24 July 1863, aged 2 years, at Geanies Street, Tain. The informant was his father William. Caroline May Rose McKenzie died on 4 February 1864, aged 45 years, at Geanies Street, Tain. The death certificate recorded that she was the daughter of Thomas Price[138], master linen draper, and Mary Price, maiden surname unknown.

The 1871 Tain census detailed the family at Dunrobin Street as follows: William McKenzie, widower, aged 53, a watchmaker; Louise, 16; Mary Ann, 14; and Edward, 12 years. All three children were recorded as scholars. Their home was described as two rooms, ie rooms with one or more windows.

William McKenzie, master watchmaker, and widower of Caroline Mayrose Price, died on 23 December 1879, aged 62 years, at Dunrobin Street, Tain, and was buried on 25 December 1879 in St Duthus Cemetery. The informant was his daughter, Mary Ann McKenzie.

He marked silver 'W[M] M[C]KENZIE', with a pellet below the [M] & [C].

JAMES HOUSTON c1810-c1850

Little is known of James Houston. He was mentioned in the Tain 1841 census noted as a jeweller, aged 30, living in Writers Lane; he was not born in Ross-shire. The *Small Debt Record Book* for the County of Ross recorded on 30 May 1849: 'James Houston Jeweller late in Invergordon now residing in Tain P.' pursuing a debt of £6-6-10d. On 27 August and 21 September 1849 claims were made against him in the Small Debt Book; on both occasions he was referred to as John Houston Jeweller Tain.

JOHN MACKENZIE AND COMPANY 1854

The *Small Debt Record Book* for the County of Ross recorded, on 21 June and 23 October 1854, claims for debts made by John MacKenzie and Company Jewellers in Tain.

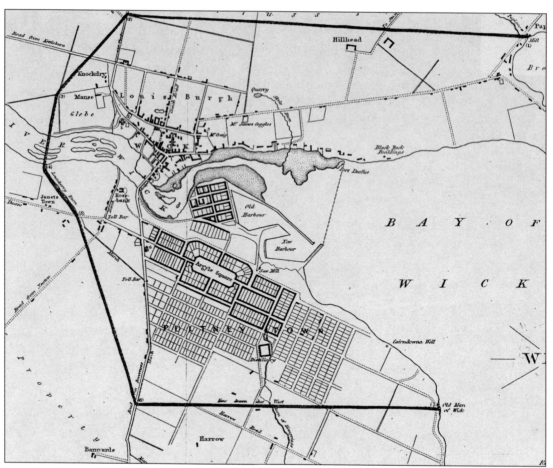

Town plan of Wick

*View of Wick harbour
showing curing stances*

CHAPTER SIX

WICK CRAFTSMEN

John Sellar 1801-86

The Royal Burgh of Wick is the principal burgh of Caithness and owed its growth in the nineteenth century to the herring industry when, at times, there were up to 1,000 fishing boats working from the harbour. The herring was exported in barrels to Germany, Russia, Poland and to ports around the Baltic. In its heyday fifty companies produced kippers in Wick.

Lt Dawson's survey in 1832 reported:

> WICK has increased considerably of late years, and Pultney Town, which is situated on the opposite side of the Harbour, and connected with Wick by a Bridge, has been entirely built within the last twenty-five years, on land feued by the British Fishery Society. Having a good Harbour, these Towns enjoy a considerable trade, and form the greatest station in the North for the prosecution of the Herring Fishery; from 1,500 to 2,000 boats remaining there during the Summer months for that purpose. Grain, Wool and the proceeds of the Fishery are the principal Exports, and furnish Cargoes to a number of Trading Vessels; but there is no Manufacture of any importance. Both Towns are in a very thriving condition.

The 1821 census of the Burgh and Parish of Wick gave a population of 6,713 and for 1831 9,850.

John Sellar 1801-86

John Sellar was born in Forres, at Millfield, on 16 December 1801; his father, also John, was a vintner, and his mother was Helen Donaldson. He was the second eldest of a family of two girls and six boys. John was probably apprenticed to a watchmaker in either Elgin or Forres, and it appears that he set up his own business as a watchmaker, in Forres, for a short time in about 1820; he was listed as such in *Pigot's Directory* of 1821-22 and 23. Shortly after this he moved to the Royal Burgh of Tain and on 8 March 1822 he married Jane/Jean Grant, of Forres, the marriage being recorded in both parishes.

WATCH AND CLOCK MAKING.

'JOHN SELLAR begs leave most respectfully to return his sincere thanks to the Inhabitants of Tain and
the surrounding country, for the liberal encouragement he
has experienced since he commenced Business, and, from
an assiduous attention to Orders, hopes to merit a continuance of their favours. And he further begs to mention,
that he intends, In addition to the above line, to carry on
the Gold and Silver Smith Work, in all its branches, having engaged an experienced hand, who has wrought a considerable time in Edinburgh. Jewellery neatly repaired,
Watch Cases, Snuff Boxes, finely Gilded, Engraving, &c.

J. S. has on hand a neat Assortment of Clocks, Watches,
and Jewellery. N. B. An Apprentice Wanted.

John Sellar advertised his business in the *Inverness Journal*, on 10 and 17 May 1822 (above). At least one longcase clock by John Sellar is known from this period; it is in a private collection.

The Tain Parish Register recorded the birth of a son, John Donaldson Gearr Sellar, to John and his wife on 30 August 1823.

John Sellar was a watchmaker who employed a silversmith/jeweller journey-man to make silver articles and used his initials 'J S' to mark the silver. A set of silver fiddle pattern tablespoons was displayed in the Tain and District Museum in September and October 1997; most were made by Alexander Stewart but the set also contained several spoons marked with 'J S' only. The spoons were engraved with a local family's initials and had been in their care for many years. The mark is, however, different from that used in Wick and different again from the one he used whilst in Elgin from 1836. Very recently a tablespoon was found (now owned by Mr N R Shaw) which had the same 'J S' mark but also included 'TAIN', proving almost conclusively that the illustrated punch (top left) is that of John Sellar whilst working in Tain.

Shortly after the birth of his son, John, he was recorded in *Pigot's Directory* 1825, in Bridge Street, Wick, as a watch and clock maker and jeweller. By 1830, however, the business had moved to High Street. It is not clear why he left Tain, although possible competition from an established watchmaker and Alexander Stewart, the silversmith in the town, might have forced the move. At least one of his clocks, a longcase, is known from Wick and is on display in the Wick Heritage Centre in Bank Row.

The *Wick Parish Register* recorded the baptisms of four daughters and two sons to John and his wife whilst in Wick; they were: Sophia Grant, born 18 April 1825; Helen (Donaldson), 15 March 1827; Flora, 12 April 1829; Jamima Annand, 6 February 1831; William Peter, 6 March 1833, and, George Grant 10 March 1835.

John O'Groats Journal
2 February 1836

STOCK TO BE SOLD OFF.

John Sellar,

JEWELLER, WICK,

BEGS to return his best thanks to the Inhabitants of Thurso and surrounding country, for the liberal support formerly received; and now informs them that he intends opening Shop in Thurso, on the 15th current, with a large Stock of Jewellery, Watches, Clocks, Fancy Goods, and Hardware.

As J. S. intends leaving Caithness, to enter into another line of Business, the whole Stock in hand will positively be sold off without reserve; and as his time is limited to fourteen days, he earnestly solicits an early call.

NOTICE.

All those having Watches, &c. in Mr. SELLAR's possession for Repairs, will please call for them immediately, as he intends to shut up his place of business next week.

Wick, 2d February, 1836.
(One concern.)

John Sellar advertised in the first edition of the *John O'Groats Journal*, of 2 February 1836 (above), that he 'intends leaving Caithness, to enter into another line of Business, the whole Stock in hand will positively be sold off without reserve'. Sellar and his family left Wick for Elgin between March and June 1836. In the Elgin Courant of 15 July 1836, John advertised that he had opened 'that

*John Sellar & Sons'
Bill Head for Elgin*

INVENTOR
OF THE ELECTRIC CLOCK AND THE
ELECTRIC PRINTING TELEGRAPH

ALEXANDER BAIN

WAS BORN AT WATTEN, CAITHNESS IN 1810
PART OF HIS APPRENTICESHIP AS A CLOCKMAKER
WAS SERVED WITH JOHN SELLAR, WATCHMAKER
IN THIS BUILDING IN 1829 - 1830.

Workshop of
ALEXANDER BAIN
Electric Clock and Telegraph Appliances
Born 1810 - Died 1877

*Plaques Commemorating Alexander
Bain in Wick and Edinburgh*

*Wine Funnel by John Sellar,
marked* WICK.
Inverness Museum and Art Gallery. Ewen
Weatherspoon

Mug by John Sellar, later decorated.
Private collection. Ewen
Weatherspoon

large Shop, in High Street, on the corner with Batchen Street'. In his new shop he was to sell gold and silver watches, bracket clocks, silver spoons and forks, hardware and ironmongery goods. He also stated that he would make and repair clocks and watches having 'engaged a thorough-bred workman from London'. (For further details of John Sellar's life in Elgin see *The Provincial Silversmiths of Moray*). The Elgin silversmith, recorded in *Jackson's Silver and Gold Marks*, as John Seller was in fact John Sellar from Forres, Tain and Wick. He died on 2 March 1886, aged 84, at Viewpark, Elgin.

During John's stay in Wick, a young man, Alexander Bain, was taken on as an apprentice from 8 January 1830 for seven years. John Sellar's workshop was in High Street, between London Close and Wares Lane; the site of this workshop is commemorated by a plaque on the wall, which is illustrated (p176).

Alexander Bain was born in Watten in 1810 and died in Kirkintilloch in 1877; he was the inventor of the electric clock, facsimile machine and the telegraph, among other advances. Bain became interested in heat, sound and electricity after attending a lecture in the Masonic Hall, Thurso, in 1830. His enthusiasm for the subject and his desire to learn more about electricity eventually led him to break his indenture with John Sellar on 21 July 1834. He went to Edinburgh, where he later finished his apprenticeship. A photograph of the engraved stone in the wall of his workshop in Hanover Street, Edinburgh, is illustrated (opposite top right). To

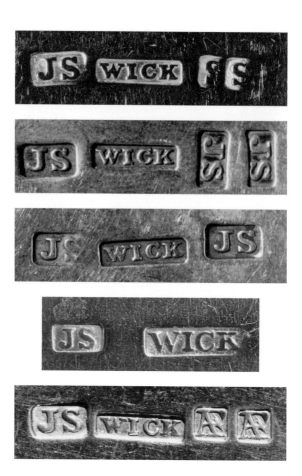

break an indenture was a serious matter and his father John Bain, farmer, Peter Bain, pensioner, Andrew Begg, farmer, and William Munro, farmer, who had acted as cautioners, had to pay £20 plus costs to John Sellar for the broken agreement. It is said that Alexander Bain later repaid the money.

While in Wick, John Sellar used six known sets of marks, they are as follows: 'J S, WICK, S, S,', 'J S, WICK, J S,', 'J S, WICK, J S, J S,' (upto three 'JS' have been noted), 'J S, WICK, THISTLE', and 'JS, WICK, AF (conjoined) twice'.

Another set of Wick marks (p179), 'DF WICK, DF'; may, possibly belong to Donald Fraser, from Inverness (see p50); the items of silver date from around 1820. At a Phillips, Edinburgh, auction held on 20 May 1983, three lots were recorded with the 'DF' mark, all with the family initials 'IML'; they were lots 262 and 263, both fiddle pattern sauce ladles, and lot 264, a fiddle pattern punch ladle or small soup ladle. Lot 262 was sold for £320; lot 263 was unsold and lot 264 was sold for £400. The David Morris Collection, auctioned by Christies of Glasgow on 3 July 1984, listed lot 63, a small fiddle pattern soup ladle, again with the 'DF' mark and the family initials 'IML'; this sold for £480. It is worthy of note that the family initials 'IML' are often seen on John Sellar's silver.

The 'J S' punch has sometimes been attributed to James Sinclair but he was a clockmaker who worked from premises in the Market Place around 1860. Other

watch and clockmakers and jewellers who worked in Wick during the nineteenth century include Thomas Cordingly (c1836-90), John McGregor (c1837) and William Bell (c1837-60).

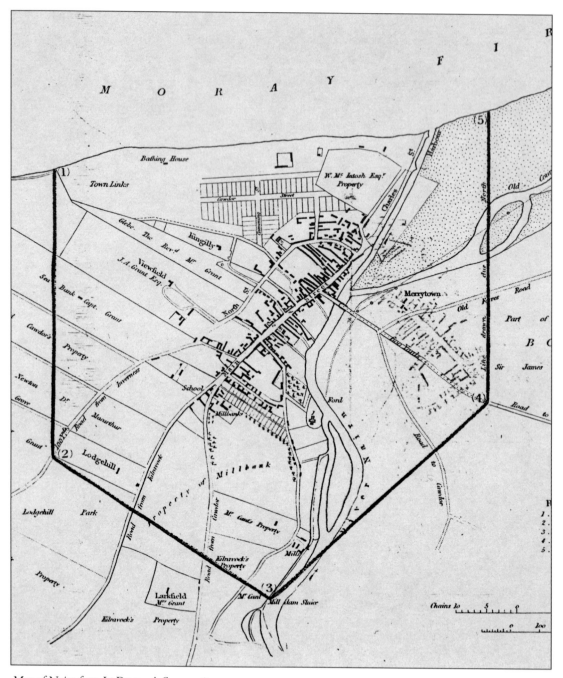

Map of Nairn from Lt Dawson's Survey 1832

CHAPTER SEVEN

NAIRN CRAFTSMEN

DANIEL FERGUSON 1814-92

WILLIAM FRASER 1851-62

Nairn is a Royal Burgh and seaport at the mouth of the river Nairn, fifteen miles east of Inverness and twenty-one miles west of Elgin. In the early years of the nineteenth century it was a considerable spa town and was popularly known, for a time, as the 'Brighton of the North'. Dawson in his 1832 survey:

> NAIRN, the County Town of the small Shire of that name, is an ancient Royal Burgh. The principal Street is tolerably spacious, but all the others are narrow and confined. Some good Houses have been erected within these few years to the South-west; also a Town House, and large Inn, by subscription of the neighbouring Proprietors. The Harbour is formed by the Mouth of the River Nairn and some years ago large sums were expended in the erection of Piers to improve it; but soon afterwards the floods destroyed part of these erections, so that Vessels of very small tonnage only can now enter it. The imports are Coal and Lime, and Merchandize for the supply of the surrounding District; which, however, is very limited, as the Highlands commence at a short distance South of the Town, and Inverness and Findhorn supply the adjoining Coast Districts. There are a good many Fishing Boats belonging to the Town, and a Building for curing Herrings. Several Villas have been built in the neighbourhood; but it cannot be considered as being in a thriving state, nor is there much probability of its increase.

The 1821 census calculated that the population was 3,228; in 1831 it was 3,266.

DANIEL FERGUSON 1814-92

Daniel Ferguson was born in Nairn on 7 April 1814; his father was Charles Ferguson, a mason, born in Cromarty, and his mother Anne Mackintosh, born in Daviot, Inverness-shire. The Riverside Church Yard, Nairn, contains a lair (No 90) which holds Charles Ferguson, mason, died 31 December 1852, aged 72; Ann MacIntosh, died 29 June 1855, aged 72, and Charlotte Ferguson, died 19 May 1886, aged 69. No other information has been found concerning Daniel's early years and we have not established with whom he served his apprenticeship as a watchmaker.

Daniel Ferguson was not recorded in *Pigot's Directory* 1837; however, we do know that he commenced business in Nairn in 1837. He appears to be the only watchmaker and jeweller to have marked silver known to have been manufactured in Nairn. Many years later he had a journeyman silversmith/jeweller who worked for him and made the silver brooches; this will be discussed further.

Daniel Ferguson's name appeared in the 1841 Nairn census with his parents, in Cumming Street, as follows: Charles Ferguson, aged 50, mason; Ann, 60; Daniel, 26, a watchmaker; John Leslie, 16, watchmaker's apprentice, and Ann Leslie, aged 10.

Daniel married Margaret McBean on 7 October 1848, in Nairn; both were living in the Parish. Margaret was born at Moss Side, Nairn, on 27 April 1824; her father was Donald McBain, and her mother Ann Rose. Daniel and Margaret Ferguson lived in Cumming Street until at least 1858. They had six known children: Ann, born 25 August 1849 (who married Arthur Medlock); Charles, born 28 January 1854; Margaret, born 8 January 1856, at 4 Cumming Street; twins Charlotte and John[139], born 15 July 1858, at 4 Cumming Street, and, Daniel[140] born 27 April 1862, at High Street, all born in Nairn.

The 1851 Nairn census for 4 Cumming Street recorded Daniel with his parents thus: Charles Ferguson, aged 69, a retired master mason, born in Cromarty; Ann, his wife, 73, born in Daviot, and, Daniel, 36, a watchmaker who employed one man, born in Nairn. Daniel was married at the time, but his wife, Margaret, and daughter, Ann, were not to be found in the Nairn Town census. However, a search for her parents' farm, in an area called Newton, located the following: Donald McBean, aged 66, who was a farmer, of 60 acres, employing 3 labourers; Ann, his wife, aged 60; William, a son, aged 25; Margaret Ferguson, daughter, and watchmaker's wife,

Nairnshire Telegraph
14 April 1858

ESTABLISHED 1837.

DANIEL FERGUSON,

WATCH-MAKER,

IN returning thanks to his numerous Customers and Friends since he commenced Business in 1837, begs to acquaint them and the Public that he has secured the services of a superior Working JEWELLER for a limited period, and will now be able to execute all descriptions of work in that Department in a superior manner.

He is regularly adding to his Stock of Ironmongery Goods and Household Furnishings, to meet the increasing demands of his Friends.

All Watches supplied by him are purchased with Cash from the first London Makers, and are warranted to give satisfaction, and Sold at lowest remunerating Prices.

High Street, Nairn,
12th April, 1858.

and, Ann, granddaughter, aged 1 year, all born in Nairn. The household was completed with two labourers and a house servant.

The *Slater's Directories* 1852 and 1860 recorded his business, under watch & clockmakers, at 74 High Street[141], Nairn.

The Nairnshire Telegraph, of 14 April 1858, carried an advertisement for the business which was headed: 'ESTABLISHED 1837 (opposite). It was probably from this time that the brooches, which bear Daniel Ferguson's mark 'D F, NAIRN', were made.

The 1861 Nairn census found him living with his wife and family at 94 High Street; Daniel, aged 44, a clock and watchmaker; Margaret, his wife, aged 30; Ann, 10; Charles, 7; Margaret, 5; John, 2; Charlotte, 2, and Daniel's unmarried sister, Charlotte, aged 44 years. There was also Margaret Fridge, a house servant, aged 18, and Thomas Sellar, 17, a clock and watchmaker's apprentice, who was born in Leith. Daniel's last business address in Nairn was recorded as 92 High Street (it had previously been 74). This was possibly due to renumbering the High Street rather than a change of shop.

The *Nairnshire Telegraph* of 30 April 1862, advertised:

CLEARING SALE OF HARDWARE GOODS. ... DANIEL FERGUSON, WATCHMAKER, begs to inform his Friends and the Public that he has made arrangements for leaving Nairn at the term of Whitsunday first, and commencing business at NO. 4, INGLIS STREET, INVERNESS; and, as he does not intend carrying on the Ironmongery business there, he has begun to dispose of his whole Stock in that department at greatly reduced prices. The Goods, which are of the best quality, and well selected, consist of a great variety of Household Furnishings, Carpenters' Tools, and Fancy Articles; and, as the whole must be disposed of previous to Whitsunday, they will be sold cheap, without reserve, to effect a clearance. Nairn, 4th March, 1862.

Nairnshire Telegraph
17 July 1862

REMOVAL:

DANIEL FERGUSON, WATCHMAKER and JEWELLER, in returning his most sincere thanks to his Friends and the Public who have so kindly patronized him since he commenced business in Nairn, begs to acquaint them that he has Removed to No. 4 INGLIS STREET, INVERNESS, which premises he will open with a large and well-selected Stock of Goods of every description in the Trade, recently selected by himself in the London markets. The Goods, being purchased with cash, will be disposed of at very reasonable prices; and INSPECTION is very respectfully solicited.

In reference to the above, D.F. begs to solicit from the inhabitants of Inverness and neighbourhood, a share of their patronage and support, and to assure them that nothing will be wanting on his part to give satisfaction to those favouring him with their orders, which shall have his most careful and prompt attention.
July 9, 1862.

Another advertisement, in the *Nairnshire Telegraph* of 7 May 1862, stated:

THE CLEARING SALE OF THE STOCK OF Hardware, Miscellaneous, & Fancy Goods, MUSICAL INSTRUMENTS, JEWELLERY &C., AT DANIEL FERGUSON'S, WATCHMAKER, IS STILL GOING ON.

The family moved around Whitsunday, in May 1862, to Inglis Street, Inverness, and Daniel's shop was at No. 4 until February 1872. The *Inverness Courier* of 17 July 1862, carried an advertisement:

REMOVAL TO INVERNESS. DANIEL FERGUSON, WATCHMAKER and JEWELLER, in returning his most sincere thanks to his Friends and the Public, who have so kindly patronised him since he commenced business in Nairn, begs to acquaint them that he has Removed to NO. 4 INGLIS STREET, INVERNESS, which Premises he will open with a large and well selected Stock of Goods of every description in the Trade, recently selected by himself in the London markets.

Luckenbooth by Daniel Ferguson, Nairn.
National Museums of Scotland

Another advertisement, in the *Nairnshire Telegraph* of 13 August 1862, recorded:

NOTICE OF REMOVAL. DAVID MACLEAN, BREAD AND BUISCUIT BAKER, Would intimate to the inhabitants of Nairn and its vicinity, that he has removed from No 2 Leopold Street, to that Shop, 92 HIGH STREET, lately occupied by Mr D. Ferguson, Watchmaker, where he intends to carry on the business in all its branches as formerly. D. M^cL. having erected a Brick Oven on the newest and most approved principles, and fitted up his Bakehouse with a Kneading and Rolling Machine, feels assured he will be able to supply his Customers with Pure Bread of the very best quality. 92 High Street, 26th May 1862.

Daniel Ferguson's business was noted in the *Inverness Courier* of 30 July 1863, with a simple entry that stated: 'DANIEL FERGUSON, WATCHMAKER & MANUFACTURING JEWELLER, 4 INGLIS STREET, INVERNESS.

Jewellery box top

Luckenbooth by Daniel Ferguson, Nairn.
Private collection

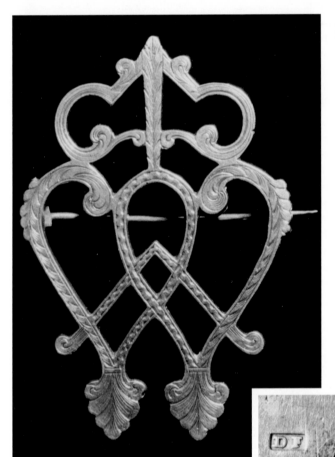

The *Inverness Directory* 1866/67 listed his working and home address as 4 Inglis Street, and *Slater's Directory* 1867 also recorded the business.

The family was recorded in the 1871 Inverness census living at 6 Inglis Street: Daniel Ferguson, aged 55, a watchmaker; Margaret, his wife, aged 43; Margaret, 15; Charlotte, 12, and Daniel, 8 years. All three children were scholars.

The *Inverness Courier* of 4 January 1872 carried an advertisement:

PREVIOUS TO REMOVAL TO 33 UNION STREET, INVERNESS. DANIEL FERGUSON, JEWELLER and WATCHMAKER, in returning his most sincere thanks to his Friends and the Public who have so liberally patronised him since he commenced Business in Inverness, begs to acquaint them that before REMOVAL he is to SELL OFF, at GREATLY REDUCED PRICES, his present Stock of JEWELLERY, CLOCKS, WATCHES, &c., &c. 4 Inglis Street, Inverness, 19th December 1871.

The *Inverness Courier* of 21 March 1872 (below) ran a similar advertisement to the above, with the exception that the sale was now over and the removal complete.

The *Inverness Courier* of 26 June 1873 advertised his business at 33 Union Street, Inverness, and the *Inverness Directory* 1873/74 confirmed this and also gave his home as 6 Inglis Street.

The *Inverness Courier* of 20 July 1876 carried an advertisement for Daniel Ferguson at 33 Union Street:

Respectfully requests the inspection of his Customers, and TOURISTS visiting the Capital of the Highlands, to his large and varied assortment of JEWELLERY made up in his Establishment, consisting of Ancient HIGHLAND BROOCHES, in Gold and Silver, and PENDANTS, CROSSES, &c., set in Cairngorms and Amythists.

By the 1881 census the family had moved to 12 Innes Street; Daniel senior was absent but his wife and two younger sons were listed, John, a watchmaker, and Daniel junior, a jeweller.

Slater's Directory 1882 recorded Daniel Ferguson working at 33 Union Street; he was listed under Jewellers & Manufacturers of Highland Ornaments, as well as Watch and Clockmakers.

Daniel and his wife were listed in the 1891 census at 12 Innes Street; he was recorded as a watchmaker and employer. He died at this address on 31 October 1892, aged 77; he was listed as a watchmaker and jeweller, the informant was his son, John, who lived at Maryann Cottage, Ardross Place, Inverness. The *Scottish Highlander* of 3 November 1892, and *Elgin Courant & Courier* of 15 November 1892 recorded his death.

Inverness Courier
21 March 1872

DANIEL FERGUSON, JEWELLER AND WATCHMAKER, respectfully begs to intimate that he has removed to 33 UNION STREET, and in doing so, returns his sincere thanks for the liberal support he has received from his friends and customers for the past ten years ; trusting to receive a continuance of their favours, he assures them that nothing shall be wanting on his part to meet their commands, having a large and varied Stock of JEWELLERY, WATCHES, &c., to select from. All orders, repairs, &c., shall have his personal care and attention.
33 Union Street, Inverness, Feb. 1872.

The family gravestone was located in Tomnahurich Cemetery; the inscription read:

Erected by Margaret McBean in memory of her husband. Daniel Ferguson Watch-maker Inverness Died 30 Oct 1892 Aged 78 Also of her beloved children Charles died 15 June 1875 aged 21 and Margaret died 12 Oct 1877 aged 21 Also in memory of Mary Ann Charlotte Youngest and beloved daughter of John Ferguson Watchmaker, Inverness died February 1895.

Margaret Ferguson died on 28 June 1902, aged 78, at Ashlyn, Crown Drive, Inverness, her daughter's home; the informant was Arthur Medlock, watchmaker, her son-in-law.

Daniel Ferguson's marks were 'D F' and 'NAIRN' in full (p184-5). It appears whilst in Nairn his main output, apart from clocks and watches, was hardware. However, there is no doubt that brooches were produced in his Nairn workshop, but very few survive today (p184-5 and below).

Daniel Ferguson was known to have trained at least two apprentices: John Leslie, noted in the 1841 Nairn census, aged 16, and Thomas Sellar, in the 1861 Nairn census, aged 17, who was recorded as born in Leith. It is also possible that Arthur Medlock was apprenticed to Daniel Ferguson.

While in Inverness Daniel Ferguson's marks were thought to be 'D. F over INS', but our recent research attributes that mark to Donald Fraser. His true Inverness marks were 'D F, INV[ss]' (below). There has been a suggestion that whilst in Inverness he also used the marks 'D FERGUSON, INV[ss]'; these latter marks have not been seen by the authors.

Heart Brooch by Daniel Ferguson, Inverness.

WILLIAM FRASER 1851–62

William Fraser, watchmaker and jeweller in Nairn, was found recorded on the following occasions:

The *Nairnshire Mirror* of 26 April 1851 advertised: 'SALE OF WATCHES, JEWELLERY, &c. SELLING OFF at the SHOP, NO. 102, HIGH STREET, Nairn, lately occupied by William Fraser, Watchmaker and Jeweller.' It continued, 'Parties indebted to Mr Fraser are requested to make immediate payment of their accounts to Mr. John Donaldson, Merchant, High Street, Nairn, who is authorised to discharge the same. 102, High Street, Nairn, 26th April, 1851.'

The *Nairnshire Telegraph* of 7 August 1861 carried an advertisement (below). The same paper of 7 May 1862 reported, 'At Wilson's Court, Nairn, on the 27th ult., the wife of Mr William Fraser, watchmaker, of a son.'

The *Nairnshire Telegraph* of 25 June 1862 carried a further advertisement: 'WILLIAM FRASER, WATCH MANUFACTURER AND JEWELLER (From London), Begs to intimate that he has REMOVED to that Shop in HIGH STREET, lately occupied by MR GILBERTSON, Shoemaker.' It concluded, 'Watches or Jewellery sent to any part of the kingdom post-free. Nairn, June, 1862.'

It is not clear whether this was the same William Fraser who set up business at 1 High Street, Inverness, in 1869.

*Nairnshire Telegraph
7 August 1861*

WILLIAM FRASER,
WATCH MANUFACTURER AND JEWELLER
RESPECTFULLY intimates that he has resumed business in Nairn in that Shop,
24 HIGH STREET,
Directly opposite the National Bank; and, from his thorough knowledge of every department of the Trade, acquired by long experience in the first Manufactories in London, he hopes, by careful and prompt execution of orders, and moderate charges, to merit a share of public support.

Watches of every description made to order on the premises.

LADIES' WATCHES.
Silver, £2 to £20.   Gold, £5 to £50.
GENTLEMENS' WATCHES.
Silver, £4 to £30.   Gold, £7 to £70.
Verge Watches converted into Lever Watches at from 20s to 50s.

An extensive Stock of JEWELLERY, in Brooches, Rings, &c., at all Prices.

Any Article not in Stock ordered by post without extra expense to the purchaser.

Watches sent to any part of the kingdom post-free.

Nairn, August 5, 1861.

CHAPTER EIGHT

MODERN CRAFTSMEN

John Fraser

Alan Roy Baillie

Colin Alexander Campbell

Douglas Scott

Keith Sim

John Fraser

John Fraser was born at 44 Church Street, Inverness in 1923, son of Hector Fraser, a butcher, and Helen Main. John was apprenticed to James Craik in 1937 for seven years followed by a further three years as an improver. John Fraser, engraver and jeweller, married Mary (Marie) Margaret Crichton in 1952 in Stornoway. Marie Crichton was born in Vancouver, British Columbia, Canada.

His business was started in 1960 in Castle Street and the Market Hall shop opened in 1961. *MacDonald's Scottish Directory* 1965-66 recorded the concern as Silvercraft, at 51 Castle Street, under silversmiths. The present establishment in the New Market shop was opened in 1971 and is still called Silvercraft; this remains at 5/7 Market Hall, with the workshop in Castle Street. John Fraser's mark is illustrated (below). He still marks larger items of silver with 'J. F, INS'.

Over the years John Fraser has completed many private commissions and Chains of Office for town officials, plus trophies for town clubs. Additionally, he has completed special pieces for royalty and local dignitaries. John Fraser must be considered as the last of a long line of Inverness-bred silversmiths, having been born in the town and having served his apprenticeship with Medlock and Craik.

Alan Roy Baillie

Alan Roy Baillie was born in Edinburgh in 1957, attending the Edinburgh College of Art from 1976 to 1980. Along with silversmithing, his other love was sculpting which possibly underlies his interest and aptitude for chasing.

On leaving Art College he worked in various sectors of applied art before joining Hamilton and Inches, of Edinburgh, as a silversmith, in 1990. Hamilton and Inches was then a family owned firm and one of the most prestigious silverware manufacturers in Scotland. As part of a small team, Alan specialised in the creation of individually crafted sgian dubhs and this continues to be one of his specialities. The manufacture of sgian dubhs requires woodcarving, silversmithing and leather-working techniques and there are few individuals with the expertise in all these fields to produce them.

Alan left Hamilton and Inches in 1994 and moved to Inverness to establish his own business as a designer silversmith. Much of his work is by commission and he continues to produce many items of Highland dress-ware, eg kilt pins, sporrans and waist-plates. Self-employment has given him the freedom to create and produce his own designs and his work is increasingly moving towards more contemporary silver-ware. Recent commissions have included a quaich for the Queen Mother, a trophy for the Inverness Music Society and a 12" silver quaich for a golf tournament in Hawaii. Alan has been a regular exhibitor at the Royal Highland Show.

An example of his mark 'A R B' is illustrated (above).

COLIN ALEXANDER CAMPBELL

Colin Campbell, born in Glasgow in 1949, was apprenticed in 1964, for six years, with Gordon & Carter, Gordon Street, Glasgow. This business was a traditional jobbing workshop, collecting and delivering daily parcels of work from shops around the city. They undertook every kind of jewellery manufacture, repair and alteration.

Until the 1980s the equipment used in jewellers' workshops had changed little over the centuries. Colin Campbell recounted:

> The first thing an apprentice had to master was soldering. This involved the use of a blow pipe, through which a constant flow of air was directed by mouth onto the gas flame of a Bunsen burner which produced a stronger and more even temperature. The technique of blowing out through the mouth and breathing in through the nose at the same time was an art in itself! Most jewellers of my age had veneered teeth or chipped eye-teeth from biting down on the blow pipe and all dreaded a head cold. Everything that was produced was fabricated from basic materials. Even a simple connecting ring was made by drawing down wire through various gauges to the required thickness. Nowadays, many pieces of jewellery are simply made up of component parts.

As a time-served journeyman he worked for two years with a Glasgow antique dealer, specialising in restoring and repairing antique jewellery. Much of the work was bought and sold at jewellery auctions, and Colin learned a great deal from beautifully constructed Victorian and Edwardian pieces which were, at the time, plentiful and inexpensive.

In 1971 Colin Campbell bought John Muir's old jewellery workshop and premises at 75 Buchanan Street, Glasgow (complete with black-out windows). This was a time of many changes in the traditional workshop. The first came with the arrival of town gas, which meant re-learning blow-pipe techniques; the second was the disruption caused by two and three day electricity strikes. Colin was fortunate in that his father-in-law had a tyre and battery business and he was 'kept going with the regular arrival of half-dead men bringing six car batteries at a time up four flights of stairs. Car headlights were used over the benches with bottled calor gas.'

Colin continued:

> In those days, jewellers used a drill called an Archimedes drill, a piece of equipment as old as the name suggests. This drill was a one-handed contraption with a string which enabled the bench jeweller to drill out a setting, for a stone, with a pumping action, while holding a ring in the other hand; nowadays a pendant drill would be used.
>
> The first piece of technology which had a real impact on the trade was the micro-welding machine. Adding chemicals to this electronic machine created a high temperature gas, similar to a mini oxyacetylene torch. It provided a constant high temperature and different nozzles created variations on the flame size.

After about five years in Buchanan Street, Colin sold his business to his apprentice and for the next four years worked from the attic at home, either collecting and delivering work or dealing by post, with retail shops. Being able to conduct his business from any location, in 1978 he decided to take his family north; they settled in Drumnadrochit and he worked from an old cottage in the garden.

In 1979 he was asked to cover a temporary vacancy at Craft Point, Beauly; this he undertook whilst still running his own business in parallel, an undertaking which eventually ran to six months. Craft Point was a Government funded centre, the purpose of which was to improve and promote Scottish products and provide a gathering point for all craft workers to exchange ideas. It set up the Aviemore Trade Show and helped fund many individual exhibitors to show and export to other countries, under the umbrella and shared expense of one Scottish stand.

Over the next couple of years he tutored a number of 'stepping stone' courses, designed to ease Art School students into a realistic work schedule. This was just one of many courses which disappeared with the closure of Craft Point.

Through Craft Point Colin Campbell was commissioned, by Father Basil Robinson of Pluscarden Abbey, between Elgin and Forres, to make a set of ceremonial robe fastenings for Pope John Paul's visit to Britain. They were made in bronze and the clasp took the form of eagle's claws.

His son, Paul, joined the business in January 1998 to learn the trade 'at the bench'. His wife operates the 'modern technology', the computer for administration and the fax machine. Without this technology he would not have been able to carry out commissions, in the time scale, from places as far apart as Vancouver and Hong Kong. Additionally, computer technology is used to ensure exact continuous patterns in varying finger sizes and widths for such items as intricately patterned Celtic gold wedding rings.

Colin Campbell's business is now conducted at Market Brae, Inverness; no longer working for the trade but open to the public. In 1996 he was granted permission, by the Edinburgh Assay Master, to incorporate the old Inverness mark 'INS' alongside the Edinburgh assay marks together with his own 'C A C'.

DOUGLAS SCOTT

Douglas Scott was born in his granny's house in Springburn, Glasgow in 1948. He attended school in Haghill and moved to East Kilbride when he was thirteen. He left school at fifteen and started work as a sheet metal apprentice and continued in this trade for the next nineteen years.

From an early age Douglas developed a general interest in history, astronomy, archaeology and the arts; as his skills grew, he began to experiment with Celtic designs in copper with the vague idea of creating a small business at some point in the future.

After being made redundant three times in the first half of the 1970s Douglas and his wife, Rita, moved north to Tain, following the birth of their first daughter, Sian, and to a new job, in 1976. A further two redundancies followed, the last when the Invergordon Aluminium smelter closed. It was at this point he decided it was time to put his plans into action and start the Tain Silver business.

For the next five years he struggled; however, he exhibited his handmade items of silver jewellery at the Aviemore Highland Trade Fair, and somewhat to his surprise his business began to take off. The late 80s and early 90s were years of success, Douglas being 'really busy' supplying the trade, but following a dip in sales due to the recession of the early 90s, he opened his shop in Tain. He presently exports all over the world, sells to the public from his shop and supplies the trade with silver and gold brooches, earrings, pendants and most kinds of jewellery.

Douglas Scott's punch is 'D S' together with the 'TAIN' mark which was approved by the Edinburgh Assay Office.

KEITH SIM

Keith Sim was born in India in 1958, where he lived until, at the age of five, his family returned to Scotland. His education commenced in Aberdeen, but, after a further move to Tighnabruaich, on the Kyle of Bute, was completed in Argyll.

On leaving school he was employed by Scotia Manufacturing Jewellers, Dunoon, for nine years, during which time he completed an apprenticeship. Whilst at Scotia he learnt tool making, enamelling, machine engraving, stone setting and mounting.

In 1986 he left this employment to become Workshop manager at Highland Craft Point, Beauly; he travelled a great deal offering advice to the many businesses in the Highland and Islands. After three years at Craft Point he set up his own business as Keith Sim, Goldsmith in Inverness. He uses the punch 'K S'.

APPENDIX

Here follows a full transcript of the Act of Sett dated 11 September 1676 and the amendment to the Act dated 13 October 1709:

11 SEPTEMBER 1676 ACT OF SETT
At Inverness the Eleventh Day of September one thousand Six Hundred & Seventy six years. The Decreet underwritten Conform to the Ordinance therein Contained is Insert & Registrate in the Burrough Books of Inverness Whereof the Tenor follows;

At Inverness the second Day of September one thousand six hundred Seventy Six years.

Anent the Act of the General Convention of Burroughs holden at Edinburgh upon the Seventh Day of July one thousand Six Hundred and Seventy Six years Last by past, by the Commissioners of Burroughs Mentioning That where the Convention being truly Informed of the great Debates Divisions and Confusions that are both within the Council and amongst the Inhabitants of the Town of Inverness in Relation to the Election of Magistrates and Councillors of the said Burgh. And Considering that it is the desire of all Parties Interested in the saids Debates that the present Convention would take the Same to their serious Consideration and to take such Effectual course therein as may preveen Such Dangers and Inconveniencies as may prove fatal to the said Burgh if not timeously Composed. And the Convention considering that it ought to be their chief Care, as it is the principal Design of their Institution that the Inhabitants of the Royal Burroughs should Live together in amity, peace, and an good understanding amongst themselves. And when any Division arises amongst any of the Royal Burroughs it is their Constant Custom to appoint Some of their Number to Setle and Determine their Differences. Therefore and for the particular Care and Respects they bear towards the Burgh of Inverness. Have appointed Likeas be thir presents appoint Sir Patrick Threapland present Provost of Perth George Brown present Provost of Dundee, Gilbert Mollison present Baillie of Aberdeen, Alexander Miln present Provost of Linlithgow, Robert Renold present Provost of Montrose, David Donaldson Commissioner for the Burgh of Brechin Captain James Bennet Commissioner for Inverkeithing Archibald Wilson Baillie of Queensferry and Mr. James Rochead General Clerk to the said Burroughs Together with James Ross Burgess of Nairn, Sir Robert Dunbar Provost of Forres, Ronald Bain late Baillie of Dingwall and Alexander Graham Provost of Fortrose or any seven of them to meet at Inverness the Last Day of August next to come with Continuation of Days and to call before them all persons within the said Burgh whether Magistrates Councillors or other Inhabitants and to hear what each party has to alledge either for or against the form and model of the present Custom of their Burgh in the Election of their Magistrates and Council, and after hearing of the samen to determine Settle, and Compose all their Differences in order to their future Elections as far as possible can be to the general Satisfaction of all parties concerned, with full power to them if needs bees to establish and set an Plat-form and Government of the said Burgh which shall be most agreeable to the Laws of the Kingdom, Example of the best Governed Burroughs of the Nation, and to the particular Constitution of the said Burgh, Wherein the saids Commissioners are to proceed and Determine without partiality and in Singleness of heart having nothing before their Eyes but the true and Solid Interest of the Common well of the said Brugh. And in regard the Convention has been at so great pains for the good and peace of that Burgh, And that the foresaids Commissioners are to be at so great trouble and Expences as to go to the said Burgh of Inverness for their quiet and Settlement. Therefore the Convention Requires and obtests the haill foresaids persons who are any ways concerned in the said Debates & Divisions to Lay aside all partiality, Animosities, humour and their own private Interests in the said affair, and to give all give all due respect Deference and Submission to what shall be appointed and Determined be our saids Commissioners on the Premises as if the Samen had been Enacted and ordained by this present Convention. Declaring that in case a Quorum of our saids Commissions do not meet at the said Burgh before their Election according to their preceeding Custom. Then declaring that the present Magistrates and Councillors shall proceed to their Election according to their preceeding Custom. And Ordains them to Report their Diligence herein to the next General Convention and this to be an head of the next missive, Whereanent thir presents shall be a sufficient warrand to the saids Commissioners. As the said Act of Burroughs of the Date foresaid under the Sign and Subscription manual of Mr. James Rochead General Clerk of the saids Burroughs at more Length bears. Conform to the appointment of the said Act. They are met and Conveened at Inverness the several Commissioners of the Burroughs afternamed upon the Last day of August last by past for taking notice of and Rectifying the Differences betwixt the Saids Magistrates of the Saids Burgh and others. To witt Sir Patrick Threapland Provost of Perth, George Brown Provost of Dundee, Gilbert Mollison Baillie of Aberdeen, Alexander Miln Provost of Linlithgow, Robert Ronald Provost of Montrose, David Donaldson for the Burgh of Brechin, Archibald Wilson Baillie of Queensferry, Sir Robert Dunbar Provost of Forres, Ronald Bain Late Baillie of Dingwall and Alexander Graham Provost of Fortrose who being met and Conveened as said is They for the more & orderly procedure in the matter underwritten Have made and Chosen Sir Patrick Threapland Provost of Perth as Preses in the said meeting. And the saids Commissioners have nominate and chosen Mr. Alexander Edward writer in Edinburgh as their Clerk to Serve them in their meeting And also have Called and Conveened before them the foresaids present Magistrates, Gildrie & Tradesmen and having perused the Council Books and read over the Contract or bond betwixt the present Magistrates Gildrie and Trades, and having heard the Grievances and objections against one another hine inde, and they being ripely and well advised therewith, The saids Commissioners with one Consent and assent Conform to the ordinance and Act of Burroughs of the Date Tennor and Contents above written Do for the peace and tranquility of the said Burgh of Inverness, and for the amicable Setting all Differences betwixt the present Magistrates and Gildrie and tradesmen in all time Coming, and for avoiding further Strife, Debate or any ground of Contention in all time hereafter, and conform to that point of the said act Impowering them to setle and Compose all Differences in order to their future Election as far as possible can be, and to Establish an Sett and Plat-form of Government of the said Burgh most agreeable to the Laws of the Kingdom Example, of the best Governed Burroughs of the Nation and particular Constitution of the said Burgh. Have Decerned and Ordained and hereby Decerns and Ordains That at the next Election of the Magistrates & Council of the Burgh of Inverness and yearly at their Elections in all time Coming there shall be strictly kept & observed without the Least change or alteration the Rules & ordinances following To witt.

Primo That the Number of the Town Council of Inverness shall consist of Twenty one Councillors and no more whereof the then present to be an part of the number, and which is conform to the Sett made by the Town Council of Inverness in anno one thousand Six hundred and forty eight years. And in respect that the great Complaint of this place has been Continuing the Council these many years by gone. Therefore and for Rectifying the Samen the said Commissioners has Ordained for this next ensuing year only, That this present Council shall Elect and choose their Councillors for the next ensuing year the persons following VIZ'. John Polson, John Barbour, John Stuart, William Thomson, William Paterson, Donald McLean, John Cuthbert, and Alexander Clunes who are to come in place of eight of the present Council to be put off and Discharged be the present Magistrates and Council. And after the eight old Councillors are put out, and the new eight put in the Council to make choice of the present Provost, Baillies, Dean of Gild and Treasurer, and in case of their not acceptance with power to them to make choice & Leet other Magistrates to Continue for the next ensuing year. And Ordains that in all time coming that the Model Sett and Platform shall be as follows To Witt. Primo that they shall Change five new Councillors every year and the five old Councillors being removed, the Council shall out of their own number every year make a Choice of their Magistrates.

Secundo The Provost of Inverness hereafter to be chosen to Continue at the most in the office of Provostry but the space of three years together and if he shall continue the whole three years but Interruption, he shall not be capable to be upon the Leet of the Provostry for the fourth year, and this is but prejudice to the Magistrates & Council to Choose him yearly as they shall think fit. Likas it is declared to be but prejudice to him to be chosen the fifth year or at any time thereafter. And it is hereby Declared that the Provost of the Burgh shall have two votes in Council which makes in the whole twenty two.

Tertio The saids Commissioners have Decerned and Ordained That the Baillies Dean of Gild and Treasurer shall at most continue but two years in their office together, And if they continue so long with out Intermission in the said offices, then in the third year they shall not be Capable to be Leeted & chosen to officiate in these offices the third year thereafter. And it is hereby Provided that the Magistrates and Council has power to Elect and choose them yearly as they think fit, but prejudice also to them to be Chosen the third year or any other time thereafter. And for the more clearing the former Sett it is hereby Declared that the Provost Baillies Dean of Gild and Treasurer shall Continue Councillors the next year after their bearing charges and offices of Magistracy ex officio. And they have Ordained that the persons to be Chosen Councillors or Magistrates in time coming within this Burgh shall be actual Residenters within the samen and Liberties thereof and actual trafficking Merchants or Maltmen allenarly, And for the more form settling the peace of this Burgh. The saids Commissioners have Decerned and Ordained for the Encouragement of Trades and tradesmen within this Burgh That the several Trades following, Providing that each one of the Incorporations underwritten Consist of seven freemen, Burgesses VIZ'. The Hammermen, Wrights, Shoemakers, Taylors, Skinners and Weavers, shall be Incorporated within themselves with power to them for their further encouragement.

First That they shall yearly give in an Leet of three of their Number to the Magistrates and Council who shall choose one of the three to be visitors or overseers of each one of their respective trades for the next ensuing year.

Secondly That one of the saids visitors or overseers being Informed that any extraneous persons does encroach upon the Privileges of any of the Respective trades by working within the freedom of this place, Then and in that case they are to apply themselves to the Magistrates of the place who are hereby obliged to fyne the persons Dilinquents as they shall think fit, and to Discharge the saids persons from encroaching upon the privileges of the respective Crafts, and to cause them Enact themselves under a penalty to do so no more in time coming.

Thirdly That the apprentices of any of the foresaids Trades being Lawfully admitted apprentices Whose names are holden to be Booked in the Council Books, and who serve their apprenticeships faithfully and have Discharges of their Indentures shall be holden and accepted of as Burgesses of this Burgh they paying their ordinary Dues and are to be Received as freemen within their respective trades. And is hereby Declared and Decerned that it shall not be Leesome to any Master of the foresaides trades to take in an prentice but one in three years time except upon the Death or running away of another prentice.

Fourthly That in case any of the foresaid tradesmen shall Transgress in their said Calling then and in these Cases it shall be Leesome and Lawful to the overseers or in making any unsufficient work or in keeping up any persons work too Long, or shall otherways transgress in their said Calling, then and in that case it shall be Leesome and Lawful to the overseers or visitors of any of the respective trades after tryal made of the foresaid faults to fine the Delinquents, the fine not exceeding ten shillings Scots, and which fines are yearly to be Counted for to the Magistrates and Council of the Burgh by the visitors and overseers, that they may see the same applied to the maintainance of the poor or other pious uses of the respective Incorporations from whom the fines are taken.

Fifthly That any freeman within the respective trades or any of their Children or apprentices after expiring their apprenticeships actually quitting their trades and take themselves to merchandizing, then they shall be admitted freeman of the Gildrie they paying the ordinary dues of the Gild brethren, and shall be capable of being Elected their Councillors or Magistrates of this Burgh. And in respect that the great Stents and Impositions and way of Imposing the samen has been one of the great grievances of this place. Therefore the saids Commissioners has Ordained and Ordains that it shall not be Lawful for the Magistrates or Council to Stent or Impose Taxations upon the Inhabitants of this place without their own Consent or at Least the most part thereof Except the Stents Imposed by public Authority and in case there is a necessity for imposing any Stents upon the Inhabitants of this Burgh then and in that case the Magistrates shall give notice to the Inhabitants what is the cause of the samen by tuck of Drum and of the time place and manner how the same is to be Imposed. And for the more Regular and equal way for Imposing the Samen they Ordain that the Magistrates and Council of this Burgh shall nominate and Elect fifteen persons of best fame and repute within this place to be Stentmasters who shall be holden to give their oaths in presence of the Council de fideli. Whereof Eleven of the fifteen shall be a quorum who shall meet in the Tolbooth of this place and no person to be Supported to be with them but one of the Magistrates, and after the same is Imposed and Collected the Magistrates and Council of this place shall be obliged to make it appear that the Stent is bestowed and Expended to the end for which it was Imposed. And Because it is Informed to the saids Commissioners that the Town is in Debt in the sum of Eight thousand merks or thereby and that there is no other way for paying the Samen but by Imposing Stents upon the Inhabitants of the place they do Seriously Recommend to the Inhabitants of the said Burgh to Concur with the Magistrates thereof for Stenting the Neighbours in order to the payment of the said Debt of the Town and to Leoy and Raise the saids Stents at Such times as they may best do with their Convenience and that no vestage or Memory be left of former differences. And for taking away all grounds of Dissentions and diversions in the place, the saids Commissioners finally ordain all actions and pursuits of Law betwixt the present Council Gildrie and trades to be presently Destroyed and Cancelled in their presence. And inlike manner the saids Commissioners Witts and Declares that the above written Decreet in all points shall stand and Continue Inviolable unchanged in all time Coming Certifying the Breakers thereof that the Royal Burroughs will notice the breakers of the Samen and punish them accordinly and State themselves as parties against them. And the saids Commissioners Ordains that thir presents shall in force in all time coming for the Rule and Government of the said Burgh of Inverness. And that Extracts shall be given forth thereof be the Preses. And that the above written Decreet is to be Insert and Registrate in the Town Court Books of Inverness In Testimony whereof The Principal is Subscribed by the said Sir Patrick Threapland Preses and the said Mr. Alexander Edward Clerk in name and at the desire of the Remanent Commissioners above written.

Extracted forth of the Records of the Royal Burroughs of Scotland by William Forbes

Submission with regard to the Sett by the Magistrates, Council and Trades of the Burgh of Inverness, to a Committee of the Royal Burroughs and Decreet Arbitral following thereupon.

The blank on the other side hereof is to be filled up be the final sentence and Decreet Arbitral of John Rose of Braidley Provost of Nairn, William Ross of Easterfearn, Kenneth Mackenzie Junior Baillie of Elgin and William Tolmie Baillie of Fortose (sic) as a Committee of the Convention of Royal Burroughs Appointed by their Act of the date the twelfth day of July last for the ends therein specified and Submitted to be Simon Mackenzie and William McLean Goldsmiths in Inverness James Porteous Taylor there Robert Miller Coppersmith there for themselves and be James Vaus visitor of the Glover Trade of the said Burgh David Munro Visitor of the Taylor Trade thereof James Dick visitor of the Shoemaker Trade, thereof Mathew Moor visitor of the Squarewright Trade thereof, James Petrie & John Mcinteer Smiths there and Andrew Denoon Peutherer there all of them for themselves and in name and behalf of the respective Incorporations of the Hammermen Glover Taylor Shoemaker Squarewright or Couper trades and the other trades of the said Burgh Submitters.

Annent the differences arisen betwixt the Magistrates of Inverness and the saids Trades conform to the respective Informations and Representations to be given in be the saids Magistrates and them hinc inde with the Instructions and Documents thereof and answers to be given in hinc inde be both parties which are declared to be as sufficient as if here Insert Renouncing hereby any Advocation and disclaiming and passing from all Process of Declarator, Reduction intended or raised orinaises be them in the said matters Like as the saids Members of Committee have accepted this present Submission & Decision of the premisses in and upon them and faithfully promise to give their final Sentence & Decreet therein betwixt and the Last day of October instant, and whatever the said Committee agreeing together in one voice shall Decide Determine & for their final Sentence and Decreed Arbitrall in the premisses give and pronounce twixt and the day above mentioned the fornamed persons Submitters for themselves and in name and behale foresaid Bind and Oblige them and their Successors in their respective Incorporation above written to stand to and abide thereat and perform and fullfill the same on their part without and fivider (sic) Process Appial or Plea of Law under the penalty of Six hundred pounds Scots money by and alloivr fullfilling of the said Decreet Consenting to the Registration hereof in the Books of Council and Session or others competent within this Kingdom That Letters of Horning and all other Ececutonalls needful may pass hereupon in form as Effeirs & Constitutes.

These Pre'nt In witness whereof the said parties Submitters have subscribed thir presents & blank on the other side hereof Likas the said Committee in Token of their acceptance have Subscribed thir presents (written be Mr. Charles McLean Town Clerk of Inverness) At Inverness this thirteenth day of October One Thousand Seven hundred and nine years before these witnesses Alexr Mackintosh of Fermil Merchant in Inverness George McKilligan Apothecary Burgess of Inverness William Ross Messenger there & the said Mr. Charles McLean and James Cuthbert Junior Merchant there (Sic subscribitur) Simon McKenzie William McLean, James Porteous Mathew Moor, Ja: Vaus, Andrew Denoon, James Dick, Robert Miller, accepts William Ross Accepts Kennith McKenzie junior Accepts Jo: Rose Accepts William Tolmie Demandato duti Jacobi Petrie Joannis Mcanteer et Davidis Munro Scribere nescien ut asserinent ut mihi notum est Calarnum tangeno Ego Johannes Taylor Notarius Publicus cum Co Notario Suberibenti Subscribo Jo: Taylor N. P. De mandalis quibus supra ut mihi notum est Scribere nisciend ut assercicre Calarnum Tangend Ego Magister Carolus McLean Co: Notarius publicus requisitus subscribe Ch: McLean N. P. George McKilligan Witness, William Ross witness James Cuthbert Witness, Alex Mackintosh Witness.

–The Committee of the Royal Borroughs within designed to whose decision the Magistrates and Councellors of the Burgh of Inverness by a Judicial Act and the trades of the said Burgh by the within Submission have submitted the Determination of the differences within written having Considered the representations, Informations and Petitions given in hine inde with the answers thereto and the Documents and verifications thereof. The said Committee for settling the Peace of this Burgh and removing all grounds of difference and debate that has arisen upon the Act of Sett give their finall Sentence and Decreet as follows Viz[t]

Primo the Committee finds that any Burges acting in the double capacity of tradesmen & Guildbrother at the same time is Contrair to the fifth Article of the Act of Sett and the Custom and Constitutions of the Borroughs, And Therefore Ordains all Burgesses acting in both Capacities to betake themselves to the One or other allenarly in all timecoming. And that they appear befor the Town Council when required and make their Election which of the freedoms they shall Continue in, and Enact themselves accordingly, But prejudice of any tradesman to have the Priviledge of Renouncing his trade, and being thereon admitted Guild brother and Capable of being Councellor, and Magistrate in the terms of the Act of Sett And Declares that the Privilidge of meeting is only Competent to Burgisses Guild brothrin and that tradesmen are Debarred therefrom by the said Act of Sett.

Secundo the said Committee finding that the Hammermen have assumed several Crafts as branches of their Incorporation, who were not in the Place the time of the Act of Sett and that the number of each Craft so assumed is not now Sufficient to serve the Burgh. Therefore the Committee Ordains that the Crafts afternamed shall be allowed at least in all time comeing the number of Persons following Vis The Black Smiths seven, Silver Smiths two, Coppersmiths three, Peutherers three Armourors three, sadlers three, Gunn Smiths three Brasiers two white Ironmen two and when any of the saids Crafts falls to be fewer then the Incorporation of Hammermen shall be obliged to admit any man Compleat in his Craft who shall offerr himself to make up the said number upon payment of the ordinary dues to the Burgh for his admission as Burgess and of a Sum not exceeding Eight pounds Scots to the Trade for his freedom.

Tertio The Committee finds that the visitor of any trade cannot poind or away take the work, or work Looms of an extraneous person or unfreeman at his own hand but must apply to a Magistrate who is obliged to Stop such persons from working and to fine them, and cause them Enact in terms of the Act of Sett.

Quarto The Committee finds that each Incorporation of the Trades may meet separately by themselves for regulating the sufficiency of work and exorbitancy of prices receiving of Freemen and doing such other things as lend to the encouriagement of the trade, and may Employ an Clerk and officer for these purposes. But finds that they are not warranted by the Act of Sett to have general meetings or General Preses (sic) or Overseer, nor to Levy money upon any pretext whatsomever except the sums accressing to them by Entry of Prentices and admission of Freemen and the fines mentioned in the fourth Article of the Act of Sett, which sums so accressing are to be applied for the uses of the Trade and compted for to the Magistrates yearly in time coming.

Quinto The Committee Ordains that the privelege granted by the Act of Sett to the weavers be allowed them and when they amount to the number of Seven Burgesses that the Magistrates do appoint them a Visitor in terms of the Act of Sett Allowing the Magistates because of the present paucity of sufficient workmen of that Craft at any time within two years, to bring into their Incorporation such a number of the best accomplished Workmen of that Craft as may be sufficient to serve the place.

Sexto That the Magistrates shall be Obliged to Admitt the sons of such as has been or shall be Burgesses Residenters of this Burgh or have served or shall Serve their Prenticeships with

Burgesses therein unto the freedom of Burgesships upon their Application and payment of the ordinary dues.

Septimo That the Skinners in time coming do not traffick in foreign Trade, or other merchant ware except Skins, Furrs, wool and such other things as are proper for their own Craft and manufactury.

Octavo The Committee Ordains That no Tradesman while continueing such shall be admitted or Chosen a Member of the Council or Magistrate of this Burgh,

Nono Ordains that when any Jeweller, founder or any other Tradesman applys to be admitted of whose craft there is none in the place for the time the said Tradesman shall be received on such terms as the Magistrates shall see reasonable.

Decimo And for Removing of differences & debates and settling peace and unanimity in all time coming. The Committee Ordaines the Incorporation of Hammermen to give in a Leet or List of three of their number qualified in the terms of this Decreet to the Magistrates and Council the first Council day of which number the Council shall choose to be visitor of that Incorporation for this year And that the Magistrates Remitt and discharge the fynes imposed by them on James Porteous William McLean, Simon McKenzie and Walter Denoon for their illegally away taking of Silver spoons from George Leith, upon consigning the said Spoons in the hands of the Magistrates to be delivered to the true owners. And Appoints the Magistrates to return their Burges Tickets to the said persons and to Robert Miller Coppersmith upon their making their Election & Ennacting themselves in the terms of the first Article of this Decreet and for the better encouragement of the Skinners to observe this Decreet, Appoints the Magistrates freely to remitt and discharge the fynes imposed on some of their number by Decreet dated the fourth of May One thousand Six hundred and ninty Seven years. And to deliver up to them the Bond granted relative thereto. And in case any debate arise hereafter betwixt the Magistrates and the Trades and their Constitution, Act of Sett or any other article of this Decreet. The Committee Ordains both parties in the first instance to apply to the Convention of Burroughs or their Commission Sitting for the time under the penalty of Two thousand pounds Scots money And Lastly The Committee humbly requests the next General Convention of Burroughs to grant a Ratification to this present Sentence and Decreet, at their next General meeting And for the more Security the said Committee do ordain that the present Decreet with the within Submission be Registrate in the Books of Council and Session or Town Court Books of Inverness or other books competent. that Extracts thereof may be given to the Parties concerned and that Letters and Exec' needfull may pass hereon in form as Effeirs In witness whereof the said Committee and John Taylor Notar Public their Clerk have subscribed these presents (written be Thomas Fraser writer in Inverness) At Inverness the fifteenth day of October one thousand Seven hundred and nine years before these witnesses Mr. John McIntosh Advocate, Mr. Charles McLean Town Clerk of Inverness James Dunbar younger, & Kenneth McKenzie Merchants There and the said Thomas Fraser writer foresaid (Sic Subscribitur) Kenneth McKenzie Junior Elgin, William Ross for Tayne Simon McKenzie William McLean James Porteous Robert Miller John Rose Nairn Mathew Moor Jo Vaus And Denoon, James Dick Ch: McLean N. P. Wm Tolmie Fortrose John Taylor Clerk to the committee Ch: McLean Witness Alex^r McIntosh witnes Kenneth McKenzie witnes, Thomas Fraser witnes James Cuthbert witnes George McGilligan witnes William Ross witnes De mandatis quibus infra Ego Joannes Taylor Notorius Publicus cum Co Notario Subscribente Subscribo Jo Taylor N. P. Extracted forth of the records of the Royal Burroughs of Scotland by William Forbes Conjunct General Clerk to the saids Royal Burroughs (Sic Subr) Will: Forbes Extracted from the Records of the Borough of Inverness By Cam' Mackintosh.

*Three Inverness Quaichs, (left to right) by
Jameson and Naughten, unknown, marked
'R I' (see p26 and 27), by Robert Naughten.*
Private collection. Ewen Weatherspoon

THE QUAICH

The word quaich, in Gaelic 'cuach', means drinking cup. Used as everyday vessels, quaichs were of various sizes and were originally made from solid wood or other natural materials. They normally have two lugs but occasionally three or even four. Some wooden quaichs were constructed of staves, tongued and grooved to make them watertight. Metal, often silver, was frequently used around the rim, feet and on the lugs, mainly for decorative purposes. They are sometimes engraved on the inside of the base with the words 'squab ase' which means literally 'sweep it up' or 'drink it up'.

When silver quaichs were first made they were designed to resemble their natural counterparts; lines were engraved to give the impression of staves. Early examples were often engraved with tulip and rose motifs which, as Ian Finlay noted in *Scottish Gold and Silver Work*, 'irresistibly suggests a judicious blend of Orange and Jacobite'. A fine example of this type, made in 1685 by James Penman of Edinburgh, is held by the National Museums of Scotland. The bowl measures approximately 15 cms, the overall measurement, including the lugs, being approximately 25 cms; it stands 5½ cms high. The size of the later Inverness quaichs was usually around 7½ cms across the bowl, 14 cms overall, including the lugs, and 3 cms high.

The lugs of silver quaichs were hollow and were frequently decorated with hatch marks or a leaf-like design around the edge. Quaichs were often given as gifts, especially at a marriage, in which case the initials of the couple would be added to the lugs.

Early Inverness examples by Robert Elphinston, Simon McKenzie and William McLean are known to exist. John Baillie and Thomas Borthwick made many quaichs later in the eighteenth century and the one on the front cover of this book indicates a change to a plainer style which was carried through to the turn of the nineteenth century by Alexander Stewart and Charles Jameson. The shape of the foot and lugs, and the depth of bowl varied with changing fashions; an example of about 1825 showed 'dropped lugs' and a Robert Naughten quaich of this period used a shorter foot than seen previously.

Marks were usually struck on the underside of the base, but have been seen under the lugs or the outside of the base rim (the latter on a quaich made by the partnership of Jameson and Naughten, opposite).

The silver quaich was thought to have originated in the Highlands; this is not the case, as some of the earliest extant examples are from Edinburgh. Thus, Inverness appears to be the town of its adoption rather than its origin.

BIBLIOGRAPHY

PUBLISHED SOURCES

BURNS, Rev Thomas *Old Scottish Communion Plate* (1892) R & R Clark, Edinburgh

DOUGLAS, R *Annals of Forres* (1934) Elgin Courant & Courier

FINLAY, Ian *Scottish Gold and Silver Work* (Revised 1991) Strong Oak Press

FULLARTON, A and Co *The Topographical, Statistical, and Historical Gazetteer of Scotland* (1848)

HOW, RN, Cdr. G E P *Notes on Antique Silver* (1951) How (of Edinburgh, Ltd)

JAMES, I E *The Goldsmiths of Aberdeen 1450-1850* (1981) Bieldside Books, Aberdeen

MACDOUGALL, Margaret O *Inverness Silversmiths* (1955) Inverness Museum and Art Gallery

MACGILL W *Old Ross-shire and Scotland as seen in the Tain and Balnagown Documents* (1909) The Northern Counties Newspapers and Printing and Publishing Company Limited

MITCHELL, Alexander *Inverness Kirk-Session Records 1661-1800* (1902) Robt. Carruthers & Sons

MOSS, G P *Provincial Silversmiths of Moray* (1994) Quartet, London

MUNRO, R W & J *Tain Through the Centuries* (1966) Tain Town Council

NICOLSON, Alexander *History of Skye*

Ordnance Gazetteer of Scotland c1892

PICKFORD, Ian *Jackson's Silver & Gold Marks of England, Scotland and Ireland* (1989) Antique Collector's Club

PORTEOUS, Alexander *The Town Council Seals of Scotland* (1906)

QUICK, Estelle *A ballance of Silver - The story of the silversmiths of Tain* (1997) Tain & District Museum Trust

ROSS, Alexander *Freemasons in Inverness* (1877) Courier Office Inverness

URQUHART, R M *Scottish Burgh and County Heraldry* (1973)

DIRECTORIES

Edinburgh Directories: 1793-to date

Inverness Burgh Directories: 1866-67, 1873-74, 1899-1929, 1956-57, 1960-61

Glasgow Directories: Taits 1783, *Jones* 1789

Glasgow Post Office Directories: to date

Kelly's Scottish Directories 1928

MacDonald's Scottish Directory with Gazetteer. 1935-36, 1936-37, 1941-42, 1965-66

Murray's Aberdeen, Inverness and North of Scotland Trades Directory: 1936-37, 1941-42

Pigot's Scottish Directories: 1821-22 &23; 1825; 1837

Slater's Commercial Directories of Scotland: 1852, 1860, 1867
Slater's Royal National Commercial Directory of Scotland: 1882, 1889, 1893, 1896, 1900, 1903, 1907, 1911, 1915, 1921

NEWSPAPERS

Aberdeen Journal
Banffshire Journal
Edinburgh Gazette
Elgin Courant
Elgin Courier
Highland News 1883-1953
Highland News Group
Huntley Express & Advertiser for the Counties of Aberdeen, Banff & Elgin
Inverness Advertiser and Ross-shire Chronicle 1849-1885
Inverness Courier 1817- to date
Inverness Journal & Northern Advertiser 1807-1848
John O' Groats Journal
Nairnshire Telegraph and General Advertiser for the Northern Counties
Northern Chronicle & General Advertiser for the North of Scotland 1881-1969
Northern Scot & Moray & Nairn Express
Scottish Highlander 1885-1897
Strathspey News & Grantown Supplement

ARCHIVES

Census Returns
Aberdeen, Dingwall, Edinburgh, Elgin, Glasgow, Grantown-on-Spey, Inverness, Keith, Nairn, Tain and Wick.

Church of Scotland Parish Registers
Aberdeen, Dingwall, Edinburgh, Elgin, Forres, Glasgow, Grantown-on-Spey, Inverness, Keith, Kirkwall, Nairn, Tain and Wick.

Monumental Inscriptions
Inverness Chapel Yard, Inverness Old High Churchyard, Inverness Tomnahurich Burying Ground, Elgin Cathedral Burying Ground.

Registers of Deeds
Inverness 1627-1873 (incomplete)
Tain 1812-84
Cromarty 1819-1932
Dingwall 1794-1889

Sheriff Court Books (These include Small Debt Claims and Sequestration Records)
Inverness, (SC29); Tain, (SC34); Wick, (SC14); Nairn, (SC31); Dingwall, (SC25).

Records of Processes
Inverness 1669-1964

Commissary Court Records (include Testaments and Inventories)
Caithness (CC12); Inverness (CC11); Nairn (CC16); Ross and Cromarty (CC19).

Miscellaneous Records
Records of the Incorporation of Edinburgh Goldsmiths
Edinburgh Assay Office Records
Inverness Town Council Books 1619-1975
Inverness Burgh Court Books 1621-1683 & 1776-1863
Inverness Burgh Treasurer's Accounts Book
Inverness Registers of Sasines 1602-1869
Inverness Dean of Guild Court Books 1788-c1792 & 1806-1837
Inverness Roman Catholic Registers
Inverness Kirk Sessions Minutes
Minute Book of the Hammermen Incorporation of Inverness 1690-1862
Presbytery of Inverness Minute Book 1670-1688
Record of Apprentice Indentures Inverness 1738-1846
Records of the Guildry of Tain 1738-1832
Register of Voters Ross and Cromarty 1832-33 & 1834-37
Town Council Minute Books of Tain 1776-1787 & 1814-1839
Balnagown Papers
Pitcalnie Papers

NOTES

[1] This is now generally not accepted.

[2] The camel is no longer to be found on the Coat of Arms. The second supporter on the old arms was an Elephant.

[3] *Jackson's Silver & Gold Marks* illustrates the mark 'MAC over MAS' with a 'cornucopia' punch which appears similar to that used by Robert Naughten.

[4] Goldsmith who worked in Aberdeen, Banff and Elgin.

[5] Member of the Trade Council (in this instance).

[6] Abreviated form for 'sixteen hundred' used by writers in the 17th century.

[7] Deacon (in this instance).

[8] Tax or rate.

[9] VOL.III. 1705-1723. (Archives. Forres).

[10] Built 1685; washed away in 1849.

[11] Baptised 22 August 1689 in Orkney, Kirkwall & St. Ola; Father Alexander Geddes and mother Jean Mudie.

[12] Probably Kenneth and Kathrine.

[13] Probably Alexander.

[14] The reason for 'the discipline of Aberdeen' was not given, but being brought by the Presbytery was obviously very serious. See *Kirk Session Minutes for St. Nicholas, Aberdeen.*

[15] It is interesting to note that a George Leith was Provost of Banff in 1691 and 1693. (The Annals of Banff. William Crammond. 1891-93).

[16] Margaret MacDougall, in her notes for *Inverness Silversmiths*, stated that, on 5 August 1702 William McLean submitted his essay to the Hammermen's Craft, which was approved, and at the same meeting he was admitted to membership of the said Craft. As previously mentioned the *Hammermen Minute Book* is now missing, and the existing microfilm copy of the Book cannot confirm the above.

[17] The 'Inverness Kirk Session Records. 1661-1800.' by Alexander Mitchell, 1902, recorded that the goldsmith was Wm McBean - the original entry definitely states Wm Mclean.

[18] These cups seem to have disappeared. (Alexander Mitchell).

[19] There were two possible baptisms in Old Machar, Aberdeen; Kath on 2 September 1673 and Catheron on 6 January 1680. On both occasions the father was given as Robert Low.

[20] A tax or rate.

[21] Abbreviated form for 'seventeen hundred' used by writers in the 18th century.

[22] No day was recorded.

[23] Baptised 2 April 1702 as recorded in the *Colinton Parish Register*. Her father was

Robert Tait, tenant in Comiston, and her mother Grissell Cleghorn. Witnesses were John Cleghorn and James Tait.

[24] Possibly named after James Tait, William's master in Edinburgh.

[25] p381

[26] William Livingston was described as a journeyman goldsmith in Edinburgh.

[27] This Edward Livingston became the goldsmith in Dundee.

[28] This time would be consistent with his entry as an apprentice in 1714, but would not account for his time in Elgin and Glasgow.

[29] Opened by the Incorporated Trades, (Craftsmen), of Edinburgh in 1704, (Town Council Minute, 3 May 1704). It was a Hospital School boarding and clothing the pupils and providing education. Entry was by petition to the Incorporated Trades by children of 'decayed or deceased' burgesses and guild freemen of the City.

[30] Margaret MacDougall in her notes for *Inverness Silversmiths*, states that John Baillie was admitted to his burghal freedom, gratis, on 3rd October 1727.

[31] Janet was baptised 2 December 1719; father James Anderson, Merchant in Inverness.

[32] This baptism was between two dated entries, one 4 December and the other 7 December 1738.

[33] Married Alex'r Simpson, 'Rector of the Gramer School', on 24 December 1781.

[34] The date does not agree with the *Parish Register*. However, this may be explained by the death occurring on the 18th and burial 19th May 1753. The year, 1757 for 1753, is either an error by the mason or his informant, or, a misreading of the inscription by the compiler of the Index.

[35] Her father was James Anderson of Knocknagial, or Knocknagiel.

[36] Overseer.

[37] Portioner/portionar: One who has a share of something. The dictionary definition is: 'A proprietor of a (comparatively small) piece of land once forming part of an estate thus divided into portions.'

[38] This was an error; it should have read Robert.

[39] Registered a mark at the Sheffield Assay Office in 1788.

[40] It is likely that he bought the ladle in and added his marks; also possible, however, is that he acquired the ladle at a later date, and then marked it.

[41] The *Aberdeen Journal* of 30 January 1839 reported, 'Died at her house in Church Street, Inverness, on 12th instant, Mrs KATHERINE INGLIS relict of the late CHARLES JAMESON, Esq, merchant, aged 83 years.'

[42] Died at Greenock on 12 April 1857; 'Mrs Elizabeth Hepburn, eldest daughter of the late Mr Charles Jameson, Jeweller, Inverness.' (*Inverness Advertiser* 21 April 1857).

[43] Died 4 February 1858, in Inverness, (Mary Smith, widow).

[44] Died at Calcutta, on 16 November 1826, aged 27, 'eldest son of Mr Charles Jameson, Goldsmith, Inverness.' (*Inverness Journal* 11 May 1827).

[45] Died 24 November 1862, in Glasgow.

[46] Tax or assessment.

[47] Alexand(e)ra or Alexanderena.

[48] *Inverness Journal* issue No. 5.

[49] Entered as McGoorman in the *Inverness Parish Register*, at his baptism.

[50] In Donald McGuirman's Testament he was described as sometime farmer in Inverness, residing on the Barnhill; it also named his wife as Elizabeth or Betty Kerr alias MacGuirman.

[51] The same date that Charles Fowler's apprenticeship to Charles Jameson in Inverness was registered following it's completion.

[52] The clues to link the two names are Thomas's death certificate and the naming of Thomas's second son. Additionally, Donald McGuirman's Testament and Inventory, registered 30 August 1825, detailed that the sum of £142 11s 8d was owing by Thomas Stewart, goldsmith in Elgin, and his wife, which 'is considered desperate'.

[53] Clerkenwell Green where Richard Lockwood worked was one of the most charming and unspoilt early nineteenth century areas of London EC. The green has gone, but the houses remain grouped as they were.

[54] The wording in his father's Testament and Inventory of 1825 suggested that Thomas Stewart was in financial difficulties earlier.

[55] No record of her baptism has been found in the *Elgin Parish Register*.

[56] There were two McRae' jewellers and silversmiths working in Inverness at this time and the baptismal name given to this child may indicate where Thomas Stewart was employed.

[57] Naughty was synonymous with Naughten. The family probably changed their name to Naughten around 1810.

[58] Robert's death certificate stated his father was Thomas Naughten, a barley miller, and his mother was Elspeth Clunes.

[59] He did not use the name Davidson during his life-time.

[60] Born c1799 in Inverness; her daughter's death certificate recorded her as a domestic servant, deceased.

[61] Her death certificate stated she was the widow of Suther Sutherland, grocer, illegitimate; her reputed father was ...... Naughton, jeweller, and her mother was Catherine McKenzie.

[62] There is no other record of this marriage nor is there any record of children born to this relationship.

[63] An advertisement in the *Inverness Courier* of 13 July 1876 stated that the business of Robert Naughten had been established sixty years.

[64] This was the first so-called 'accurate census' as far as age was concerned, but Robert would have been aged 65.

[65] This date of birth does not agree with the parish records or his death certificate, and appears to be a mistake by the mason or informant.

[66] There are 2 Kilmuir's on Skye; one 4 miles north of Uig and the other ½ mile south of Dunvegan.

[67] Which is 9¼ miles north east of Inverness.

[68] Campbeltown or Ardersier, a village in Ardersier and Petty parishes, NE Inverness-shire, on the coast of a picturesque bay of the Moray Firth, 1½ miles SE of Fort George, this being 9½ miles NE of Inverness. A burgh of barony under the Earl of Cawdor, it took its designation of Campbeltown from his lordship's family name.

[69] Witnessed by Hugh Faulkner (sic), (wife's father?), and Alexander McRae (silversmith?).

[70] Witnessed by William Munro (silversmith?) and Donald Mackenzie (silversmith?).

[71] Alexander Falconer married Christine Munro; he was a jeweller in High Street and may have been the brother of Alexander McLeod's wife. He died in 1837.

[72] Against this entry was the following, 'McKiligan absconded only served a year & a half'.

[73] At Greenbank, Academy St, Fortrose, aged 84. (Death certificate).

[74] Devonshire Street was the name of the present day Devonshire Row, which runs between Bishopsgate and Devonshire Square in the City of London, opposite Liverpool Street Station.

[75] The 1851 census recorded that she was born in Dingwall and was a 'Teacher of Music'.

[76] From the 1851 census we know she also became a music teacher; she died on 10 May 1877, aged 49.

[77] Flora married John B. Fyfe on 18 January 1855; she was recorded as aged 23, her father was Alex. McRae, writer, and her mother Lydia Davies (sic). Flora died 20 August 1885, age given as 45, and her father listed as Alexander Macrae, mercantile clerk.

[78] *Pigot's Directory* 1821-22 & 23 recorded Jonathan Wells, iron founder, in 'Green'; the 1825 Directory listed him as an ironmonger and hardwareman, in Muirtown Green. The 1837 Directory detailed a John Wells, iron founder, in Friars' Place.

[79] This appears to be an error by the mason or the informant.

[80] A county which is now East Lothian.

[81] Knockbain is a parish on the Black Isle, 3 miles north from Inverness.

[82] This appears to be a mistake by the enumerator.

[83] This must have been Ann as she was not listed in the 1861 census.

[84] Originally registered as David on 7 November 1859, but name altered on 27 December 1859.

[85] Pencaitland was a parish within Haddingtonshire, (East Lothian); not Fife, as stated in the census.

[86] Isabella was married at King Street, Pollokshaws, on 19 November 1868, to Thomas Hill; her parents were recorded as John and Margaret McRae.

[87] Jane Mason married Alexander Ferguson in Inverness on 24 July 1856. Alexander was, by that date, a 23 year old jeweller working in Glasgow and the elder brother of James and William who were to form the firm of Ferguson Brothers in Inverness ten years later. The Post Office Directory of Glasgow for the year 1857-58 shows Alexander Ferguson living at 118, Union Street, a jeweller. In the 1858-59 Directory he is at 87, Union Street, where he is listed as a goldsmith. In the general section he is listed as a manufacturing jeweller. In 1859-60 details remain the same; however, he is missing from the following year's Directory.

[88] Died 18 July 1862; he was recorded as an engraver. Address was 41 Huntly Street.

[89] Married Helen Munro on 24 October 1866; died 29 September 1881, aged 49.

[90] Married John Cook Gordon on 26 December 1866.

[91] Must have died by 1846; a second Donald was recorded in the *Parish Register* but only the latter was listed in the 1851 census.

[92] Spelt many ways, in contemporary records, but generally Farlaha or Farlaw.

[93] One of the witnesses was John McRae.

94 No details of the birth or baptism have been found.

95 Gravestone, incorrectly, gives date of death as 7 November 1857.

96 North America.

97 Alexander Pratt Stewart, illegitimate son of Annabella Pratt, domestic servant, born 6 October 1869.

98 Annabella Pratt married Alexander McIntosh, journeyman cabinet maker, on 20 November 1874.

99 Mary Naughten's death certificate recorded her father as a master mason.

100 The baptismal entry added Kintail after Gairloch and if this refers to the Parish of Kintail, also in Ross-shire, it lies some considerable distance from Gairloch.

101 Who died before 1851.

102 Who died in Inverness on 3 December 1884, aged 74.

103 Born in Edinburgh c1845.

104 Presumably John, his eldest son, aged 13 years.

105 Who died in Inverness in 1884, aged 74.

106 Isabell (sic) used her maiden name. Her husband was not at home on the night of the census.

107 Name was Evan MacDonald.

108 Died at 4 Hill Place, Inverness. Recorded as a law book keeper.

109 Born 27 July 1846.

110 Born 28 October 1849.

111 Which is 13 miles south east of Elgin and 12 from Keith.

112 Her birth certificate states she was born 5 February 1860 at 74 Broad Street, Fraserburgh, daughter of Farquhar Smith, teacher, and Elizabeth Cardno.

113 On her death certificate she was described as the 'widow of John Medlock, labourer'. At his son John's marriage he was described as a butler. At his daughter Grace' marriage he was recorded as a house steward.

114 Polton Street had 20 inhabited houses containing 55 males and 51 females, including children.

115 The adjoining parish to Cockpen.

116 Arthur Medlock was, for the first time, described as a master watchmaker on the certificate for the birth of Daniel John.

117 Note the dates over the business address in the photograph (p132) are 1876-1930.

118 He was to manage this business.

119 This was the son of James MacBean, the MacBean of Ferguson & MacBean.

120 Note the dates over the business address in the photograph are 1876-1930.

121 William Taylor's brother, who ran the clock and watch side of the business, had been apprenticed to Brook & Son, Edinburgh.

122 It would appear that James Jack died about the same time as Jessie Ann was born.

123 There were two Hugh Ross', both silversmiths; they were probably father and son.

124 This could be Alexander Stewart senior, or his son.

125 The Luckenbooth, a silver and sometimes gold heart-shaped brooch, which was given as an betrothal gift or love token and named after a booth or covered stall which could be locked up (locked booth) in 17th century Edinburgh, and other

medieval Scottish towns. Also named as 'Witch Brooches' when pinned to children's clothing to ward off evil spells and the evil eye!

[126] Born around 1776 and died c1845.

[127] The exact wording on the cups is as follows: '*GIFT FROM* JOHN BAILLIE *HOUSE CARPENTER TO THE KIRK SEFSION INVERNEFS*'.

[128] It has been suggested that this indicated wares retailed in the Burgh of Cromarty, but no positive evidence has been found to support the theory.

[129] Taken on the night of 11 January 1852.

[130] On Richard Maxwell Wilkie's death certificate his father was recorded as a hosier and glover.

[131] Born at Bloombury Cottage, Church Lane, Edinburgh. Died on 18 November 1940, at 260 Marionville Road, Edinburgh; recorded as a retired Insurance Clerk, unmarried.

[132] Scotland.

[133] Born in London c1819.

[134] Down Lodge was 200 metres from Down House, which was the home of the Victorian Naturalist, Charles Darwin, from 1842 to 1882.

[135] Christie's Scotland catalogue of 26 May 1998, lot 95; Silver-mounted Oak Casket. The lock-plate was inscribed William Ross, Silversmith, Tain.

[136] Born Tower Buildings, Tain.

[137] Born Tower Buildings, Tain.

[138] This was at odds with her marriage certificate.

[139] In the Inverness 1891 census he was listed with his wife and four children at 5 Mary Ann Court. He was recorded as a watchmaker, aged 32 years.

[140] In the Inverness 1891 census he was listed as a jeweller, aged 28, living as a lodger at 22 Union Street.

[141] No number in the High Street was given in the 1860 Directory.

INDEX